E. Angela's letter to her grandparents has twelve mistakes in capitalization. Use proofreading marks to correct each mistake.

1237 Kelley street

Dubuque, Iowa 52001

September 15, 2000

Dear grandmother and grandfather,

Thanks again for coming to help us out. That was a nasty spill Mom took on my skateboard in the memorial day parade. I hope her cast will be off so that she can drive us to see you on the fourth of July.

Love,

Angela

Score: _____ Total Possible: 12

F. Correct nine mistakes in the inside address and body of the business letter below. Then write the letter correctly on another piece of paper. Add your address, the date, and a proper greeting and closing. Sign your name.

Inside Address:

Ms. Jessica Kline

5 Cash Street

San Antonio, Texas 78227

Body:

I saw an ad for Geo videotapes in your magazine. I'm interested in buying the tape about the denali national park in alaska. Could you send my Father and me information about it?

Score: _____ Total Possible: 9

REVIEW SCORE: _____ REVIEW TOTAL: 62

9 Punctuation: Periods

✏ *Think about it! What if there were no periods? Reading would suddenly be a lot more difficult.*

9/13/01

······················· Did You Know? ·······················

A period should follow a sentence that makes a statement or gives a direction.

> I don't like cold weather, unless there's snow.
> First, turn on the computer.

Titles of respect, such as *Mister* and *Doctor*, are abbreviated when they are followed by a person's name. A period should follow the abbreviation.

> Dr. Jonas Salk developed a vaccine for polio.
> Mr. and Mrs. Casey are James's uncle and aunt.

Initials are also followed by periods.

> John F. Kennedy was the thirty-fifth president.
> My friend's name is Katherine Colleen, but she uses her initials, K. C.

If an abbreviation appears at the end of a sentence, you need only one period.

···

Show What You Know

Read the paragraph below. Add periods where they are needed. Circle them so they are easier to see.

Have you decided how you will sign your name when you are famous?

Many well-known writers and artists use their first and last names. For example, Tasha Tudor is the author and illustrator of books for children. On the other hand, a photographer whose pictures are in a book about Ms Tudor uses one name and one initial. He is Richard W. Brown. A well-known writer of children's books, R. L. Stine, uses just initials and his last name. The amazing Dr. Seuss doesn't use his real name at all, just a title and a made-up name.

Score: _____ 5   **Total Possible: 10**

Proofread

The report below has seven mistakes in the use of periods. Use the proper proofreading mark to show where each period should be used.

Example: Mr⊙Greenthumb owns the garden store⊙

Three all-time favorite movies for children are *The Little Mermaid*, *The Wizard of Oz*, and *Peter Pan*⊙Each of these films is based on a book⊙Hans Christian Andersen wrote *The Little Mermaid*⊙L⊙Frank Baum wrote a series of books about Dorothy and her visits to Oz⊙James M⊙Barrie first told the story of Peter Pan, Wendy, and the dog Nana⊙

Practice *nice story but you didn't follow directions*

NSYNC

Write a story that you think would make a great movie or television show. Include at least one character with a title, such as Dr., Mr., Mrs., or Ms. Include a character who uses his or her initials. Be sure your sentences are correctly punctuated.

Once There was a guy Named Justin who Dreamed of Becomeing a Profeshinol Basket Ball Player. Justin didn't Think it was so hard. But all his friends said it was very hard. But to him it wasent. Justin Dreamt. One day it finnally came True Justin was a Profshionall Basket Ball Player. Justin Love Playing Basketball he had a great Time.

Tips for Your Own Writing: Revising

Choose a piece of your own writing and look it over carefully for the use of periods. Be sure you used a period at the end of each sentence and after every initial and abbreviation.

✏️ *Use periods correctly to make your writing clear to your reader.* NSYNC.

23

10 Punctuation: Abbreviations

Mrs. Brief moved to Pine Ave. on Thurs., Jan. 3. There was a mix-up with the movers; her furniture didn't arrive until Fri., Jan. 4.

.... **Did You Know?** ....

The names of some months of the year may be abbreviated in an informal note or where there is little space. A period should follow each abbreviation. May, June, and July are not abbreviated.

> Call me after **Apr.** 3, please. I'll see you on **Dec.** 27.
> I'm free anytime after **May** 12.

The names of the days of the week may be abbreviated in an informal note or where there is little space. A period should follow each abbreviation.

> Make your appointment for **Mon.** or **Thurs.**

....

Show What You Know

Read the diary entries below. Add periods where they are needed. Circle them so they are easier to see.

Dear Diary,

This is the last Mon in Feb, and I'm going to write to you every day this week

except Wed, because I have to go to swimming class and band and won't have

time. I got you last Tues as a tenth birthday present. I'm glad to have you here.

Dear Diary,

I didn't write any more during Feb I had poison ivy. I've stopped scratching, and

now I'm back to you. I'll be deep-sea fishing during Mar and Apr and most of

May. Then I'm going on vacation for all of June and July to my aunt's ranch in

Colorado. Yea!

Score: _____   Total Possible: 7

Proofread

This photographer's list of appointments has five mistakes in punctuation. Use the proper proofreading mark to show where each period should be used.

Example: I have a haircut appointment on Wed⊙ Sept⊙10, at 3 o'clock.

Superman	Tues	May 8	6 P.M.
Princess Jasmine	Fri	Jan. 12	3 P.M.
Aladdin	Mon.	Feb 3	4 P.M.
Minnie Mouse	Fri	Apr 9	10 A.M.

Practice

Create a calendar that begins on Monday and ends on Friday. Use abbreviations for the days of the week. The calendar can be used to keep track of your activities. On the lines below write the months of the year and their abbreviations.

_____

_____

_____

_____

_____

Tips for Your Own Writing: Proofreading ....

Choose a piece of your own writing in which you used abbreviations. Be sure you used abbreviations only in informal writing or in charts, calendars, and other places where you have little space. Check your use of periods.

A period at the end of an abbreviation tells your readers that you've stopped short of writing the whole word.

11 Punctuation: Question Marks, Exclamation Points

✏ *Little punctuation marks can make a big difference in your writing! Do you know how to use them correctly?*

·························· **Did You Know?** ··························

A sentence that asks a question ends with a question mark.

What's your favorite kind of weather**?**
Why are you watching that pointless television show**?**

A sentence that expresses a strong feeling, such as surprise, disgust, or great pleasure, ends with an exclamation point.

Don't say that again**!**
What a terrible plan**!**

An exclamation point also follows a single word that expresses strong feeling.

Amazing**!** Beautiful**!**

Show What You Know

Read the paragraph below. Circle the periods that are correct. Draw a line through the ones that are incorrect and write the correct punctuation mark above each.

Do you enjoy learning about animals. You can do it in your own neighborhood. Watch that house finch, the small bird with a bright red cap and neck. Do you hear his pretty, clear song. That tiny bird makes so much noise.

Is there a cat in your neighborhood. Watch quietly as it stalks a bug or butterfly. Now close your eyes. Can you imagine a lion or cougar stalking a small animal. Amazing. The small cat and the large one make the same moves.

Do you want to learn more. Your librarian may be able to help you find books published by the National Geographic Society. You can also watch National Geographic programs on television. What a great way to learn new things.

Score: _____   **Total Possible: 15**

Proofread

Three sentences in the report below are not punctuated correctly. Use the proper proofreading marks to add two question marks and one exclamation point.

Example: How do you like my new shoes?

How did people live in America long ago. About two thousand years ago, a group of farmers experimented with new kinds of seeds. Do you like corn on the cob, peanuts, tomatoes, and beans. All of these were grown in the parts of North America that we call Mexico, Arizona, and Colorado. How wonderful that these farmers gave us such important foods.

Practice

Write two questions about animals. Then write the answers to the questions in complete sentences. In your answers, include at least one sentence or word that expresses strong feeling. Punctuate your questions and answers carefully. You might want to exchange questions with a friend and share what you know about animals.

1. _____

_____

_____

2. _____

_____

_____

Tips for Your Own Writing: Revising ....

Choose a piece of your own writing and look carefully at the kinds of sentences you used. You may be able to make the writing more interesting by including a few questions and perhaps even an exclamation.

If you use the proper punctuation signals, you will always be heading in the "write" direction!

12 Punctuation: End Marks

Every sentence ends with some type of punctuation, doesn't it? It's up to the writer to know which type is correct.

································· **Did You Know?** ·························

A period follows a sentence that makes a statement or gives a direction.

> You are probably anxious to get started.
> Turn on your computer.

A question mark follows a sentence that asks a question.

> Why did you choose this program?

An exclamation point follows a sentence or phrase that expresses surprise or any strong feeling.

> No way would I ever buy that software!

Show What You Know

Read the following paragraphs. Add the correct punctuation where it is needed. Circle the periods.

In order to build a kite, you must first decide on the type of kite you want Would you prefer a two-stick kite, a box kite, or a flexible kite The two-stick kite is probably the simplest

The materials for a two-stick kite are inexpensive and easy to locate Find two straight, lightweight, strong sticks of approximately the same length You will need twine to lash the sticks together in the form of a † You also will need a paper cover to catch the wind Would you like your kite to be very simple Then newspaper makes a good cover

In addition to these materials, you will need a tube of glue and a ball of strong, light string to make a flying line Choose a bright ribbon for the tail, and you are ready to put your kite together Then go fly your kite

Score: _____   **Total Possible: 12**

Proofread

Six of the following sentences have incorrect end marks. Use proper proofreading marks to delete the incorrect punctuation marks and add the correct ones.

Example: A giant sequoia is huge?

Many redwood trees and giant sequoia trees are more than two thousand years old! One bristlecone pine tree is believed to be almost six thousand years old. Now, that's old. But can trees be hurt. Yes, they can, and you will want to prevent that. Never injure a tree by cutting it, putting nails into it, or breaking its branches? Take care of trees near you. Be sure they get enough water? Remove dead and dying branches. Call a professional tree doctor if your tree is not doing well!

Practice

Write four sentences about the tree in the picture. Write at least one question and one sentence that ends with an exclamation point.

1. _____
   _____

2. _____
   _____

3. _____
   _____

4. _____

Tips for Your Own Writing: Proofreading ....

Choose a piece of your own writing and look it over carefully for the use of end punctuation. If you find mistakes, copy the writing, correcting mistakes.

 Do you feel sure about how to use end punctuation? Good!

13 Punctuation: Sentences

Who do you know who talks without stopping? Maybe you do! When you write without stopping, though, you aren't helping your readers.

.... Did You Know? ....

Some writers put sentences together that do not belong together. Using end punctuation and capital letters correctly will help you avoid this.

> **Incorrect punctuation:** Mr. Aono is Jodi's father, he is an actor in Chicago.
> **Correct punctuation:**   Mr. Aono is Jodi's father. He is an actor in Chicago.
> **Incorrect punctuation:** We watched the skaters in the park, aren't they good.
> **Correct punctuation:**   We watched the skaters in the park. Aren't they good?

Show What You Know

Rewrite the following paragraphs. Use correct end punctuation and capital letters to correct sentences.

There is only one place in the United States where four states meet, the four states are Colorado, Utah, New Mexico, and Arizona they meet at a place called Four Corners.

At Four Corners, you can see mountains and deserts, you can also visit parks and campgrounds, it is one of the most beautiful regions in the United States.

_____

_____

_____

_____

Score: _____   **Total Possible: 8**

Proofread

Use proper proofreading marks to show where four end marks and two capital letters should be used to correct the sentences.

Example: We went to a Chicago Bulls game⊙/they won!

Megan finally had the camera she had asked for, it was a little heavier than her old one. She watched the dancers fly past her. She had never been to a polka party before, would she be able to get any good pictures. Everyone danced so fast. Megan just knew she would end up with blurred pictures.

Practice

Write four sentences about a place you would like to visit. It may be a real place or an imaginary one. Make your sentences interesting by using questions and exclamatory sentences as well as statements. When you have written your sentences, read them very carefully to be sure you do not have two or more sentences joined together.

1. _____

   _____

2. _____

3. _____

4. _____

Tips for Your Own Writing: Revising ....

Choose a piece of your own writing and look it over carefully for incorrect sentences. Rewrite any incorrect sentences that you find. Be sure you use correct end punctuation in your sentences.

 A period can help you stop a sentence from running on and on and on!

14 Punctuation: Sentence Fragments

As a good writer, you know where to put end punctuation. Do you know there may be times when you need to take out some punctuation?

⋯⋯⋯⋯⋯⋯⋯⋯⋯ Did You Know? ⋯⋯⋯⋯⋯⋯⋯⋯⋯

Some writers break sentences into parts, leaving one part that is not a complete sentence. These pieces of sentences are called sentence fragments. Using end punctuation and capital letters carefully will help you avoid sentence fragments.

Sentence and fragment: Please stay with me. Until the work is done.

Corrected sentence: Please stay with me until the work is done.

Sentence and fragment: We planned to go on a picnic. After it stopped raining.

Corrected sentence: We planned to go on a picnic after it stopped raining.

Show What You Know

Read the following paragraph. Underline the four sentence fragments.

For a long time, people believed that they had to eat a lot of meat. In order to be healthy. They ate meat. Whenever they could. Today we eat more whole-grain foods. Like bread, cereal, rice, and pasta. Fruits and vegetables are also important. For a healthy diet.

Score: _____   Total Possible: 4

Proofread

Find three sentence fragments in the paragraph below. Correct the sentence fragments by using proper proofreading marks for end punctuation and capitalization.

Example: I love to eat candy, Whenever I can.

　　Wendell and his sister Jessica like games. Although they like different kinds. Wendell spends most of his time throwing a ball around. He can move so fast in his wheelchair. That his sister can't keep up with him. Jessica is always looking for someone to play Scrabble with her. She doesn't often ask her brother. Because he can't spell very well. Sometimes they get together and have a swimming race.

Practice

Read the sentence fragments in the box below. Then write four sentences. Use one fragment in each sentence. End punctuation can help make your sentences clear and correct.

after the game	wondering what happened
not a competitor	no way to know

1. _____

2. _____

3. _____

4. _____

Tips for Your Own Writing: Revising ....

Choose a piece of your own writing and look it over carefully for sentence fragments. Then make corrections. Use end punctuation and capital letters correctly to help you make complete sentences.

 Did you see the sign on the good writers' clubhouse door? It read: No Fragments Allowed!

15 Review: Punctuation

A. Use proper proofreading marks to add eight periods to the following paragraph.

There's always something interesting going on in my neighborhood Early this morning, Ms Bonnie Blair challenged me to a race around her Olympic-sized skating rink I took a few swings in the batting cage of Mr Cal Ripkin, Jr Mr David Robinson recently built a new basketball court Last week, he invited Mr Michael Jordan over to shoot some hoops.

Score: _____   Total Possible: 8

B. Use proper proofreading marks to show where seven periods should be placed in this paragraph.

Keith is the busiest friend I know. On Sat he had dinner with the President. Tues morning he recorded a CD with the Atomic Artichokes. He'll be on a world tour from Nov to Feb He plans to finish his new book in early Apr Keith knows he'll be tired out by Sept—he's planning to relax for one hour every Fri morning!

Score: _____   Total Possible: 7

C. Add seven question marks and three exclamation points to the sentences in the following paragraph.

What a happy story that is Didn't Jeannie always want to be a teacher Why was that a problem Didn't she have arthritis when she was a kid Of course she did But didn't she finish college anyway Yes, and didn't she become a teacher She made it, so hurrah for Jeannie Do you think her students will understand how hard she worked Couldn't we tell them

Score: _____   Total Possible: 10

D. **Add three periods, one question mark, and two exclamation points where they are needed.**

In the eighteenth century, lead was discovered in southwestern Wisconsin Miners from Cornwall, a place in Great Britain, came to work in the mines Why did the Cornish people come here They were miners whose mines had closed. What a great opportunity Later on, the Wisconsin mines closed, too How awful

Score: _____   Total Possible: 6

E. **Use the proper proofreading marks to correct three sentence fragments.**

1. Last week we saw a Winnebago storyteller she used signs to tell her story.

2. What do you mean, she used signs, you can't tell stories with signs.

3. This woman did it was just beautiful.

Score: _____   Total Possible: 7

F. **Rewrite the following sentences to correct sentence fragments.**

1. The traffic in any large city is terrible. Because there are so many cars.

2. Why don't people ride the bus? When they need to go downtown.

3. Someday there will be different forms of transportation. Because the air is getting so polluted.

1. _____

_____

2. _____

_____

3. _____

_____

Score: _____   Total Possible: 3

REVIEW SCORE: _____   REVIEW TOTAL: 41

16 Punctuation: Commas in Series and Introductions

 Commas help make a sentence clear.

·························· Did You Know? ·························

Words in a series should be separated by commas.

> The five planets nearest the sun are Mercury, Venus,
> Earth, Mars, and Jupiter.
> Mars, Earth, and Jupiter have satellites.

An introductory word is separated by a comma from the rest of the sentence.

> Yes, those are some facts about the planets.
> No, Mercury and Venus don't have satellites.
> Well, let's find more information about planets.

···

Show What You Know

Read the report below. Add commas between the words in a series and after introductory words.

Some modern structures are best known for their great size. The tallest dams in the United States are in Colorado Arizona Idaho and Nevada. The dams in the United States that hold the most water are in Arizona Montana and South Dakota. The United States also has three of the world's longest bridges. They are in New York California and Michigan.

Yes there were also huge structures in the ancient world. Among these were statues gardens sphinxes and temples. No not all of these are still standing, but you still can see the Egyptian pyramids. All of these structures were the results of work by ancient artists architects engineers and laborers.

Score: _____   Total Possible: 15

Proofread

Six sentences in the following paragraph contain mistakes in the use of commas. Use a caret to add commas where they are needed.

Example: I have my towel, swimsuit, and sunscreen.

Last year Lauren Brody's family tried a different kind of Labor Day celebration. Like many Americans, they usually celebrate with family trips picnics and swimming parties. Last year they traveled to Michigan to take a long walk across the Mackinac Bridge. On Labor Day, the bridge is closed to cars, buses vans, and other vehicles. Walkers runners and wheelchair racers line up to cross the bridge, which is more than 3,800 feet long. The Brodys who planned to do the walk were Lauren, Michael Mother, Dad and Grandpa. The day was warm, sunny and breezy. Yes they all finished the walk and liked the new way to celebrate.

Practice

On another piece of paper, list three of your favorite hobbies or sports. Then use your list to help you write three sentences with words in a series. Begin at least one sentence with the word _well, yes,_ or _no_. Use commas correctly.

_____

_____

_____

_____

Tips for Your Own Writing: Revising ....

Choose a paragraph from a piece of your own writing that you could improve by using names of places, words, or activities in a series. Rewrite the paragraph, using commas to make your series clear for your reader.

**W**ell, now you know ways to use commas in lists, after introductory words, and in a series of ideas!

17 Punctuation: Commas in Dates, Addresses, and Direct Address

Wendy the warrior writer says, "Use commas to divide and conquer your sentences."

Did You Know?

A comma in a date separates the year from other words in the sentence.

On July 4, 1976, the U.S. celebrated its 200th birthday.

A comma in an address separates the name of a state from the rest of the sentence.

The movie was filmed in Cheyenne, Wyoming.

When a person is addressed by name, that person's name is separated from the rest of the sentence by a comma.

William, that movie was so boring I fell asleep.

Show What You Know

Read the letter below. Add commas where they are necessary.

72809 East Saddle Road

Omaha Nebraska 68102

October 5 2000

Dear Andrew and Jennifer,

Andrew you have to come next month to ride with us in the parade. Afterward, we can go to Council Bluffs Iowa for a picnic. Jennifer you wanted to see Arbor Lodge. That's in Nebraska City Nebraska and not far away. We can also go there if you come.

Your friend,

Jerry

Score: _____   **Total Possible: 8**

Proofread

Use a caret to add seven commas in the letter below.

Example: Grandpa‸I understand you're coming for a visit on July 11‸1999.

712 Albert Avenue

Kansas City Missouri 67153

June 6 2000

Dear Grandma,

Mom, Dad, and I have moved around a lot, haven't we? The first time I remember moving was August 5 1993, when we moved into a huge house in Chicago Illinois. I didn't start third grade until after we moved on September 3, 1998. That move was to Kansas City, Missouri which is my favorite place so far. I guess that's all for now Grandma.

Love

Angela

Practice

Write a funny story about these travelers. Use direct address, at least one date, and the name of one or two cities and states.

_____

_____

_____

_____

_____

Tips for Your Own Writing: Proofreading ....

The next time you write a letter, check your use of commas. Use proofreading marks to show changes that you need to make.

 Isn't a comma a convenient little mark?

18 Punctuation: Commas in Dialogue

When writers include people in stories and reports, they often use dialogue to help readers "hear" these people. A comma separates the speaker's words from what is said.

Did You Know?

Dialogue is conversation between two or more persons. Dialogue is always separated from the rest of a sentence by a comma. Notice that the comma is always before the quotation marks.

"I'd like to make a box with three sides," Latisha said. "Then use this pattern, cut it out, and fold it into a box," Jorge told her.

The words that someone says are always separated from the rest of the sentence by a comma.

"I'm sure you all know how to tie a knot," the mathematician told us.

Show What You Know

Read the dialogue below. Add commas to separate each speaker's words from the rest of the sentence.

When Arthur and his friend Albert get together, they often end up having a duel with weird facts that they have read. "It's a fact that picky eaters grow up to be an inch shorter than less fussy eaters" Arthur read while reaching for chips.

"Less fussy doesn't mean eating all the time" mumbled Albert.

"If you eat lots of sugar, you might have low intelligence" Arthur continued.

"You'll eat four tons of potatoes in your life" volunteered Albert.

"You'll drink two thousand gallons of milk in your lifetime, too" said Arthur.

"Don't eat pasta for lunch. It can make you sleepy" Albert mentioned.

"Yeah, but sleeping helps you grow" responded Arthur.

Score: _____   Total Possible: 7

Proofread

Use a caret (∧) to add five commas to these sentences.

Example: "Please read us a book∧" begged the students.

"This is a great mystery story" Miss Lacy said.

"Tell us what it's about" Judith requested.

"Well, all I can tell you is that there is a treasure hidden somewhere here in

Minneapolis" the teacher told them.

"People have looked for it for years" Laura explained.

"The clues to find the treasure map are in chapter five" Miss Lacy told the

class as she held up the book with the bright cover.

Practice

Write a dialogue at least four sentences long for the girls in the picture.

_____

_____

_____

_____

_____

_____

_____

Tips for Your Own Writing: Revising ....

Choose a story you have written that could have dialogue added. Rewrite the story, adding dialogue. Use a comma to separate the speaker's words from other parts of each sentence.

 "I can't imagine a story without dialogue," said Gertie Grammar. Peter Punctuation agreed, "It would surely be boring!"

19 Punctuation: Commas and Sentences

You can often combine two sentences, but be on the alert for two sentences that shouldn't be punctuated as one.

.... **Did You Know?** ....

Two or more sentences written as though they were one sentence are hard to read. To correct this kind of problem, use a comma before the word *and* or *but* to separate the two short sentences.

Incorrect punctuation: I need a world map there's one in here.

Correct punctuation: I need a world map, and there's one in here.

A comma alone is not strong enough to join two sentences. It must be used with the word *and* or *but*.

Incorrect Sentence: I needed a book on iguanas, they were all checked out.

Correct Sentence: I needed a book on iguanas, but they were all checked out.

Show What You Know

Read the report below. Add five commas to correct the sentences.

North America is an interesting continent and it has great variety. There are many types of landforms, such as mountains, deserts, and prairies. Many kinds of animals live here but there are not as many as there used to be. There are still many wide-open spaces in North America but there are crowded cities, too. The United States and Mexico are part of North America. Canada is also in North America, and it is the biggest of the three countries. Farming is important in these countries but more people work in industry. Central America is a part of North America and it is made up of seven countries. In addition, there are many islands in the Caribbean that are considered to be part of North America.

Score: _____   Total Possible: 5

Proofread

Use a caret (^) to show where five commas should be added to correct the sentences in the paragraph below.

Example: One of my favorite sports is basketball ^ but I also like football.

Basketball has become one of America's most popular sports and it can be played outside or indoors. Basketball became an Olympic Game in 1936 but it was invented in 1891. Behind the basket is a backboard and this is usually made of a special type of glass. A team player's name is sometimes printed on his jersey and so is his number. A basketball is filled with air but it cannot weigh more than 22 ounces.

Practice

Match a sentence in Part I with a sentence in Part II to create a new sentence. Use commas and the words *and* or *but* to combine the sentences.

Part I
A hippopotamus is the third-largest land animal.
A hippopotamus has a good sense of smell.
The word *hippopotamus* means "river horse."

Part II
The animal is more like a hog than a horse.
Its vision is only fair.
Only the elephant and rhinoceros are larger.

1. _____

_____

2. _____

_____

3. _____

_____

Tips for Your Own Writing: Proofreading ....

Choose a piece of your own writing. If you have used any incorrect sentences, rewrite them. You might add commas and words like *and* or *but*.

 Commas can help you keep your words from running into each other!

Lesson
20 Review: Commas

A. Use the proper proofreading mark to add six commas to the sentences below.

1. Well anyone who wants to learn about birds should begin with a good book.

2. Yes Chris bought one last week.

3. She told us that she has seen finches woodpeckers blackbirds and sparrows in
her yard.

4. No she hasn't seen a large bird yet, but she hopes that she will.

Score: _____   Total Possible: 6

B. Use the proper proofreading mark to add three missing commas in this E-mail letter.

Sharon in my last note I told you about the visit to the Raven House in Fargo

North Dakota. Let me know if you want to see the pictures I took. The

photographs were taken January 1 2000.

Score: _____   Total Possible: 3

C. Read the paragraph below. Use the proper proofreading mark to add three commas where they are needed in three sentences.

The meanings of some words will surprise you and you can learn a lot about
words you use all the time. An example is the word *margarine*. Until about a
hundred years ago, there was nothing like the margarine we eat today. People
used butter or lard on their bread and for cooking. Good lard was pearly white
and people began to call it "margarita." *Margarita* is the Latin word for "pearls."
In 1854 a scientist named it *oleomargarine* but this word was too long. Soon
people were calling it margarine.

Score: _____   Total Possible: 3

D. Read the following quotations carefully. Use the proper proofreading mark to add eight commas where they are needed.

"Once a lion fell asleep in the woods" I told my sister Emma. "A little mouse came along and crawled up on him" I said in a scary voice.

"The lion's going to get that mouse!" Emma exclaimed.

"When the lion felt those feet on him, he woke up and roared" I went on. "I'll bet you'd get out of this trouble if you were the mouse," I said to Em.

"That mouse isn't as smart as I" she reminded me.

So I went on. "The mouse told the lion he would help him someday" I said, smiling at my sister.

"I guess he is pretty smart," she said.

"The lion thought that was pretty funny, so he didn't hurt the mouse" I said.

"I can't imagine a mouse helping a lion" said Emma.

"We're both glad he got away, though" I said, and Emma nodded.

Score: _____   Total Possible: 8

E. Use the proper proofreading mark to add fourteen commas where they are needed in the book review.

On July 20 1969 Vivian and Gil Staender flew to the Brooks Range of Alaska. They were flown north from an area near Fairbanks Alaska in a small plane but the pilot of the plane who took them returned right away to the south. They planned to stay for a year in this Arctic spot. Yes it took courage but the Staenders had planned well. After the plane left them, Gil spoke. "It certainly is quiet here" he said. Everything was new. "Viv listen" Gil would often say. They were soon able to hear the sounds of moose bears wolves hawks and falcons.

Score: _____   Total Possible: 14

REVIEW SCORE: _____   REVIEW TOTAL: 34

21 Punctuation: Quotation Marks and Commas in Dialogue I

Quotation marks that point out a speaker's exact words help readers make sense of a piece of writing.

···················· Did You Know? ····················

A quotation begins and ends with quotation marks.

> "Somebody cut down all the milkweed," Dr. Alvin complained.
> "I don't like that. The monarch butterflies won't come," said Kwok.

When a comma separates the quotation from the rest of the sentence, the comma comes before the closing quotation mark.

> "Well, let's plant more milkweed," suggested Alicia.

Show What You Know

Read the dialogue below. Add quotation marks before and after each speaker's words.

Cathal and his sister Colleen were searching a book of names for babies. I'm glad we get to name the twins, said Colleen.

Me, too, agreed Cathal.

Here's a great name, cried Colleen as she held up the book. We could call the girl Melissa.

I want to call the boy Collin, Cathal said.

OK, then we'll call the girl Constance, his sister stated firmly.

We'll all have the same initials, warned their dad.

Score: _____   Total Possible: 14

Proofread

Use proper proofreading marks to add eight quotation marks where they are needed.

Example: "Monarch butterflies feed on milkweed," said Alicia.

1. It took more than thirty minutes for that storm to pass, Joe said nervously.

2. "This is our home, so we are used to these storms, Agnes told him.

3. Look, the moon is rising now, Grandmother pointed out.

4. That means there will be no more storms for a while," Agnes stated quietly.

5. Parts of the Southwest where you live, Joe, have few storms, but they can be strong ones, too," Grandmother warned.

6. When you live here in the mountains, you get used to severe weather," Agnes added.

Practice

Write four statements about the weather where you live. Then write a dialogue between you and a visitor from a place that has different weather. Use quotation marks and commas to show the exact words of both speakers.

_____

_____

_____

_____

_____

Tips for Your Own Writing: Revising ....

You can often make a written report stronger and more interesting by adding quotations. Find a piece of your own work that could be improved by adding quotations or dialogue. Rewrite the piece. Use commas and quotation marks carefully.

 A story without dialogue is like a day without playtime!

22 Punctuation: Quotation Marks and Commas in Dialogue II

Quotation marks and commas help your reader keep tabs on who's saying what to whom.

·························· **Did You Know?** ·························

A quotation can be divided into parts. In a divided quotation, use a comma to separate both parts of the quotation from the rest of the sentence.

> **Undivided:** "Geese can travel all day without stopping until evening," the scientist told us.
>
> **Divided:** "Geese can travel all day," the scientist told us, "without stopping until evening."
>
> **Undivided:** "We often hear them coming, and they head directly for our cornfield," the farmer said.
>
> **Divided:** "We often hear them coming," the farmer said, "and they head directly for our cornfield."

Show What You Know

Read the paragraphs below. Add quotation marks and commas where they are needed.

We're here because we know we need clean water the group leader began and we're worried that it's becoming polluted.

My dad says they used to drink water from the creek a girl from a ranch told us but I certainly wouldn't do that today!

We get all of our drinking water from a well behind the house a boy from a small town said and some days I think it smells funny. I'm afraid it won't be good much longer.

Some days a city kid announced our tap water is sort of gray.

Well the leader agreed it looks like we all need some help.

Score: _____   Total Possible: 30

Proofread

Use proper proofreading marks to add five commas and nine quotation marks to the dialogue below.

Example: "Spiders have eight legs, said Ms. Web, and they spin silk."

"It has wings, six legs, and a light body," Miss Brave Bird said, so it's a butterfly." She looked right at me. "Is that right?" she asked.

Well, sure I answered that's what butterflies look like." For some reason, a few kids were giggling.

"Listen to this sentence then she said and see if you agree with it, too.

"If it has wings, six legs, and a light body" she repeated, it's a moth.

"I'd better look it up," I told her. Miss Brave Bird smiled.

Practice

Rewrite these quotations as divided quotations.

1. "A lepidopterist studies insects, including butterflies and moths," I told Mother.

2. "I know butterflies are out in the day, but I don't know about moths," she said.

3. "Butterflies fold their wings vertically, and moths fold theirs horizontally," I added.

1. _____

_____

2. _____

_____

3. _____

Tips for Your Own Writing: Proofreading ....

Choose a story you have written using quotation marks. Have you used quotations that might sound better if you rewrote them as divided quotations? If so, revise your work.

Divided quotations and undivided quotations in the same story will give your sentences some variety and keep your writing from being dull.

23 Punctuation: Quotation Marks in Titles

Quotation marks are used for more than quotations.

Quotation marks are used to set off the titles of reports, short stories, and poems.

> The class put together a report on caring for the environment. They called it **"Take Care of That!"**
> They had read Mitsumasa Anno's story, **"The King's Flower,"** about respecting little things.
> They also read a poem called **"Song of the Pop-Bottlers"** by Morris Bishop.

Show What You Know

Add quotation marks around titles of reports, poems, and stories in the paragraphs below.

Do you like to read stories? Stories come from all over the world. Abiyoyo is about magic and comes from South Africa. Remaking the World is a story told by the Brule Sioux. The Fox and the Grapes is a fable from Greece.

Perhaps you love poems. People seem to write poems about anything, even sometimes about weird things. Aileen Fisher wrote Noses after looking into her mirror. Things To Do If You Are a Subway is a poem by Bobbi Katz. Rudolph Is Tired of the City is a poem by Gwendolyn Brooks.

If you ever write a report about the kinds of things you like to read, you'd have to think of a title. Titles should get the reader's attention. Here are two titles—Mixed-up People with Mixed-up Tales and Reading I Liked—that could be used for a report. Which one would attract your attention?

Score: _____ **Total Possible: 16**

Proofread

Use proper proofreading marks to add ten missing quotation marks to the titles below.

Example: When I was very young, my favorite nursery rhyme was ˇLittle Boy Blue.ˇ

1. "Narcissa is a poem by Gwendolyn Brooks.

2. Rudyard Kipling's The Way Through the Woods" is a serious poem.

3. My two favorite poems are Silver and Bones by Walter De La Mare.

4. Small Star and Mud Pony is an old Pawnee tale.

5. Did you read the story The Thirteen Clocks" by James Thurber?

6. Gotcha" is a very interesting report on new books.

Practice

Think of four people or animals you know who would be good subjects for a funny poem or story. Write one sentence about each one. Then write a great title you might use if you decide to write the story or poem.

BEWARE OF GOOSE

_____

_____

_____

_____

_____

_____

_____

Tips for Your Own Writing: Proofreading ....

Choose a report, short story, or poem you have written. Use proofreading marks to show where quotation marks should be placed.

 Have you read the new report "A Thousand and One Uses for Quotation Marks"?

51

24 Punctuation: Book and Movie Titles

Do you write with a pen or on a computer? It will make a difference when you write some kinds of titles.

.... **Did You Know?** ....

There are special rules for writing titles of books and movies.

When the name of a book or movie is published, or is printed on a computer, the title is shown in italic type like this: *Babe.*

> *How to Make a Mummy Talk*
> *Where in the World Is Carmen Sandiego?*

When the name of a book or movie is written by hand, the title is underlined.

> How to Make a Mummy Talk

Show What You Know

Circle the titles of books and movies in the story.

For her tenth birthday, Rosa Garcia's mother bought her a book about a ten-year-old girl who was also named Rosa. Rosa de Jong lived in Holland during World War II, more than fifty years ago. The name of the book about her life is Dancing on the Bridge of Avignon. Then Rosa Garcia found a paperback book about a boy who had also lived during World War II. Yankele lived in Poland. That book's title is Along the Tracks. Rosa thought both books were sad but very interesting, so she and her mother watched an old movie about the war. The movie's title is Mrs. Miniver, and it helped Rosa see the war through an Englishwoman's eyes. Together, Rosa and her mother read another book about two kids escaping from the war. The title is She Flew No Flags. It was harder to read, but Rosa thought it was exciting and romantic and not as sad.

Score: _____   **Total Possible: 4**

Proofread

Underline the titles of two books and two movies below.

Example: They have made the book <u>The Hunchback of Notre Dame</u> into a movie.

Two books I'd like to read are:

1. Strange Journey Back by Paul McCusker

2. Stranger in the Mirror by Allen Say

Two videos I'd like to see are:

1. Strangers in Good Company

2. D2: The Mighty Ducks

Practice

Make a list of two favorite books and two movies you enjoyed. Write a sentence describing each one. Perhaps you can share your list with a friend.

_____

_____

_____

_____

_____

_____

_____

Tips for Your Own Writing: Proofreading ....

Choose a report you wrote on a book or movie. Are all titles written correctly?

When you're typing on a computer, remember to use italic type for titles of books and movies. When you write, underline them!

25 Punctuation: Friendly Letters

Do the friends and relatives who get letters from you see that you know how to write a really good letter?

.... **Did You Know?** ....

A friendly letter has five parts. You will use some type of punctuation in four of the five parts.

> **Heading:** Place a comma between the name of the city and the state. In the date, place a comma between the day and the year.
>
> **Greeting:** Place a comma after the name of the person to whom you are writing.
>
> **Body:** Use commas and other punctuation correctly in every sentence.
>
> **Closing:** The last word in the closing should be followed by a comma.
>
> **Signature:** No punctuation is needed.

Show What You Know

Add ten commas where they are needed.

Heading →
  4224 North 24th Street
  Chicago Illinois 60409
  June 3 2000

Dear Andrew ← **Greeting**

Body

  Yesterday I was in Olean with Dad, and we visited your grandparents. They took us out to lunch in a nice restaurant. They laughed when I ordered just a hamburger. Yes I also ordered ice cream. Dad had pasta bread salad ice cream and coffee.

  Your grandparents talked about you a lot and they really seemed to enjoy having visitors who knew you. Come to our house for a week this summer. Then maybe we can go to see them together.

Closing → Your friend

Signature → *Jake*

Score: _____   Total Possible: 10

54

Proofread

Find the punctuation errors in the letter below. Use proper proofreading marks to add four commas and a period.

Example: Gina‸can you meet me in Denver‸Colorado, on May 16?

18 Western Boulevard

Butte Montana 59701

October 16, 2000

Dear Grandmother

    Remember when you read <u>Jumanji</u> to us? Well now it's a movie. If

you see it, let me know if you liked it. I loved it.

    You should come here next summer We'd have a lot of fun.

Love

Susan

Practice

Write the body of a letter to a friend or relative who lives in another town. Tell about something that made you think of him or her. Copy the letter onto another piece of paper, adding the other four parts.

_____

_____

_____

_____

_____

Tips for Your Own Writing: Proofreading ....

Look at the letter you just wrote. Check to see that you used commas appropriately in the heading, the greeting, and the closing of your letter.

 Punctuation helps you make your point!

26 Punctuation: Business Letters

✏️*A business letter is a formal letter. It must be clear and have no errors in capitalization or punctuation.*

.... **Did You Know?** ....

A business letter has six parts.

1. **Heading:** Put a comma between the name of your city and state and between the day and the year.
2. **Inside Address:** Put a comma between the name of the city and state and add any punctuation marks used in the name of the company or person to whom you are writing.
3. **Greeting:** Put a period after the abbreviation for a person's title, and a colon after the name or the greeting *Sir* or *Madam.*
   Example: Dear Mr. Watson:
4. **Body:** Use commas and other punctuation correctly.
5. **Closing:** A comma follows the last word.
6. **Signature:** No punctuation is needed except for initials.

Show What You Know

Add six punctuation marks where they are needed.

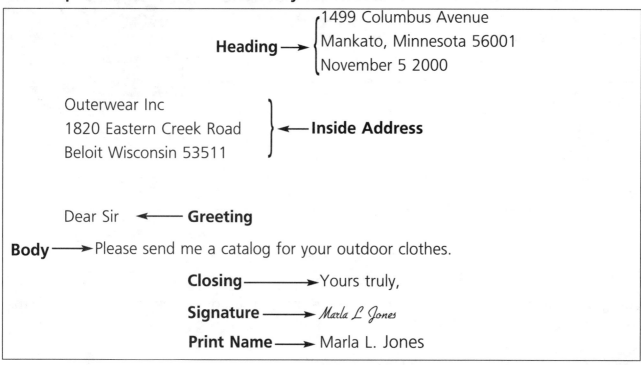

```
                                    ⌈1499 Columbus Avenue
              Heading ──→ ⎨Mankato, Minnesota 56001
                                    ⌊November 5 2000


Outerwear Inc                          ⎫
1820 Eastern Creek Road      ⎬──  Inside Address
Beloit Wisconsin 53511         ⎭



Dear Sir  ←─── Greeting

Body ──→Please send me a catalog for your outdoor clothes.

              Closing ─────→Yours truly,

              Signature ───→ Marla L Jones

              Print Name ──→ Marla L. Jones
```

Score: _____   **Total Possible: 6**

Proofread

Find five punctuation mistakes in the letter below. Use proper proofreading marks to show corrections.

Example: We live in Grand Rapids∧Michigan⊙

1929 May Boulevard

Kansas City Kansas 66106

October 1 2000

Games for You

12 Rush Street

Grand Junction Colorado 81501

Dear Ms. Green

    Thank you for sending your catalog. I want to order Item 6682, the game "Let Me Help." A check from my father is enclosed

        Yours truly,

        Joey Waters

Practice

Write the body of a business letter to the President of the United States. Tell the President what you like best about the nation. Copy the letter onto another piece of paper, using the correct form for a business letter.

_____

_____

_____

_____

_____

_____

Tips for Your Own Writing: Proofreading ....

When you write a business letter, check your punctuation carefully. Did you use commas in the heading, the inside address, and the closing? Did you use a colon in the greeting?

 People won't take your letters seriously if the letters have lots of mistakes.

27 Review: Quotation Marks

A. Use proper proofreading marks to show where eight quotation marks should be placed in the following sentences.

1. Everybody likes watching basketball on TV, Aki said.

2. I think you're wrong, Jessica told her.

3. Carl said, Jessica is right, because I'd rather play than watch.

4. Well, we're watching it now, anyway, Aki told them.

Score: _____ Total Possible: 8

B. Use proper proofreading marks to show where to add five commas and ten quotation marks in the following sentences.

Winds can reach 65 miles an hour during a storm here a ranger told us as

we set up camp.

A tent won't be any protection in that kind of storm Angela said.

We'll turn on our radio several times a day Mr. Simon promised her. He said

That should warn us in plenty of time if a storm is coming.

The ranger added Then you will all come to the cabins if the weather gets bad.

Score: _____ Total Possible: 15

C. Use proper proofreading marks to show where to add ten quotation marks.

Yaeko wrote a report called Something to Do This Weekend. He listed two

poems and two stories he thought his friends would enjoy.

Stories

Blue Moose by Manus Pinkwater

The Case of the Stolen Yacht by Walter Myers

Poems

The Bat by Theodore Roethke

Explanations by Aliki Barnstone

Score: _____ Total Possible: 10

D. Underline fourteen titles in the sentences below.

1. If you liked <u>Morning Girl</u> by Michael Dorris, you will love his newer book, which is called <u>Guests</u>.

2. You'll find mystery stories by Walter Dean Myers in <u>Smiffy Blue, Ace Crime Detective</u>.

3. Shel Silverstein wrote and illustrated a book of poems called <u>A Light in the Attic</u>.

4. If you liked J.K. Rowling's book <u>Harry Potter and the Sorcerer's Stone</u>, you can find other books by the same writer.

5. Gail Carson Levine's book, <u>Ella Enchanted</u>, offers a twist on the Cinderella story. Is it as good as her other book, <u>The Princess Test</u>?

6. Do you read science fiction? Try <u>The Arkadians</u> by Lloyd Alexander.

7. Carol Fenner's book, <u>Yolonda's Genius</u>, is about an African-American girl.

8. If you read aloud to younger kids, try <u>Twist with a Burger, Jitter with a Bug</u> by Linda Lowery and <u>A Drop of Rain</u> by Wong Herber Yee.

9. Lois Lowry has written many popular books. <u>Number the Stars</u> and <u>The Giver</u> both won Newbery awards.

10. Try <u>The St. Patrick's Day Shamrock Mystery</u> by Marion M. Markham if you want something easy and fun to read.

Score: _____   Total Possible: 14

E. Write a one-sentence movie review for two of your favorite movies. Underline each movie's name.

1. _____

2. _____

Score: _____   Total Possible: 2

REVIEW SCORE: _____   REVIEW TOTAL: 49

59

28 Usage: Verbs—Came/Come, Rang/Rung, Sang/Sung

Today we sing. Yesterday we sang. We sang a song we had sung before. Verb forms tell you when something has happened.

.... **Did You Know?** ....

Some verbs have two forms that you can use to tell about past actions. Notice how the spelling of these verbs changes when the verb has a helping word with it. Three of the most common helping words are *have*, *has*, and *had*.

I **came** home late yesterday.
Have you ever **come** too late for something important?

I was late because the school bell **rang** early.
It **had rung** early in the morning, too.

My cousins **sang** a great song.
They **had sung** it before, but I hadn't heard it.

Show What You Know

In each space below, write one word from the pair of words at the top of the paragraph.

came, come

Summer has _____, and the goat herders are moving their flocks. In
                    1
earlier years, when summer _____ early, they moved the animals sooner.
                          2

rang, rung

Many years ago, one goat often wore a bell. The flock would follow the

bell. If the bell had _____ from far off, the herder knew something was
                     3
wrong. A bell that _____ nearby signaled that the flock was near.
                  4

sang, sung

Cowhands are herders, too. There are stories about cowboys who sing to

their herds to keep the animals calm. Many of the songs these herders

_____ are well known today. Perhaps you have _____ them in school.
5   6

Score: _____   Total Possible: 6

Proofread

Read the sentences. If an underlined word is not used correctly, draw a delete mark through the word and write the correct word above it. There are four mistakes.

Example: She had ~~sing~~ very nicely.
sung

All of Megan's friends had <u>come</u> to a party to help her celebrate getting
₁

well again. Megan's grandmother <u>come</u> late from work, but she was glad to see
₂

everybody.

At the party they ate and ate and ate, and then they <u>sang</u> songs. Everything
₃

that they had <u>sang</u> was new to Grandma. "I bet you learned all of those songs
₄

from your CDs," she said.

Just as the party was getting really fun, the doorbell <u>rung</u>. Terri's Dad had
₅

<u>come</u> to take her home. Soon, the doorbell had <u>rang</u> for every guest, and only
₆   ₇

Megan and her family were left.

Practice

Write a story, a poem (some of the words in this lesson rhyme), or sentences. Use each of these verbs at least once: *sang, sung, rang, rung, came, come.*

_____

_____

_____

_____

_____

Tips for Your Own Writing: Proofreading ....

Choose a piece of your own writing and look for verbs used in this lesson and for other verbs that have several forms. Did you use helping words such as *has* or *had* with forms such as *rung* and *sung*?

 Have you (sang, sung) a song to celebrate finishing this lesson?

61

29 Usage: Verbs—Took/Taken, Gave/Given, Ate/Eaten

In the right place at the right time—the right verb form will get you there.

.... **Did You Know?** ....

Some verbs have one spelling when they tell about the past without a helping word and another spelling when they follow a helping word. Some helping words are verbs such as *have, has, had, was,* and *were.*

We each **took** an apple for the horses to eat.
We **have taken** apples with us every time we have gone to the farm.
Eva, though, **has taken** a box of sugar cubes before.

Eva **gave** her favorite horse some sugar cubes.
She **has given** all the best treats to that lucky horse!

The horses came to the fence and **ate** the apples.
When all the apples **were eaten,** we went for a ride.

Show What You Know

In each space below, write the correct word from the pair of words in parentheses at the end of each sentence.

1. Public television has _____ viewers many nature programs. (gave, given)

2. If you have _____ advantage of these programs, you probably know a lot

about animals in distant places. (took, taken)

3. One nature program _____ exciting facts about lions and hyenas. (gave, given)

4. Viewers learned that these animals often _____ the same foods. (ate,

eaten)

5. After the lions have _____, they are ready to sleep. (ate, eaten)

6. Students who _____ time to watch these programs found them

interesting. (took, taken)

Score: _____   Total Possible: 6

Proofread

Look at the word in bold type in each sentence. If a word is used incorrectly, draw a delete mark through it. Then write the correct form of the word above it. There are five mistakes.

Example: The horse had ~~ate~~ eaten all the hay.

1. "Who **given** us the directions to get here?" Michael asked.

2. "Well, I was **gave** the wrong ones," complained Jennifer.

3. "Yes," agreed Karl. "If I had **took** those directions, I'd be lost."

4. "I **took** them," said Colin. "And I got here!"

5. "Well, you're so late that we have already **ate.** Ask Mom for more sandwiches if you're hungry," Maggie told them.

6. "I've **ate,** so I'm not hungry," Michael replied.

Practice

Write a paragraph of at least four sentences about the picture. Use at least one of the words _gave_, _given_, _ate_, _eaten_, _took_, and _taken_ in each sentence.

_____

_____

_____

_____

_____

_____

Tips for Your Own Writing: Proofreading ....

Read aloud a piece of your writing. Do all of your verb forms sound right? Check to see that you used the correct verb form.

Have you (took, taken) care to use verbs correctly? You have been (gave, given) rules in this lesson.

30 Usage: Verbs–Began/Begun, Fell/Fallen, Went/Gone

✏️ **W**riters with good timing learn the verb forms that tell when in time the action takes place.

······················ **Did You Know?** ························

Began, begun, fell, fallen, went, and *gone* are among the words that need special attention. One in each pair of these words needs a helping verb. Some helping verbs are *have, has, had, was,* and *were.*

> Marilyn **began** to enjoy poetry.
> She **had begun** reading poems a year ago.

> Marilyn says a book of poetry **fell** in front of her.
> Do you think she would read math all the time if a math book **had fallen** at her feet?

> Anyway, she **went** right to the poetry section.
> She liked the poems so much that she **has gone** to that section often.

··

Show What You Know

If the underlined word is used correctly, write C in the space. If it is used incorrectly, write the correct form of the word.

1. It was October, and leaves <u>began</u> to fall. _____

2. That meant the cranes had <u>began</u> traveling south. _____

3. Along the Platte River, cottonwood leaves <u>fell</u> into yellow piles. _____

4. Soon, visitors arrived, kicking through leaves that had <u>fell</u>. _____

5. As the cranes <u>began</u> to arrive, more visitors came to watch them. _____

6. Scientists <u>went</u> to the river, too. _____

7. They stayed until the last cranes had <u>went</u> south. _____

Score: _____   Total Possible: 7

Proofread

Read the story below. If the word in bold type is used incorrectly, draw a delete mark through it. Then write the correct word above it. There are five mistakes.

went
Example: They ~~gone~~ to the store.

Bryan watched all day, but no snow **fell.** First, he had **went** to the kitchen, then he **went** to the window in the front room. Still, no snow had **fell.** Finally, Bryan **gone** to the basement to get his toboggan. He found it in the corner, covered with dust. He filled a pail with some warm, soapy water and **begun** to wash the toboggan. "Well," he said, "if it ever does snow, I'll be ready." Bryan put the toboggan back in the corner and **went** upstairs. Passing the kitchen door, he looked out. Snow had **began** falling!

Practice

Choose one pair of words: *began, begun; fall, fallen;* or *went, gone.* Write a story in which you use that pair of words at least one time.

_____

_____

_____

_____

_____

_____

Tips for Your Own Writing: Proofreading ....

Next time you write about something that happened in the past, check carefully for verbs that change their spellings when they are used with helping words. Remember, a dictionary can help you find the correct spellings for these verbs.

 Did you ever fall into the trap of mixing up the words fell *and* fallen?

65

Lesson
31 Review: Verbs

A. **Write in the blank the word that correctly completes each sentence.**

1. Scientists have _____ to the ocean to study the dolphins. (came, come)

2. Last year many _____ from far away. (came, come)

3. At the oceanarium, trainers have _____ bells to have dolphins do tricks.

   (rang, rung)

4. In the ocean, no bells _____ as the beautiful animals circled gracefully.

   (rang, rung)

5. Those who listened said the dolphins _____. (sang, sung)

6. They have always whistled or _____ to talk to one another. (sang, sung)

                                    Score: _____   **Total Possible: 6**

B. **Write in the blank the word that completes each of the six sentences.**

(took, taken)

   A diver _____ a camera underwater. He has _____ a tank with
                    1   2

enough air to keep him safe for an hour.

(gave, given)

   He knows these dolphins and has _____ them names. He says they
                                        3

_____ one another names long ago.
       4

(ate, eaten)

   The dolphins _____ as they swam together. When dolphins have
                        5

_____ the food in one area, they will move away.
       6

                                    Score: _____   **Total Possible: 6**

C. Write in the blank the word that correctly completes each of the six sentences.

1. People's interest in dolphins _____ long ago. (began, begun)

2. Scientists had _____ studying the intelligent animals. (began, begun)

3. They noticed that the number of dolphins had _____ in some areas. (fell, fallen)

4. Why the number _____ was not known. (fell, fallen)

5. Sometimes the dolphins simply _____ away. (went, gone)

6. Where, and why, had they _____? (went, gone)

Score: _____   Total Possible: 6

D. Write in the blanks the ten words that correctly complete each sentence.

The audience had known the program would be good because the students

had _____ concerts before. Students holding handbells had _____
   1(gave, given)   **2**(rang, rung)

the bells in perfect order. Then the chorus had _____ winter songs.
                                         3(sang, sung)

As the audience _____ home, they said they were glad they had
                 4(went, gone)

_____.
5(came, come)

    Most of those who _____ were friends and families of the students.
                   6(came, come)

They knew the children worked hard every time they _____ a concert.
                                            7(gave, given)

They _____ their handbells at long practices and _____ hard
    8(rang, rung)   **9**(sang, sung)

songs over and over to get them right. The students had _____ to a lot
                                                  10(went, gone)

of work for this concert.

Score: _____   Total Possible: 10

REVIEW SCORE: _____   REVIEW TOTAL: 28

67

32 Usage: Verbs—Sit/Set

Sometimes people spell words the way they hear them pronounced. Say the words sit *and* set *until you can hear the difference.*

.... **Did You Know?** ....

Sit means "to take a seat." **Sitting** and **sat** are other forms of **sit**. **Sitting** shows an action that is going on. **Sat** shows an action that happened in the past.

> Do you **sit** in the same seat on the bus every day?
> I **sat** there yesterday.
> I **have sat** there every time I have taken the bus.
> Are you **sitting** there now?

Set means "to put something in a place." **Set** has one other form: **setting**.

> Please **set** the pizza on the table.
> I **have set** the plates on the table already.
> You should be **setting** the glasses on the counter.

Show What You Know

Write *sit, sat, sitting, set,* or *setting* in each space in the following paragraphs.

Do you know the story of Jack Sprat who _____ down at the table and
₁

asked for lean meat? His wife, who was _____ across from him, said she
₂

would eat the fatty parts. They were the kind of people who always ate the

same food and _____ in the same place. Maybe they would have had more
₃

fun if they had _____ at a different table and eaten different food.
₄

Then there's the story of Dr. Foster who went to Gloucester when it was

raining. He _____ his foot down in a big puddle. The story says Dr. Foster
₅

wouldn't go to Gloucester anymore. What if he had _____ his foot in a dry
₆

spot? I don't think that _____ your foot in one puddle should make you
₇

dislike a whole town. Of course, the story says that the puddle was "up to his

middle." I guess he really had _____ his foot in a puddle!
₈

Score: _____   **Total Possible: 8**

68

Proofread

Draw delete marks through the five words in bold type that are not correct. Write the correct form above each word.

set
Example: He has ~~sat~~ the table for dinner.

The crystals in the geology museum were **set** out in rows on a table. "No two crystals are exactly alike," said a guide who was **sitting** labels next to the crystals. He pointed to the label of a green crystal as he **sat** it down. The label said "Beryl Crystal." A white crystal with needlelike edges had been **set** inside a closed glass box. "This is like asbestos," the guide said as he **sat** its label down next to it. "Its needles are soft."

A boy who was **setting** at the table said he owned a crystal with hard needles. "It's gray, not silvery like this one," he said. He **sat** there a long time, examining every crystal. Some museum visitors were invited to **set** on the floor to listen to a lecture on crystals.

Practice

Write four sentences. Use *sit, sat,* and *set* at least one time each.

1. _____

   _____

2. _____

3. _____

4. _____

Tips for Your Own Writing: Proofreading ....

Next time you write about someone *sitting* or *setting,* stop and ask yourself, "Is this person taking a seat or putting something in place?" This test will help you choose the right word.

 *D*on't just sit there! Learn the difference between sit *and* set.

33 Usage: Can/May, Of/Have

When their meanings or sounds are similar, words sometimes get mixed up.

.... **Did You Know?** ....

Can **means "to be able to."**

> **Can** you ice skate? (Are you able to ice skate?)
> **I could** skate better if I had my own skates. (I would be
> able to skate better if I had my own skates.)

May **means "to be allowed to."**

> Your mother says you **may** go skating with the class.
> (You are allowed to go.)

**The meanings of the words *of* and *have* are not alike at all,
but they can be mixed up because they sometimes sound
alike. Read these sentences aloud:**

> I **could have** gone skating.
> I thought **of** going yesterday.

**Think how most people would say the first sentence: I
could've gone skating. When you hear the sentence, it is
easy to hear *could of*. When you write, make sure you use
the correct spelling: *could've*.**

Show What You Know

Write *may* or *can* in each space in the sentences.

I'll climb the mountain if you think I _____ make it to the top! The
                                              1
ranger said we _____ have permission to camp overnight. _____ you
                      2   3
play a guitar? We want music at our campfire. I'm glad my parents said I

_____ come to this camp again.
       4

Write *of* or *-'ve* in each space in the sentences.

We would _____ skated better if it weren't so cold. We all learned a
                 5
lot _____ new skating moves, though. We all should _____ brought
        6   7
our own skates. Then we might _____ stayed longer, too.
                                     8

Score: _____   Total Possible: 8

70

Proofread

Draw delete marks through any incorrect words in bold type. Write the correct form above each incorrect word. There are four mistakes.

Example: You ~~can~~ ^{may} have some cookies.

A tornado **can** do great damage. Ask neighbors if you **can** go into their basements in case of a tornado. During the storms last summer, more people should **of** taken shelter. Earlier warning would also **of** helped people avoid injury. Have you heard **of** any tornadoes in your part of the country? Ask if sometime you **can** visit a weather center and talk about storms.

Practice

Write a sentence using *can* and a sentence using *may*. Then, write three more sentences using *should've* or *might've*, and *heard of*.

1. _____

_____

2. _____

_____

3. _____

4. _____

5. _____

Tips for Your Own Writing: Proofreading ....

Using *of* in place of *have* or *-'ve* is a common error in writing. Next time you write, remember that *have* or *-'ve* follows helping words such as *might, could, would,* or *should.*

 Should've, would've, could've—don't let of get in the way of correct writing.

34 Usage: Verbs–Let/Leave

*D*on't let these words mix you up; if you know what they mean, you can leave confusion behind.

.... Did You Know? ....

Let means "to allow" or "to permit."

> Will your parents **let** you come to the concert with me?

Leave means "to go away from" or "to allow something or someone to remain as is." *Left* is the form of the word *leave* used when speaking or writing in the past tense.

> When you **leave** the room, don't **leave** the door open.
> I hope you **left** those papers the way they were.

Leave and *let* have the same meaning in just one case. Either word can be used.

> Please **leave** me alone.   Please **let** me alone.

Show What You Know

Write *let, leave,* or *left* in each sentence below.

1. The librarian _____ us use a tape recorder to listen to Shel Silverstein's funny poems.

2. We didn't _____ a single book of his poems on the shelf.

3. My friend Harold should have _____ his other tapes at home!

4. He kept taking my tape—he wouldn't _____ me alone.

5. Knowing how to use the library catalog will _____ you find other books of poems.

6. Don't _____ the library without *A Drop of Rain* to read to a younger brother, sister, or friend.

Score: _____   Total Possible: 6

Proofread

Five of the words in bold type are used incorrectly. Draw a delete mark through each incorrect word and write the correct word above it.

Example: Please ~~leave~~ *let* us go to the movies.

The Feldman family **left** for vacation in South Dakota the day school ended.

"**Leave** me ride in the front, please," Morley said.

"We may **let** you at home," teased his father. They had planned to **let** their

dog Poppy behind. At the last minute, Sarah decided she couldn't **let** without

Poppy. Dad **let** the dog climb into the back of the car. Then Morley started

teasing Poppy.

"**Leave** him sit still," said Sarah. While driving across Iowa, Sarah said to her

family, "Now, everybody, **let** me alone so that I can read all about South Dakota."

Practice

Write a story in which you use the words *let* and *leave* at least twice. Use the picture for story ideas.

_____

_____

_____

_____

_____

_____

Tips for Your Own Writing: Proofreading ....

See if you can find a piece of your writing in which you used *let* and *leave*. To test whether you chose the right word, substitute *permit* for *let,* and *go away from* or *allow someone or something to remain* for *leave*. If the sentence still makes sense, you will know that your word choice was correct.

 Let us leave no stone unturned when looking for mixed-up words.

35 Review: Verbs

A. Write *set, sat,* or *sitting* in each blank to correctly complete each of the five sentences below.

Chairs had been _____ up for Joseph's party guests. The guests
  1
_____ in a circle around a huge birthday cake. They _____ the
  2   3
birthday gifts they had brought on a big rock nearby. Quickly, Joseph reached

out, grabbed the cake, and _____ it on the ground. The elephant paid no
                              4
attention to the guests who were _____ there, waiting to celebrate his
                                      5
birthday.

Score: _____   **Total Possible: 5**

B. Write the word *can* or *may* to complete each of the six sentences below.

You _____ use this pool only if a lifeguard is present. Members
     1
_____ bring one guest. If you _____ swim, you _____ may use
  2   3   4
the deep end of the pool. Good swimmers _____ sign up to pass
                                            5
Intermediate Tests. Swimming _____ be fun or dangerous. Be careful!
                                6

Score: _____   **Total Possible: 6**

C. Write *of* or *-'ve* in the blanks to correctly complete each of the five sentences below.

My friends couldn't find enough _____ the books they wanted to read
                                    1
yesterday. They all wanted to read *Guests,* but should _____ checked first
                                                            2
to see that there were enough copies of the book in the library. Some of them

could _____ read *Morning Girl.* Then they might _____ shared their
         3   4
ideas about the two stories. It seems that many _____ my friends like the
                                                    5
same kinds of books.

Score: _____   **Total Possible: 5**

D. Write the word *let, leave,* or *left* to complete each of the following eight sentences.

"Please _____ me alone—I need to think," said Kevin. Our parents had
_____ us at the zoo by mistake. We were supposed to go at 3:00, but we
didn't _____ the big cat house on time. "I wish the zookeeper would
_____ me feed the tigers," Kevin said. The tigers wouldn't _____ the
door where the zookeeper was preparing to feed them.

"We should go now," I said. "Mom and Dad might _____ us here."

"They would never _____ us stay here!" Kevin said, laughing. Our
parents found us where they had _____ us—at the ice cream stand.

Score: _____   Total Possible: 8

E. Complete each of the eight following sentences with one of the following: *sit, set, of, -'ve, let, leave, can,* or *may.*

1. _____ you play an instrument?

2. My grandmother wouldn't _____ me touch her new piano.

3. I knew I could _____ played it because I had taken piano lessons.

4. But Grandma said, "You _____ not play this piano."

5. "She's afraid I might break it or _____ something on the keys," I said to myself.

6. "I'll show you how to play it before you _____ today," Grandma said.

7. Later she said, "_____ here beside me." Then she pushed a button.

8. The piano began to play by itself! Now I knew why she treated it as if it were made _____ gold.

Score: _____   Total Possible: 8

REVIEW SCORE: _____   REVIEW TOTAL: 32

Lesson
36 Usage: Adjectives That Compare

✏️ *One way to compare things is to use different forms of an adjective. Use one form of an adjective to compare two things. Use another form to compare three or more things.*

.... **Did You Know?** ....

Most adjectives can be compared by adding *-er* to compare two things, and *-est* to compare more than two.

> Hyenas are **fast** runners. Gazelles are **faster** than hyenas. Cheetahs are the **fastest** of all.
> A hippopotamus is a very **large** mammal, but an elephant is **larger**. The **largest** of all is the whale.

Some adjectives are compared by placing the word *more* or *most* in front of the adjective.

> Deer are **frequent** visitors to our camp, but black bears are **more frequent** than the deer. The **most frequent** visitors are raccoons.

To compare some adjectives, change the word completely.

> Our back porch is a **good** place to watch deer.
> The park at the edge of town is **better** than the porch.
> The **best** of all places is the beach on Summer Lake.

> The mosquitoes are **bad** this year.
> Some people say they were **worse** two years ago.
> Everyone agrees the **worst** year was 1990.

Show What You Know

Write the correct form for each adjective shown in parentheses.

1. This path is _____ than that one. (safe)

2. This is the _____ view in the park. (good)

3. Would you be _____ on a raft than in a canoe? (comfortable)

4. Upsetting the canoe was the _____ accident I ever had! (scary)

5. Ms. Jason was _____ than I was. (helpful)

Score: _____   Total Possible: 5

Proofread

Draw delete marks through the four incorrect adjectives. Write the correct form above each incorrect word.

Example: That classroom is the ~~smaller~~ smallest one in the building.

My aunt's garden was more pretty than the one at home. "I'm taking gooder care of the roses this year than I did last year," she said. Just then, my cousin brought in the redder rose we had ever seen. "I may enter the best rose competition at the fair," said my aunt.

"Choosing the winner will be the easy decision in the world for the judges," I said.

Practice

Write a sentence using a comparative form of each word in parentheses.

1. (tall)

_____

2. (silly)

_____

3. (wise)

_____

4. (dangerous)

_____

5. (good)

_____

Tips for Your Own Writing: Revising ....

Choose a piece of writing in which you compared things. Rewrite your description, using as many adjectives that compare as possible. Remember to add -er or more when comparing two things, and -est or most when comparing more than two.

 Be sure to check spellings when you add endings to words in a comparison.

37 Usage: Adjectives and Adverbs

*A*djectives and adverbs are easy to mix up. Here are some ways to keep them straight.

Did You Know?

Adjectives describe nouns or pronouns. Adjectives can come just before a noun, or they can come after a verb.

The men sang a **loud** song about buffalo.
Those huge buffalo were **loud**.

Adverbs usually tell how, when, or where something happens.

The buffalo called **loudly** to one another.

Some adjectives and adverbs are very much alike. Writers and speakers must think carefully to use the correct form. Many adverbs end with -*ly*.

The beaver was **quiet**.
The deer moved **quietly** through the trees.

Show What You Know

Choose the correct word from the pair of words in parentheses and write it in each space in the sentences below.

This was the _____ picnic of the year. We _____ found a
1 (final, finally)   2 (final, finally)
nice place to eat. A deer appeared, moving _____ . All of us sat
3 (slow, slowly)
_____ and watched it.
4 (quiet, quietly)

"There aren't many deer left here," Grandfather said _____ .
5 (sad, sadly)

We were _____ as we listened to him.
6 (quiet, quietly)

"Well, we at least saw this one," Mother reminded us _____ .
7 (gentle, gently)

Score: _____   Total Possible: 7

Proofread

Draw delete marks through the five incorrect words in the following sentences. Write the correct form above the incorrect word.

                       loud

Example: The crowd was too ~~loudly~~.

"Drive careful," the officer warned everyone. "Animals crossing the road

move slow."

A bear appeared next to the car very sudden. It swung its head back and

forth angrily. "Roll the window up quick!" James shouted.

Suddenly the bear moved away. It walked silent into the trees.

Practice

Choose four of these words and write a sentence using each: *slow, slowly, soft, softly, wild, wildly*. Write something about the picture.

1. _____

  _____

2. _____

  _____

3. _____

  _____

4. _____

  _____

Tips for Your Own Writing: Proofreading ....

Look over a story you wrote in which you used dialogue. Adding adjectives and adverbs may make the dialogue more interesting and vivid for your reader.

 *T*ry not to write sentences like "Sing soft" or "Do that quicker."

38 Usage: Your/You're, Its/It's

If two words sound exactly alike, how can you tell which spelling to use? Here are some facts to help you.

.... Did You Know? ....

Your is a pronoun that shows possession. It always comes before the name of something or someone.

> We saw **your** cousin at the show yesterday.
> Was she wearing **your** hat?

You're is a contraction. It is the shortened form of the two words "you are." The apostrophe means that the letter *a* is missing from *are.*

> **You're** going to the show tomorrow, aren't you?
> I'll bet **you're** going to be early, as usual!

Its is a pronoun that shows possession. It always comes before the name of something.

> **Its** mane was huge and made the lion look scary.

It's is a contraction. It is the shortened form of the two words "it is." The apostrophe means that the letter *i* is missing from *is.*

> **It's** very clear that the lion is dangerous.

Show What You Know

Write *your, you're, its,* or *it's* in each space in the following report.

If _____ a computer user, you know that when a problem arises with
      1

_____ computer it is called a "bug." _____ a term that was first used
  2   3

more than fifty years ago when a computer malfunctioned. The programmer

found a dead moth in _____ interior. _____ presence there was
         4   5

probably not the cause of the problem. If you have a problem with a computer,

_____ not going to be able to blame moths. _____ probably not
  6   7

_____ fault, either.
  8

Score: _____   **Total Possible: 8**

80

Proofread

Read the sentences below. Draw a delete mark through each incorrectly used word, and write the correct word above it. There are eight mistakes.

Example: ~~You're~~ *Your* dog was barking.

"You're turn has come," the fox leader told Alla. She heard it's voice but could not see the beautiful red animal.

It's cool in the forest. That is why Alla and her brother Karsh had moved into it's shade.

"Your next," the leader's voice reminded them. Together, they crept slowly out of the forest, stopping at it's edge.

"Your almost there," the voice whispered. Quietly, Karsh and Alla walked toward a baby fox and its proud mother.

"Oh, its just beautiful," Alla sighed.

"You're new baby is a treasure to behold," Karsh told the fox leader.

Practice

Use *its, it's, your,* and *you're* in a story of your own. Use the picture for ideas or write from your own imagination.

_____

_____

_____

_____

Tips for Your Own Writing: Proofreading ....

Choose a report you have written and check it carefully for the four words you studied in this lesson. Remember, *your* and *its* show possession and always come before the name of someone or something. Use *you're* for "you are" and *it's* for "it is."

 You're *going to find* it's *easy to use these words correctly—with practice.*

39 Usage: There/Their/They're, Here/Hear

Words that sound alike but are spelled differently and have different meanings are called homophones.

Did You Know?

There **may mean "in that place," or it may be used to introduce a sentence before a word such as** *was, were, is,* **or** *are.* **The word** *here* **is in the word** *there,* **which may help you remember.**

> We found the treasure chest right over **there**.
> **There** were pieces of gold in the chest.

Their **means "belonging to them."**

> The pirates said the chest was **their** property.

They're **means "they are."**

> **They're** not going to like it if we take their treasure.

Here **may mean "in this place," or it may be used to introduce a sentence.**

> Let's leave the treasure **here**.
> **Here** is the map that we used.

Hear **means "to listen." The word** *ear* **is in** *hear,* **which may help you remember.**

> Didn't you **hear** the pirates' warning?

Show What You Know

Read the sentences below. Write *their, there,* or *they're* in each space.

Many people work hard to develop _____ muscles. _____ are
                                                1   **2**
some muscles that you can control. _____ called voluntary muscles.
                                            3
_____ are also involuntary muscles, which you cannot control.
  4

Write *here* or *hear* in each space.

_____ is a fact you may not know. You have about 700 muscles.
    5
Would you like to _____ more information about your muscles?
                          6

Score: _____   Total Possible: 6

Proofread

Draw delete marks through the four incorrect words in the poem below. Write the correct word above each incorrect word.

Here
Example: ~~Hear~~ are the papers you lost.

Now, here this tale of two travelers in space.

They're trip through the universe became a bad race.

"Here is the goal," one said to his friend,

"But their is a quick way to get to the end."

There still on the way and may never be found.

They found the "quick way" was the *long* way around!

Practice

Write four sentences about the travelers in the poem. Use *there*, *their*, *they're*, *hear*, and *here* at least once each.

1. _____

   _____

2. _____

   _____

3. _____

4. _____

Tips for Your Own Writing: Proofreading ....

Choose a piece of your writing and check it carefully for mistakes in the use of the three homophones *there*, *they're*, and *their.* You may want to trade writing with a friend and check each other's work. Remember, *they're* tells *who; their* tells *whose;* and *there* tells *where.*

 *T*here, they're, their, now! That wasn't hard, was it?

40 Review: Adjectives, Adverbs, Homophones

A. Write the word in the blank that correctly completes each of the five sentences below.

Lupe won the medal for the _____ vegetable garden in the
  1(better, best)

neighborhood. Joel's garden was voted the _____ of all. Donna's
  2(baddest, worst)

watermelons were the _____ on the block. Mr. Stern's corn was
  3(sweeter, sweetest)

good, but Mr. Castle's was _____. Mrs. Meloy's zucchinis were
  4(better, best)

_____ than anyone else's.
5(bigger, biggest)

Score: _____   **Total Possible: 5**

B. Write the word that completes each of the five sentences below.

1. Some plants will grow _____ in sandy soil. (easy, easily)

2. Other plants even grow _____ in plain water. (rapid, rapidly)

3. Marina sings to her plants, but not _____, though. (loud, loudly)

4. She says singing makes them grow more _____. (quicker, quickly)

5. "Just sing _____, please," her mother teases her. (soft, softly)

Score: _____   **Total Possible: 5**

C. Write *its, it's, your,* or *you're* to correctly complete each of the five sentences below.

_____ not enough just to like gardens. _____ garden will be a
    1   2

success only if you know how to grow plants. Writer and illustrator Tasha Tudor

wrote about a garden _____ sure to like. _____ bright colors are
                          3   4

exciting. _____ idea of gardens will grow if you read Tudor's book.
              5

Score: _____   **Total Possible: 5**

D. Write *their, there, they're, your,* or *you're* to complete each of the six sentences below.

Long ago _____ were gardens to help win a war. During World
          1
War II, the government asked people to grow vegetables in _____
                                                          2
gardens. If you had a garden, you shared _____ vegetables.
                                         3
   Everyone agreed, "_____ able to grow a garden if you have a yard!"
                     4
Some people even planted _____ tiny gardens in window boxes.
                         5
   "_____ being creative," their neighbors admitted.
    6

Score: _____   **Total Possible: 6**

E. Write fourteen words to correctly complete the sentences below.

Long ago, _____ was an unusual garden _____.
          1(there, their, they're)   **2**(here, hear)

_____ bed was built on the side of a hill, where _____ was
3(Its, It's)   **4**(there, they're, their)

very little room. Small bells rang _____ to keep birds away, and people
                                   5(soft, softly)

could _____ the music. The garden had the _____
      6(here, hear)   **7**(tallest, most tall)

sunflowers and the _____ tulips anyone had ever seen. _____
                   8(tiniest, tinier)   **9**(Its, It's)

success was assured because all the neighbors did _____ best
                                                  10(there, their, they're)

to help. _____ the flowers grew _____ than in the next
         11(Here, Hear)   **12**(brighter, brightest)

town. Today people still like to _____ about beautiful gardens because
                                13(here, hear)

_____ are not many of them anymore.
14(there, their, they're)

Score: _____   **Total Possible: 14**

REVIEW SCORE: _____   **REVIEW TOTAL: 35**

41 Usage: Plural Nouns

There's more than one way to write words that refer to more than one thing.

.... **Did You Know?** ....

A singular noun refers to one person, place, or thing.
> A **blackbird** lives near the pond.

A plural noun refers to more than one person, place, or thing. Most plurals are formed by adding -s.
> Those **blackbirds** are beautiful.
> The farmer has three **donkeys**.

If a word ends with *ch, x, s, ss,* or *sh,* add -es to form the plural.
> Red **foxes** are quick and quiet.
> Aren't **walruses** ugly?

When a word ends with a consonant and the letter *y*, change the *y* to *i* and add -es to form the plural.
> Six **ponies** are spotted, but one pony is not.

For some words that end with the letter *f*, change the *f* to *v* and add -es.
> Those **calves** are twins. One **calf** is brown.

Words that end in *o* are tricky. Some form the plural by adding -s. Others add -es to form the plural. Look up in a dictionary the words you need to know. Then, memorize them.
> That **burro** is small, but **burros** are very strong.
> Dad asked if I wanted a baked **potato** or mashed **potatoes**.

....

Show What You Know

On the lines below, write the correct plural ending of each underlined word.

Cut two orange _____ in half. Then slice two peach _____ or
　　　　　　　　1　　　　　　　　　　　　　　　　2

tomato _____. Cut two hard-boiled egg _____ in half and put everything on
　　　　3　　　　　　　　　　　　　　　4

dish _____. Add a few sandwich _____ and some chips if you are really hungry.
　　5　　　　　　　　　　　　6

Proofread

Draw delete marks through the seven incorrect plurals in the sentences below. Write the correct word above each incorrect word.

Example: We put all the books onto three ~~shelfs~~. *shelves*

1. The science museum is an interesting place, with tiny flys in a large glass case.

2. Pretty boxies hold valuable things, like rare watches and golden ringes.

3. Laser demonstrations were shown to large groupes every half hour.

4. Modeles of animals were exhibited in various areas.

5. On the museum bookstore shelves are studys of leaves, echoes, and elfs.

Practice

Write five sentences about detectives. Use the plurals of these words: *penny, box, key, knife, hero, radio.*

1. _____

_____

2. _____

_____

3. _____

_____

4. _____

5. _____

Tips for Your Own Writing: Proofreading ....

Next time you write, pay close attention to the plural nouns that you use. Memorize the rules for forming plural nouns so that you can automatically recognize mistakes.

 Hang on to that dictionary for the words that end in o!

Lesson

42 Usage: Irregular Plural Nouns

 For help with some plurals, make the dictionary your friend!

.... **Did You Know?** ....

Plural forms for some nouns follow no pattern.
> The **geese** flew south. One **goose** was left behind.

Some singular and plural nouns are the same.
> That **deer** has a white tail. Many **deer** live in the city.

A few plurals are formed by adding *-en.*
> Babe was a blue **ox.** Two **oxen** pulled wagons.

Sometimes abbreviations written with capital letters are used as words. To form their plurals, add a lowercase *-s.*
> The store had all the **TVs** tuned in to the ball game.

To form the plural of some hyphenated words, add *-s* **to the first part of the word.**
> Marty had two **sisters**-in-law.

Some plurals can be formed in more than one way.
> The plural of *fish* is *fish* or *fishes*.

Some singular and plural nouns both end in *-s.*
> Please bring six **scissors** to the table.
> Will you please hand me a pair of **scissors?**

....

Show What You Know

Write the correct plural form above the singular word in parentheses.

1. Presidents are also called (commander-in-chief).

2. The backyard was filled with (goose).

3. For supper we ate the twelve (fish) Grandmother caught.

4. You can get any type of music on (CD).

5. Are (ox) really as strong as they look?

6. All of the servers wore blue shirts and (pants).

Score: _____   **Total Possible: 6**

Proofread

In the sentences below, there are four mistakes in the spelling of a plural. Draw a delete mark through each incorrect word and write the correct word above it.

Example: There are many ~~gooses~~ *geese* in the pond behind my house.

José's grandfather raises oxes on his farm. José and his

brother-in-laws help take care of the crops and the farm animals. They

sometimes see deers in the fields, and they enjoy the songs of many species of

birds.

Sometimes the men like to roll up the legs of their jeans and go fishing.

They caught eight fish last weekend. José's sisters prefer watching movies to

fishing. They can watch movies on the six TVies in their house.

Practice

Write four sentences about a problem in the picture. Use at least three plural words.

1. _____

_____

2. _____

_____

3. _____

4. _____

Tips for Your Own Writing: Proofreading ....

You may not have a lot of these irregular plurals in your own writing. However, proofreading a piece of your own writing will help you catch any spelling mistakes you have made when writing any kind of plural noun. Make corrections if you find mistakes.

"Oh, give me a home where the buffalo/buffaloes/buffalos roam." Which one should it be?

43 Usage: Possessives

Nouns have a form that shows ownership or possession.

.... **Did You Know?** ....

The possessive of a singular noun is formed by adding an apostrophe and -s.

> Elena**'s** hat   Cass**'s** jeans

The possessive of a plural noun that ends in *s* is formed by adding only an apostrophe.

> the teams**'** caps   the players**'** awards

The possessive of a plural noun that does not end in *s* is formed by adding an apostrophe and -s.

> children**'s** clothing   men**'s** jackets

The possessive of a hyphenated noun is formed by adding an apostrophe and -s to the last word.

> his brother-in-law**'s** warm-up jacket

....

Show What You Know

Write the correct possessive form above each underlined word.

Liz thought it would be cool to visit the past. She thought her

<u>great-grandmothers</u> quilt was beautiful. She wondered how hard the <u>women</u>
      1   **2**

work was if they had to take time to make quilts. Did a farm <u>familys</u> day begin
                                                            3

early? Were the <u>children'</u> chores hard? Would she ever know her ancestors'
                         4

stories?

Score: _____   Total Possible: 4

90

Proofread

Use proper proofreading marks to show where an apostrophe or -'s is needed in four words in the paragraph below.

Example: That is my dad's car.

Two artists paintings hang in the museum. The paintings are by Berthe Morisot and her brother-in-law Edouard Manet. The woman picture is of a mother with two children. One child clothes are dark. Her brother-in-law work shows a garden.

Practice

Use the following words in a story about or a description of a picture you have seen or about an imaginary picture you would like to paint.

bears'   horse's   hero's   children's

_____

_____

_____

_____

_____

_____

_____

_____

Tips for Your Own Writing: Proofreading ....

Look at a story you have written and see where using possessives might improve the story. If so, make the changes. Remember, the rules for forming the possessives of singular and plural nouns are different. Read the old and the new versions. Keep the better piece of writing.

 **W**hose is it? The apostrophe will tell you where to look!

44 Usage: Plurals and Possessives

Most plurals end with s. Most possessives end with s. There's an important difference between plurals and possessives, though.

.... **Did You Know?** ....

The plural of most nouns is formed by adding -s or -es to the singular.

> boy—boy**s**   day—day**s**   store—store**s**   brush—brush**es**

The plural of many other nouns is formed by changing the last letters of the singular form and adding -s.

> knife—kni**ves**   grocery—grocer**ies**   lady—lad**ies**

The possessive of most nouns is formed by adding an apostrophe and -s.

> man**'s**   girl**'s**   shop**'s**   Mrs. Sands**'s**

The possessive of plural nouns that end in s is formed by adding only an apostrophe.

> teachers**'**   artists**'**   shoppers**'**   waiters**'**

Show What You Know

If the underlined word is plural, write *Pl* above it. If it is singular and possessive, write *SP*. If it is plural and possessive, write *PP*.

Many <u>shops</u>₁ at the mall sell <u>kids'</u>₂ shoes. A <u>lady's</u>₃ jewelry store attracts many <u>customers</u>₄ around Mother's Day. A sign on another store is for <u>gentlemen's</u>₅ hairstyles, but that shop is not very busy. <u>Teens'</u>₆ clothes are a big seller. <u>Clerks</u>₇ in these stores can help you put together outfits.

<u>George's</u>₈ two brothers work in a sporting goods store at the mall. George is always eager to visit his <u>brothers'</u>₉ store.

In the music store, <u>customers'</u>₁₀ orders are filled quickly because of the large stock. <u>Elena's</u>₁₁ favorite store is the music store. I share my <u>friend's</u>₁₂ love of music, too.

Score: _____   **Total Possible: 12**

Proofread

Each of the five sentences contains one mistake in the writing of a possessive or a plural noun. Draw delete marks through the incorrect plurals and write the correct words above them. Use proper proofreading marks (ṽ) to show where apostrophes are needed.

Example: I know where those boy's ~~watchs~~ ^{watches} are hidden.

1. Who borrowed Miss Marks copy of the big dictionary?

2. Borrower's rules are on the chart in front of the desk.

3. Please read them before you take books off the shelfs.

4. The jackets that library helpers wear are from the womens and men's

departments in the store at the mall.

5. Will you help in the library? We need volunteers to unpack boxs of books.

Practice

Write four sentences about a shopping trip you have taken. Use at least two plurals and two possessives in your sentences.

1. _____

_____

2. _____

_____

3. _____

4. _____

Tips for Your Own Writing: Proofreading ....

Next time you write, use possessives to add detail to your descriptions or dialogue. Before you write, review the differences between plurals and possessives.

 The position of an apostrophe tells you how many owners a thing has.

45 Usage: Contractions

When you speak, you may pronounce two words as if they were one. For example, instead of saying, "I have not been there," you might say, "I haven't been there." Read on to find out how to make contractions in your writing.

Did You Know?

A contraction is a shorter way to say and to spell two words. When you write, you use an apostrophe to show where you have left out a letter.

The computer store **was not** open that evening.
The computer store **wasn't** open that evening.

You are learning to use your computer.
You're learning to use your computer.

In questions, the order of words may be changed when a contraction is used.

Can you **not** understand why we need a computer?
Can't you understand why we need a computer?

Why **did** she **not** listen during class?
Why **didn't** she listen during class?

Show What You Know

Circle the two words in each sentence that can be combined to form a contraction. Write the contraction on the line at the end of the sentence.

1. The class had not visited Shedd Aquarium before. _____

2. "It is home to thousands of beautiful fish," the guide said. _____

3. "Please do not tap on the glass," she added. _____

4. "That is very disturbing to the fish." _____

5. At the Shedd, there is a giant squid hanging from the ceiling. _____

6. You can not see some of the fish because they hide so well. _____

7. You will want to go to the main aquarium at feeding time. _____

8. A diver will get into the tank; she will feed the fish. _____

9. They are from many different parts of the world. _____

Score: _____   Total Possible: 18

94

Proofread

Use proper proofreading marks to show where six apostrophes are needed below.

Example: I don̬t want to go.

Why wasn't the team on the field? The Jayhawks hadnt forfeited a game in years!

"Wheres everyone?" the coach asked.

Sam grew impatient; he didnt understand his teammates. "Weve waited a long time for this game," he said to himself. "But now theyre all late. We'll probably have to forfeit the game."

At last, the team's van arrived. "Sorry we're late," the assistant coach called.

"Im the only one who is warmed up," Sam thought. "At least Coach can count on me."

Practice

Write four sentences about the picture. Use the contraction for each of the following words at least once: *will not, should not, he will, she is, that is.*

1. _____

   _____

2. _____

3. _____

4. _____

Tips for Your Own Writing: Proofreading ....

Proofread a piece of your own writing in which you used dialogue. Look for pairs of words that might be written as contractions. Read aloud the dialogue using the contractions. Does it sound better? Dialogue often sounds more natural if contractions are used.

 Contractions are usually not used in business letters and other kinds of formal writing.

Lesson
46 Review: Plurals, Possessives, Contractions

A. There are five misspelled plurals in the following paragraph. Draw delete marks through the misspelled words. Write the correct spellings above the words.

Where I live, leafs begin to fall in the monthes of September and October. The familys in our neighborhood go to the lake for a fall picnic. One neighbor brings ponys for the kids to ride. Most of us play softball and eat sandwichs, corn, and peaches.

Score: _____   Total Possible: 5

B. Four plural words are spelled incorrectly in the following sentences. Draw delete marks through the misspelled plurals and write the correct spellings above them.

The mayor, her sisters, and her brother-in-laws march in the Memorial Day parade. The event is watched on TVes all over town. On the holiday, people dress in their old shirts and jeanes. Children play in the parks, scaring away deers and birds. Along the riverbank, people enjoy the sunshine and try to catch as many fish as they can.

Score: _____   Total Possible: 4

C. There are eight mistakes in the paragraph below. Use proper proofreading marks to show where an apostrophe or an apostrophe and -s should be added to a word.

In western Nebraska, the early settlers families faced hard times. All of the family members had to work from sunrise to sunset. A farmer land was usually sandy, so the settlers crops were often poor at first. The childrens school was far off. A womans day was filled with hard work around the home and in the fields. But many people stayed in the state dry region despite the hardships. They would even invite an uncle or a brother-in-laws family to join them in Nebraska.

Score: _____   Total Possible: 8

D. **The following report has six mistakes in plurals and possessives. Use proper proofreading marks to correct the mistakes.**

A report in our citys newspaper stated that many big store's have bad spelling habits. A photograph showed a mistake. The sign in the story said Mens Shoes instead of Mens Shoes. The writer said these are foolish mistake's. Writer's for ad company's should know better.

Score: _____   Total Possible: 6

E. **On the line at the end of the sentence, write a contraction for the underlined words.**

1. <u>Nothing is</u> more fun than taking pictures.   _____

2. "<u>Do</u> cameras <u>not</u> break easily?"   _____

3. "<u>Is</u> it <u>not</u> hard to choose the right film?"   _____

4. "I <u>would not</u> have any idea how to get good pictures."   _____

5. "Let Uncle Ed take pictures; <u>he will</u> get good ones."   _____

6. "You <u>can not</u> expect me to take a photo!"   _____

7. These are some excuses, but <u>they are</u> not good ones.   _____

8. If <u>you would</u> like to be a photographer, get started now.   _____

Score: _____   Total Possible: 8

REVIEW SCORE: _____   REVIEW TOTAL: 31

97

47 Usage: Verb Tense

 Verb forms are the clue to the past, present, and future.

.... Did You Know? ....

The past tense of a verb tells you that something happened in the past.

The past tense of most verbs is formed by adding *-ed.*

> I love to **learn** new songs. I **learned** a funny one yesterday.

The past tense of verbs that end in silent *e* is formed by dropping the *e* and adding *-ed.* If the verb ends with a single consonant, double the consonant and add *-ed.*

> The song was about a cowhand who had to **saddle** a horse.
> After he had **saddled** it, it refused to move.
> The cowhand tried to **plan** ways to make the horse move, but everything he **planned** failed.

The past tense of some verbs is formed by changing the spelling of the verb.

> I like to **sing.** I **sang** the saddle song over and over.
> I **know** that I **knew** all the words perfectly yesterday.
> I **think** I've forgotten them, but I **thought** I had them memorized.

Show What You Know

Write the correct past-tense verb above each underlined verb in the paragraph below.

I <u>think</u> television <u>is</u> unhealthy for kids. We <u>sit</u> around too much. How many
  1   2   3

of us <u>play</u> sports every single day? <u>Are</u> most teens in sports? You say that you
    4   5

<u>skate</u>? You <u>love</u> hiking? Well, most kids <u>walk</u> very short distances! We all <u>plan</u> to
 6   7   8   9

exercise, right? Next week, be able to say, "I <u>exercise</u> every day!"
                                                10

Score: _____　　　Total Possible: 10

Proofread

Draw a delete mark through each of the two verbs in each sentence below. Then write the correct past-tense form above each verb.

Example: Have you ~~play~~ the piano?
played

    The careful carpenters correct every mistake they find. The scientists work

hard and discover a new medicine. Writers create wonderful poems and

compose exciting stories. Police officers search patiently and solve many crimes.

Teachers make colorful bulletin boards and organize exciting activities. But some

people just sit around and get really lazy!

Practice

Use the past tense of *experiment, boil, write,* and *catch* in four sentences of your own.

1. _____

   _____

2. _____

   _____

3. _____

4. _____

Tips for Your Own Writing: Proofreading ....

Many stories describe events as though they happened in the past. Next time you write a story, try writing it in the present, and then write it in the past tense. Which account sounds better? Stories written in the present tense sometimes capture an excitement and suspense better than those written in the past tense. However, most stories you read are written in the past tense.

 Like magic, you can change present to past by changing the verb tense.

48 Usage: Subject-Verb Agreement I

The ending of a verb may change to match the subject of the verb.

.... **Did You Know?** ....

In the present tense of most verbs, the endings change to match the subject. If the subject is a singular noun or the pronoun *he, she,* or *it,* the verb should end in *-s.*

She **walks** with us.　　　John **walks** for exercise.
It **walks** on its hind legs.　　He **walks** with a cane.

If the subject is a plural noun, or the pronoun *I, we, you,* or *they,* you do not add *-s* to the verb.

They **walk** often.　　I **walk** every day.
You **walk,** too.　　The workers **walk** to the fields.

If the verb ends in *o, ch, sh, ss,* or *x,* add *-es* to the base word for singular nouns, or the pronoun *he, she,* or *it.*

I **fish**　　　Do you **fish?**　　Jason **fishes** every day.

Show What You Know

In the spaces below, write the correct forms of the verbs in parentheses.

1. A camel _____ heavy burdens. (carry)

2. Camels _____ in Africa. (live)

3. The camel _____ a little like some of its relatives in America. (look)

4. You _____ what a llama is, don't you? (know)

5. The furry animal _____ a little like a camel. (behave)

6. A llama, though, _____ not have a hump. (do)

7. A llama _____ a burden, just as a camel does. (carry)

8. The animals _____ many pounds at a time. (carry)

9. A herder _____ the valuable animals. (watch)

Score: _____　　　**Total Possible: 9**

Proofread

In the sentences below, eight of the underlined verbs have incorrect endings. Draw a delete mark through any verb that is spelled incorrectly. Write the correct verb above it.

enjoy
Example: We ~~enjoys~~ riding our bikes.

The cyclists works hard at practice every day. Eliza acts as team leader
        1   **2**

for the track racers. She ride at the rear of the group. She watch for riders who
        3   **4**

are not careful. Team members cycles carefully, even at high speeds. They try not
            5   **6**

to make mistakes that would lose a race. Eliza try to catch every mistake they
                          7

make. The riders feels that it is an honor to be on the team. Eliza know that it is
      8   **9**

an honor to be team leader. She wear her leader's badge proudly.
      10

Practice

Write a story about the shepherd boy in the picture. Describe how he feels about his work. Use at least three of these verbs, adding correct endings: *watch, play, carry, walk, climb.*

_____

_____

_____

_____

_____

_____

_____

Tips for Your Own Writing: Proofreading ....

Choose a piece of your own writing. Check to be sure that verb forms match subjects in your sentences. This kind of review is very important because subjects and verbs that do not agree draw the reader's attention away from your message.

A story should unwind like a ball of yarn; don't let your subjects and verbs get tangled!

49 Usage: Subject-Verb Agreement II

I practice. You practice. She practices. How do you know which verb form to use?

.... Did You Know? ....

When the subject of a sentence is one thing or one person, except *you* or *I*, add an *-s* to the verb.

Alan seems tired in the early morning.

When the subject of the sentence is made up of two singular persons or things joined by *and*, use a verb that does not end in *-s*.

Alan and his trainer seem tired when they come in.

When the subject is made up of two words joined by *or* or *nor*, add an *-s* to the verb unless the word closest to the verb is plural.

Neither **Alan nor his trainer seems** tired.
Neither **Alan nor his friends waste** time.

Take special care when a helping verb comes before its subject, as it does in many questions.

Why **do skaters and coaches** work so hard?

Show What You Know

Underline the words that make up the subject of each sentence. In the blank, write the correct form of the verb in parentheses.

Why _____ readers and television viewers get animal groups mixed up?
    1(do, does)

Often, the viewer and the reader _____ that animals are alike or
                              2(decide, decides)

different because of their appearance. Both the cassowary and the emu

_____ to the group of birds that can't fly. On the other hand, koalas
3(belongs, belong)

and kangaroos seem different, but they both _____ into the same species.
                                        4(fit, fits)

However, the bear and the koala are different and _____ their young in
                                              5(raise, raises)

different ways.

Score: _____   Total Possible: 15

Proofread

Five of the underlined verbs are not correct. Draw a delete mark through each incorrect verb and write the correct form above it.

swims
Example: The team ~~swim~~ every day.

It is dark as Nora and her mother <u>begins</u> their long train journey. Neither her father nor her uncle <u>are</u> with them. Uncle Joshua and his children <u>plan</u> to take a plane at a later date. Dad and Nora's brother always <u>drives</u> when they travel. When boarding the train, either Nora or her mother trips on the step of the train. The women, bags, and the carrying case for the cats <u>falls</u> to the ground. Neither the cats nor people <u>are</u> hurt. The train conductor and all the passengers <u>waves</u> as the train moves away. A new home and new friends <u>promise</u> a new adventure for Nora.

Practice

Write three sentences comparing the two vehicles in the drawing. How are they alike? How are they different?

1. _____

   _____

2. _____

   _____

3. _____

   _____

Tips for Your Own Writing: Proofreading ....

Choose a paragraph from a piece of your writing. Look for sentences that have more than one subject. Check the verbs. Remember which forms need *-s* and which do not.

A subject and a verb in a sentence must agree with each other. Be sure to match them correctly.

Lesson
50 Review: Verbs

A. Write the correct past tense form of the ten underlined verbs in the blank in each sentence.

Yesterday's storm <u>seem</u> _____ to come without warning. Suddenly,

the sky <u>turn</u> _____ the color of charcoal. Thunder <u>shake</u> _____ the

houses. It <u>rattle</u> _____ the windows. Lightning <u>strike</u> _____ the

biggest tree on the block. Some small children <u>cry</u> _____ in fright. When it

was over, everyone <u>celebrate</u> _____. Then some people <u>ask</u> _____

about the storm. No one <u>expect</u> _____ it! It had really <u>surprise</u> _____

them.

        Score: _____   **Total Possible: 10**

B. Use the underlined word in each sentence below to form the correct verb for each blank. Write it in the blank.

1. The swim team is supposed to <u>swim</u> daily, but Andrew _____ only weekly.

2. At the meet we want the other team to <u>chase</u> us, but Andrew always _____ the other team!

3. "<u>Smile</u> if you lose," the coach said. He even _____ at Andrew.

4. Sometimes we <u>succeed</u>. Sofia _____ when she swims one on one.

5. <u>Watch</u> the competition. A good coach _____ other teams carefully.

6. Our team likes to <u>win</u>, but the team that practices a lot _____.

7. Maybe if we <u>practice</u> two hours, we could beat the team that _____ one hour.

        Score: _____   **Total Possible: 7**

C. Write the correct verb form above each of the fourteen underlined verbs in the paragraphs below. Use the present tense.

The news arrives. President Harrison promise land to any settler who come
                                        1   2

to Oklahoma. To Jonas, April 22, 1889, seem like the most important day of
                                         3

his life. The family will have the farm Jonas want to live and work on.
                                              4

Jonas line up with his family and thousands of others. At exactly noon, a
      5

signal is given and Jonas rush across the line. With his family, he choose a good
                          6   7

section of land. His friend Alfred head to a place where he think a town will
                                   8   9

grow. While Jonas hurry to start a farm, Alfred desire to find a place for a town.
                   10   11

Elias, an Osage boy, live in the region. He ask whether his father could help
                     12   13

Jonas set up the farm. Elias know that the Osage have farmed in that area for
                             14

hundreds of years.

Score: _____   **Total Possible: 14**

D. Write the correct verb in each blank.

1. Foxes and wolves _____ out ways to get along. (works, work)

2. Foxes and wolves _____ in the same region. (lives, live)

3. _____ foxes and wolves fight one another? (Does, Do)

4. Foxes and wolves _____ at different times. (hunts, hunt)

5. However, a fox _____ some of the same things as a wolf. (eats, eat)

Score: _____   **Total Possible: 5**

REVIEW SCORE: _____   REVIEW TOTAL: 36

51 Usage: Pronoun Agreement—Compound Subjects

 A compound subject can include both nouns and pronouns.

.... **Did You Know?** ....

A subject pronoun is used when the pronoun is part of a compound subject. Subject pronouns are words like *I, you, he, she, it,* and *they*.

> Gordon Parks lived with his sister in Minneapolis.
> His sister and **he** came from a poor family.
> Both **she** and Gordon worked hard.

When the pronoun *I* is part of a compound subject, the *I* always follows the other word in the subject.

> Both Gordon and **I** are great photographers.

Show What You Know

Circle each correct pronoun in the parentheses. In some sentences, the pronoun is in the wrong order. Write the words in the correct order above the sentence.

My sister and (me, I) thought it would be funny to rewrite the story of the
                        1
"Three Little Pigs." Then my sister and (me, I) read the story we wrote to our
                                              2
parents. The story goes like this:

Well, (me, I) and my family were on a picnic and needed a can opener. Dad
        3
and (I, me) saw some houses on top of a hill. (Him, He) and I walked to the first
       4   **5**
house. We knocked at the house, but there was no answer. (Me, I) and Dad
                                                            6
knocked at the next house, but there was no answer there, either. Finally at the
third house, (we, us) found some pigs at home. The oldest pig opened the door.
              7
(Him, He) and his brothers had a can opener, but they didn't have any food. Dad
    8
and (me, I) invited them to bring their can opener and come to our picnic.
       9
Mom said that (her, she) and my sister were happy to meet them. (Me, I),
                10   **11**
my family, and the pigs had a nice picnic.

Score: _____   **Total Possible: 14**

106

Proofread

Delete two incorrect subject pronouns in the diary entry below. Write the correct form above the incorrect word. Then, in another sentence, the words should be in a different order. Draw a line through the incorrect order and write the words in the correct order above the sentence.

Example:
<u>John and I</u>
~~I and John~~ are going to the movie theater with ~~she.~~ *her*

May 24, 1857

Along the Platte River in Nebraska

Today Father and me saw a lot of buffalo. We needed meat, but I and he

shot only one because there aren't going to be many buffalo someday at the

rate we're going. That's what both Father and Buck Taylor, our guide, say.

Mother says we are lucky. Her and Marie Taylor know how to cook buffalo meat.

Practice

Write a diary entry in which you tell about an imaginary adventure you have with some of the people mentioned in the diary entry above. Use compound subjects with at least one pronoun in two or three sentences. Put the date and place at the beginning of your diary entry.

_____

_____

_____

_____

_____

Tips for Your Own Writing: Proofreading ....

Choose a paragraph from a story or diary entry in your own writing. Look for a compound subject with the pronoun *I*. Remember, in a compound subject, *I* always comes second.

He, she, *and I can be part of a compound subject, but* him, her, *and* me *cannot.*

52 Usage: Pronoun Agreement–Object Pronouns

Joey gave the book to Jan and ___. Is the pronoun I or me correct in this sentence? Don't be fooled when a compound object includes both nouns and pronouns!

···················· **Did You Know?** ····················

An object pronoun (me, you, him, her, it, us, them) is used when the pronoun is part of a compound object; that is, it comes after a verb or a preposition.

> The ranger told the hikers and **her** to watch for bears.
> He warned the campers and **us** to be careful.
> The thought of bears scared both **them** and Mary.

When the pronoun *me* or *us* is part of a compound object, *me* or *us* always follows the other word in the object.

> The huge snake scared Mary and **me.**
> No one warned the hikers or **us** to watch for snakes.

Show What You Know

Circle each correct pronoun in the parentheses.

Our class planned a geography quiz show just for (we, us). First, our teacher
₁ asked (we, us) to list the places we had read about in class. Then he formed
₂ writing groups and asked (they, them) to write questions. The rest of the class
₃ voted for contestants, and they voted for Gloria, Bob, and (I, me). The very first
₄ question eliminated (he, him). Then Gloria answered correctly. Next, the teacher
₅ asked (I, me) the name of the mountain range that runs through Peru. I said,
₆ "The Andes Mountains."

Who won?

Score: _____   Total Possible: 6

Proofread

Delete five incorrect object pronouns in the diary entry below. Write the correct form above the incorrect word. Then, in another sentence, the pronoun is in the wrong order. Delete the words in the incorrect order and write the words in the correct order above the sentence.

Example: The medal was given to ~~she~~ ^{her} by mistake.

June 30, 1857

Today Father and Mr. Taylor told Todd, Jamie, and I to stay with them

as we traveled. There are important places along the trail they wanted

me and my brothers to know about. Gracie and Annie, our older sisters,

followed along after the men and we. It was still early when Father told the girls

and we to stop and listen. I heard a hiss, then a grunt. Mr. Taylor pointed to two

spotted snakes. "Pick them up," he said to the girls and I. "They're harmless."

Gracie looked nervous, but I told she and Annie that they were safe.

Practice

Write a diary entry about an animal you see as you travel on an imaginary journey with the people in the diary entry above. Use a compound object, including a pronoun, in at least one sentence.

_____

_____

_____

_____

_____

Tips for Your Own Writing: Proofreading ································

Review a piece of your writing. Check to be sure you used the correct pronoun in a compound object. For example: Jan wrote **him** and **me** a letter. Jan wrote _him_ a letter. Jan wrote _me_ a letter.

✐ _Remember the object pronouns—me, you, him, her, it, us, them—and you'll make the right choices._

109

53 Usage: Double Negatives

No! Never! None! *are words that have a negative meaning. How many others can you think of?*

.... **Did You Know?** ....

A negative is a word that means "no." Some common negatives are *no, not, never, nothing,* and *none.*

Fishing is **not** allowed in this part of the lake.
There is **nothing** to do but fish in the other part.

Avoid using two negatives in the same sentence.

Incorrect: Susan would **not never** swim in the lake.
Correct: Susan would **not** swim in the lake.
Susan would **never** swim in the lake.

Remember that part of some contractions are negatives. Do not use another negative when the contraction already has *not* in it.

Incorrect: The city has**n't no** lifeguards at the lake.
Correct: The city has**n't** any lifeguards at the lake.
The city has **no** lifeguards at the lake.

Show What You Know

Underline the sentence in each pair that uses negative words correctly.

1. Some writers never use no rhymes in their poems.
   Some writers never use rhymes in their poems.

2. Other writers don't never write without using rhyme.
   Other writers never write without using rhyme.

3. "Warning" by John Ciardi doesn't use no rhyme.
   "Warning" by John Ciardi doesn't use rhyme.

4. Readers might think that Ciardi has no poems that rhyme.
   Readers might think that Ciardi hasn't no poems that rhyme.

5. None of the lines in Carl Sandburg's poem "Arithmetic" rhyme.
   Not none of the lines in Carl Sandburg's poem "Arithmetic" rhyme.

Score: _____   Total Possible: 5

Proofread

Draw delete marks through the six double negatives below and write the correction above each one. There is more than one way to correct each sentence.

Example: She ~~isn't never~~ going to leave again. *(is never/isn't ever)*

When Charlie visits his grandparents, he doesn't never get bored. They have a big backyard filled with birdhouses and feeders. There aren't no cats or dogs in the yard, so the birds aren't never afraid. Charlie has seen finches and red-winged blackbirds at the feeders, but hasn't ever seen a grosbeak. His grandparents said grosbeaks were there once, but none never came this summer.

Until this year, Charlie's grandparents hadn't never seen any bluebirds in the yard. But one day when Charlie was not there, one came. Now Charlie is hoping to see a bird his grandparents haven't never seen.

Practice

Write sentences that answer the following questions about the picture. Use *no, not, none, never,* or any other negative in each sentence.

1. Have you ever seen a bird this large?

2. What would you do if you did see one?

3. Could a bird like this fly? Why or why not?

_____

_____

_____

_____

Tips for Your Own Writing: Proofreading ....

Look for the negatives *no, not, never, none,* and *nothing* in a piece of your writing. Then check for contractions with *not.* They already have a negative, so do not use another negative in the sentence.

 Never, never, never put two negatives in the same sentence!

54 Review: Pronoun Agreement, Double Negatives

A. Circle the correct pronoun in each pair. In three sentences, the pronouns are in the wrong order. Write them in the correct order above the sentences.

Daria and (I, me) took a trip to the Grand Canyon National Park.
1

Me and Daria were among the three million visitors who come to the park each

year. Other visitors and (we, us) began our sightseeing. (She, Her) and (I, me)
2   3   4

walked along the South Rim of the Grand Canyon with five other visitors.

(Them, They) and (I, me) never stopped being amazed by the beautiful views at
5   6

Desert View and Hermit's Rest. Our families joined us and the others as we

reached Mather Point. Later, our families and (we, us) boarded a bus for the
7

North Rim. (We, Us) marveled at the view from Bright Angel Point and Point
8

Imperial. I and they will never forget the beauty of the Grand Canyon.

                                        Score: _____   Total Possible: 11

B. Circle the correct pronoun in the parentheses.

King Midas was kind, but many called (he, him) and his helpers foolish.
1

Midas had a daughter. He loved (she, her) and the rest of his family.
2

Once Midas helped a poor creature who granted (he, him) a wish. Midas
3

told the creature that he and his helpers had decided that they wanted

everything he touched to turn to gold.

Just then his daughter and her friends ran into the room. Midas reached out

to greet (she, her) and her friends. His touch turned (she, her) to gold.
4   5

The teller of this story has a lesson for all adults and (we, us). The storyteller
6

might be telling both (they, them) and (I, me) to be content with what we have.
7   8

                                        Score: _____   Total Possible: 8

112

C. Complete each sentence by correctly writing a pronoun in each of the five blanks.

Do you know some famous fictional pairs? What about Calvin and Hobbes? _____ and Charlie Brown and Snoopy are pairs of characters in cartoon
1
books. Of course, you know Bert and Ernie. Sesame Street was the place where
you found _____ and Big Bird. My brother and _____ have read
2   3
about Paul Bunyan and Babe, another famous pair. The librarian told our mother
and _____ about Mutt and Jeff and Ike and Mike. Oh, I must remind
4
_____ about Hansel and Gretel.
5

Score: _____   Total Possible: 5

D. Draw delete marks through the five double negatives below and write the corrections above them.

Railroad trains haven't never been through Hazel Green. There are other

towns where no trains never went. Sometimes there was a bus route, and

sometimes there weren't none. Many people in small towns couldn't never travel

far from home. Then, more and more people got cars, and soon there weren't no

places you couldn't go.

Score: _____   Total Possible: 10

REVIEW SCORE: _____   REVIEW TOTAL: 34

55 Grammar: Nouns

 *W*hen we want to name things, we use nouns.

Did You Know?

A <u>noun</u> is a word that tells who or what did the action or was acted upon by the verb in the sentence.

The **scientists** search for the **bones** of **dinosaurs**.
They use soft **brushes** to remove the **dirt**.

Nouns can be singular or plural.

They found a small **bone** next to those large **bones**.

Some nouns, called proper nouns, name a specific person, place, or thing: *Paul Sereno* and *South America*. They are always capitalized. Nouns like *fossils* are common nouns. They are capitalized only at the beginning of sentences.

Paul Sereno found many important **fossils** in **South America**.

Proper nouns may be made up of a group of words.

The **Museum of Natural History** houses dinosaur bones.

Show What You Know

Find the twenty-nine nouns in the following report. Circle each noun you find. Some nouns are made up of more than one word, like *prairie dogs*.

The Badlands National Park is in South Dakota. Its rocks, woods, and hills were shaped by wind, rain, frost, and streams. The hills are surrounded by grass. Many animals live there. Visitors can see deer, bison, antelope, coyotes, and prairie dogs. People live in the Badlands, too. Ranchers work on this dry land. Rangers patrol the park. Men and women run stores, hotels, and restaurants.

Score: _____   Total Possible: 29

Practice

Tell a story by writing a noun in each blank.

I visited a _____ in _____ last _____. I saw many _____ there
            1   **2**   **3**   **4**

and ran to the _____ when I heard a _____ that seemed too close.
           5   **6**

Later, _____ and I ate _____ and watched the amazing _____.
     7   **8**   **9**

Revise

Make the following story clearer by writing a more specific noun above each underlined noun or phrase.

The <u>men</u> who were draining the <u>body of water</u> found
  1   **2**

an <u>animal</u> living there. <u>People</u> came to watch as <u>workers</u>
   3   **4**   **5**

tried to move <u>the animal</u>. <u>The people</u> knew <u>these animals</u> will bite
         6   **7**   **8**

and that they are very strong. By the end of the day, <u>someone</u> had caught <u>the animal</u>
                                 9   **10**

and taken it to a <u>park</u> where it would be safe.
           11

Tips for Your Own Writing: Revising ....

Choose a piece of your writing. Look at the nouns you used. Could you make some of them more specific? For example: *shovel* instead of *a tool* or *daisy* instead of *a flower.*

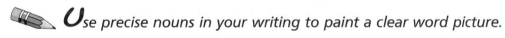 *U*se precise nouns in your writing to paint a clear word picture.

56 Grammar: Pronouns

✎ *By using pronouns, a writer can avoid repeating the same nouns and can tie the ideas together in sentences.*

.... Did You Know? ....

Writers use <u>pronouns</u> to avoid using nouns over and over again. A pronoun can refer to a person, a place, or a thing. The words *she, her,* and *it* are pronouns.

> Franny raced toward **Franny's** goal. **Franny** knew **the goal** was a mile away.
>
> Franny raced toward **her** goal. **She** knew **it** was a mile away.

The form of a pronoun changes depending upon how it is used in the sentence. The pronouns *I, myself, my,* and *me* all refer to the same person.

> **I** wanted to hike there by **myself,** but **my** parents wouldn't let **me.**

Sometimes pronouns make writing confusing. A reader cannot tell if *his* in the first sentence refers to Carl or Jacob. The second sentence makes it clear.

> Carl told Jacob to bring **his** coat.
> Carl said, "Bring **my** coat, Jacob."

Show What You Know

Underline any words that should be changed to pronouns to make the writing smoother and clearer. Write the pronouns above the nouns.

Terri was flying in a hot-air balloon faster than the leader had promised. The wind above the town felt cold. Terri felt uncomfortable and scared. This kind of flying wasn't what the leader had said flying would be, Terri thought. Then another thought came into Terri's mind. The leader hadn't said how Terri could stop flying. Terri remembered a plastic tool in a jeans pocket. Would it help?

Score: _____   Total Possible: 12

Practice

In real life, who flies? What flies? Make a list.

_____

_____

_____

Now, write a three-sentence paragraph about a person, place, or thing on your list. Use nouns and pronouns to make the scene very clear to your readers.

_____

_____

_____

_____

Revise

Delete six nouns in this story that are used too frequently, and write a pronoun above each one.

Joshua felt for the penknife Joshua had put in Joshua's jeans pocket. It would help

when Joshua had to cut branches to sleep on. Joshua did not remember what the ranger

had said about bears. Joshua hoped the ranger had said bears were not in this part of the

park. Joshua will have to spend the night here.

Tips for Your Own Writing: Revising ....

From your own writing, choose a paragraph about a person, place, or thing. Are any pronouns you used confusing? Check to be sure that the reader can clearly see to what or whom each pronoun refers.

 Use pronouns to improve your writing.

57 Grammar: Verbs

Verbs are the hardest workers in a paragraph. With wishy-washy verbs, you'll have a wishy-washy story!

.... **Did You Know?** ....

A <u>verb</u> tells what the person, place, or thing in a sentence is doing, or it links or connects the subject to the rest of the sentence. A verb might tell about being rather than acting. The words *felt and hiked* are verbs.

> The boys **felt** tired as they **hiked** on the trail.

Verbs also show whether something happens in the present, the past, or the future. The word *hike* is present tense, *hiked* is past tense, and *will hike* is future tense.

> Today I **hike.**   Yesterday I **hiked.**   Tomorrow I **will hike.**

Verbs must match their subjects. In the present tense, the verb *walk* changes when its subject is a third-person singular noun, such as *girl.*

> I often **walk** on that trail.
> Girls from my school **walk** on it, too.
> I know a girl who **walks** on the trail every day.

Some verbs express a state of being. The most common verbs that show being are *am, is, are, was, were,* and *be.*

> The cougar **was** huge, and the boys **were** terrified.

....

Show What You Know

Write a correct verb in each blank.

Mountain climbing _____ a popular sport. People _____
                   1   2

mountains for many reasons. Some people _____ the challenge of trying to
                                       3

reach high and dangerous places. Others _____ to explore the outdoors
                                     4

and _____ the beauty of nature. Whatever the reason, mountaineering
     5

_____ serious business. Every climber _____ to work with
   6   7

experienced teachers.

Score: _____   **Total Possible: 7**

Practice

Imagine standing at the top of the world's highest mountain peak. What would you do? Write three verbs to fill the blanks in this sentence.

At the top of the mountain, I _____, _____, and
                                1   2

_____.
   3

Next, write three sentences that use the verbs you chose. Add details to create interesting sentences.

_____

_____

_____

_____

Revise

Write a stronger, more specific verb above each underlined verb.

First, the frightened turtle <u>walked</u> toward the water. Then it seemed to <u>know</u> it could
                                         1   2

not <u>go</u> as fast as the dogs could <u>move</u>. The turtle pulled its head and legs into its shell.
   3   4

The dogs <u>ran</u> up and stopped. They <u>barked</u> and <u>touched</u> the turtle with their noses. Then
          5   6   7

they <u>went</u> away. The turtle <u>moved</u> again toward the sea.
    8   9

Tips for Your Own Writing: Revising ....

Reread a story or poem you have written. Replace some of the verbs to add action and interest to your story. A word like *walk* could be replaced with *march, tiptoe,* or *prance.* Each verb gives a slightly different meaning to the action and provides a different image.

 *V*ivid verbs add vitality to your writing.

119

Lesson
58 Grammar: Adjectives

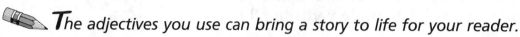 *The adjectives you use can bring a story to life for your reader.*

.... **Did You Know?** ....

**An adjective is a word that describes a noun or pronoun.
An adjective is a word that can fit in both these blanks:**

The _____ tree is very _____.

In the following sentence, the words *smooth, dark, big,* and *green* are adjectives.

The artist had **smooth, dark** skin and **big, green** eyes.

**Adjectives usually come before the words they describe.
Sometimes two or more adjectives describe the same word.
Adjectives may tell *how many, what kind,* or *which one.***

Adjectives sometimes follow a verb.

The bicycle was **rusty.**

Adjectives should be specific. They should help give the reader a clear picture of whatever is being described.

Show What You Know

Circle the twenty-three adjectives in the following paragraph. Do not circle the words *the, an,* and *a.*

The unexpected visitors left their enormous, wooden boats and waded through the rough, warm water to the shore. The visitors were tall and had pale skin. Their dark, long hair was tied back with red, blue, and brown cord. The men's bright clothing covered their bodies. Their wet faces showed that they were tired. The first man to touch shore wore a red cape and a blue hat. He carried a long, black stick, which he pointed at the surprised people standing on the sandy, white shore.

Score: _____   Total Possible: 23

120

Practice

You are visiting a workshop for gymnasts. Think of words that tell what they look like. Write five words that would fill the blank in this sentence: The _____ gymnasts practice.

_____

_____

_____

Next, write two sentences about the gymnasts, using some of the adjectives from your list. Remember, the words that describe the gymnasts are adjectives.

_____

_____

_____

Revise

Write a stronger, more specific adjective or group of adjectives above each underlined adjective that will help give the reader a clearer picture of the story.

The beach was <u>pretty</u> and the sun felt <u>nice</u>. The <u>big</u> lifeguard looked <u>funny</u> on
　　　　　　　　　1　　　　　　　　　　　　　　2　　　　3　　　　　　　　　　　4

the little jet ski, but Michael knew it would be <u>cool</u> to ride one. "Ready?" asked the
　　　　　　　　　　　　　　　　　　　　　　　　　5

lifeguard.

　　"Sure," Michael said, but suddenly he knew it would be a <u>scary</u> ride. "<u>Great</u>," he kept
　　　　　　　　　　　　　　　　　　　　　　　　　　　　　6　　　　　　7

mumbling to himself, even when he fell off the <u>fast</u> machine and swallowed a mouthful of
　　　　　　　　　　　　　　　　　　　　　　　　8

<u>awful</u> water.
9

Tips for Your Own Writing: Revising ....

Choose a piece of your writing. Replace your adjectives with ones that are more specific and interesting. You may want to use a thesaurus to help you find other adjectives to use.

 *A*dding colorful adjectives adds color to your writing.

59 Grammar: Adverbs

Adverbs add a little energy to your verbs. Even a strong verb needs help once in a while.

.... **Did You Know?** ....

An _adverb_ is a word that describes a verb, an adjective, or another adverb. Adverbs tell _how, when, where,_ and _how much._

> The children giggled **wildly** as the clowns ran past. (*Wildly* is an adverb that describes the verb *giggled.*)

> One large clown sat **very** carefully on a tiny stool. (*Very* is an adverb that describes the adverb *carefully.*)

> Another clown carried a **brightly** painted banner. (*Brightly* is an adverb that describes the adjective *painted.*)

Many adverbs end in _-ly: wildly, sadly, quickly, slowly._ However, some common adverbs do not: _almost, not, often, too, very._ Some adverbs are spelled like their matching adjectives: _hard, first, far._

Show What You Know

Find the thirteen adverbs in the following paragraph. Circle each adverb you find. Remember, an adverb will tell _how, when, where,_ or _how much._

The class had studied seriously to learn about the historically important pier. They had finally come to visit it, but it was too crowded to see much. People were packed tightly in the restaurants. The museum was completely filled with visitors. The air-conditioned bookstore felt only slightly cool inside because of the crowds. The lines for the rides were ridiculously long. Why was everybody so happy? Why were they all extremely glad that they had come to this very exciting place?

Score: _____   Total Possible: 13

Practice

Write an adverb in each blank to complete the story.

   Tess, Carol, and Jake _____ got on their bikes

1

and started down the trail. Their aunt had _____

2

agreed to meet them _____ and to take them

3

and their bikes home in her van. Taking the lead, Carol

rode _____. "Do you think we'll make the whole

4

twenty miles?" Tess asked _____.

5

   "Sure!" Jake said _____.

6

Revise

Choose a different adverb that sets a different mood and write it above each underlined adverb below. Adverbs you might choose are *eagerly*, *gently*, *hesitantly*, *rapidly*, *suddenly*, *softly*, *unexpectedly*, and *violently*.

   A canoe ride! Casey ran <u>fast</u> toward the river. Sheila moved more <u>slowly</u>. She liked to

1   2

think about things, and this chance to ride in a canoe had come too <u>fast</u>. The current

3

moved <u>slowly</u> here, so it would be safe, Sheila told herself. Then, <u>surprisingly</u>, rain began

4   5

to fall, <u>a little</u> at first, then <u>hard</u>. The girls turned and ran <u>fast</u> toward the house.

6   7   8

Tips for Your Own Writing: Revising ....

Select a piece of writing you have done. Revise it to include adverbs that help your reader know where, when, or how something happened. Remember—do not overuse the word *very*. Choose adverbs like *quickly* or *rapidly* instead.

*T*ell how. Carefully. *Tell when.* Today. *Tell where.* Outside. *Adverbs add useful details.*

60 Grammar: Articles

There are only three articles in the English language. Using the right one is easy if you listen carefully.

························· **Did You Know?** ·······················

An <u>article</u> is a kind of adjective. There are only three articles: *the, a, an.*

The is a definite article because it identifies a specific noun.

> Beryl Markham was **the** first person to fly solo across **the** Atlantic Ocean from east to west.

A and *an* are indefinite articles because they refer to any one of a group of nouns.

> **A** small plane and **an** unexpected storm made her flight dangerous.

Use the word *a* before words that begin with a consonant sound. Use *an* before words that begin with a vowel sound.

> Markham had been **a** pilot in Africa for many years.
> A compass is **a** useful tool.
> She had flown in **an** open cockpit plane through all kinds of weather.
> She waited **an** hour before taking off.

Show What You Know

Write the correct article *a, an,* or *the* in each sentence.

Elephants from Africa are _____ ones with large, fanlike ears.
1

Elephants also live on _____ continent of Asia. _____ elephant has
2   3

_____ almost hairless body. It also has _____ long, flexible trunk.
4   5

Elephants are _____ largest mammals that live on land. _____ only
6   7

larger mammals, whales, live in the ocean.

Score: _____   Total Possible: 7

Proofread

Proofread the paragraph. Circle seven incorrect articles. Write the correct article above each incorrect one.

Do you know how a moth is different from the butterfly? A butterfly has a knob on a antenna. A butterfly is active during a daytime. A butterfly has brighter colors than the moth. A butterfly folds its wings upward when it rests. A butterfly has the smooth body, and a moth may have the hairy one. Although the butterfly is a insect that almost everyone likes, many people don't like the moth.

Practice

Write *a* or *an* in each blank below.

1. _____ happy trip

2. _____ useful guidebook

3. _____ apple

4. _____ hourly schedule

5. _____ foreign country

6. _____ united group

Now write a journal entry or a letter describing your imaginary travels. Use several of the phrases you created above.

_____

_____

_____

_____

_____

Tips for Your Own Writing: Proofreading ....

Remember that the article *a* is used before words beginning with a consonant sound. The article *an* is used before words beginning with a vowel sound.

 The three most commonly used words in English are the, a, *and* an.

61 Review: Parts of Speech

A. Circle the five common nouns below. Write a proper noun to replace each article and common noun.

1. The president arrived. _____

2. The mayor is traveling. _____

3. I visited a museum. _____

4. The street is busy and noisy. _____

5. The city is large and exciting. _____

Score: _____   Total Possible: 10

B. Write the correct pronoun in each blank.

Clint's mother just told _____ about the family's vacation plans. Now
                         1
_____ is excited and is telling all of _____ about this great trip. _____
   2   3   4
are going to Disney World, a place Clint and _____ brother have always
                                                5
wanted to see. My sister and _____ told _____ mother that _____
                               6   7   8
thought a trip to Florida sounded great. _____ agreed but said _____
                                            9   10
won't happen soon!

Score: _____   Total Possible: 10

C. Underline seven verbs in the paragraph. Above each underlined verb, write a stronger verb to make the story more exciting.

The storm came. Thunder sounded. Suddenly, a bolt of lightning hit the tree

in the yard. The tree broke into pieces and fell. We came up from the basement.

The storm moved toward the next part of town.

Score: _____   Total Possible: 14

D. Make the sentences more interesting by writing an adjective in each blank.

1. The _____ car led a _____ parade.

2. The _____ event was well-attended.

3. _____ boys and girls wore _____ clothes.

4. _____ adults wore _____ jeans and T-shirts.

5. We enjoyed a _____ lunch.

Score: _____   Total Possible: 8

E. Circle an adverb in each sentence.

1. The wind blew fiercely across the sand.

2. The canvas tent flapped noisily.

3. The air seemed very cool when night came.

4. Inside the tent, Anna danced wildly.

5. She loved the wind and was too excited to mind the cold.

Score: _____   Total Possible: 5

F. Draw a delete mark through each incorrect article. Write the correct article above the incorrect word. If all of the articles in a sentence are correct, write C above the sentence. There are four incorrect articles.

1. Abiyoyo was a fearsome giant!

2. Actually, he was a ogre!

3. He danced when an ukulele was played.

4. The boy with the ukulele was an hero.

5. That boy over there is a one who saved the town.

Score: _____   Total Possible: 9

G. Write the part of speech above each word in the sentence below.

A   fat   frog   croaked   loudly.

Score: _____   Total Possible: 5

REVIEW SCORE: _____   REVIEW TOTAL: 61

127

62 Grammar: Statements and Questions

✏️ *W*riting can be used to ask and to answer questions.

······························ **Did You Know?** ························

Most sentences are statements. They end with a period.
> The weather is very nice today**.**

Statements have a subject and a verb. The *subject* tells who or what the sentence is about. The *verb* tells what the subject is doing, or it links the subject to the rest of the sentence. Usually, the subject comes before the verb.
> S   V
> **We practice** our batting and hitting.

In many questions, the subject comes between two verbs.
> V S V
> What **can I do** indoors?

··

Show What You Know

Read the paragraphs below. If a sentence is a statement, put a period in the blank. Circle the periods so they are easier to see. If the sentence asks a question, put a question mark in the blank.

We want to avoid adding to Earth's pollution_____ We want to save
                                                1

money on electricity_____ Can we do both at the same time_____ Can saving
           2   3

electricity help avoid pollution_____ The answer is yes, it can! Every time
                         4

someone uses electricity, a power plant somewhere works a little harder_____
                                                  5

This means it uses more fuel_____ What kinds of fuel do power plants
                    6

use_____ Many of them use coal_____ Some burn oil or gas_____ Some use
   7   8   9

nuclear power_____
     10

Burning any fuel can cause pollution_____ If smoke goes into the air, it
                              11

makes the air we breathe dirtier_____ Can nuclear power cause water
                    12

pollution_____ Yes, it can! Heat from a power plant can heat water in a river
   13

and kill plants and fish_____ We have good reasons to use electricity
              14

carefully_____ Work toward saving electricity_____
   15   16

Score: _____   Total Possible: 16

Proofread

Read the story below. Use proper proofreading marks to correct the five punctuation mistakes.

Example: We went to the park?

Have you ever been lost in the woods. It sounds like a great adventure, but it is not fun. I live near Lost Creek State Park, where I've been about a thousand times? On my birthday, my family went up there to celebrate. We started to hike to the falls. I was at the tail end of the group. Could I use a shortcut and get ahead of them. Suddenly I was in the forest, surrounded by enormous trees, dim light, and weird noises. I had no idea what I could do? It was very scary. Then I heard my father yell my name. I followed his voice and got out. "Was I worried?" they asked me?

"Of course not," I answered bravely.

Practice

Write four lines of dialogue for the people in the picture. Use questions and statements.

_____

_____

_____

_____

_____

Tips for Your Own Writing: Proofreading ....

Review a piece of your own writing. Check to be sure you put periods after sentences that tell something, and question marks after sentences that ask something. The order of the subject and verb will help you decide.

Periods signal that something is being stated. Question marks signal that something is being asked.

63 Grammar: Requests and Exclamations

Whether you're writing a report, story, play, or poem, the order of the words in your sentence and the punctuation you use are signals for your readers.

.... **Did You Know?** ....

A sentence that expresses strong feeling is an <u>exclamation</u>. It ends with an exclamation point. That signals that it is intended to express strong feeling.

> I can't believe it**!** Ready, set, go**!**

A sentence that gives orders or directions is a <u>command</u>. Most commands have no stated subject. "You" is understood to be the subject. The forcefulness with which the command is given determines whether an exclamation point or a period is used at the end.

> Don't throw that trash into the lake**.**
> Don't throw that trash into the lake**!**

A sentence that tells a person to do something is a <u>request</u>. A request is a polite command and is followed by a period.

> Bring my books to the car, please**.**

Show What You Know

In the following sentences, add the correct punctuation at the end of each sentence. Circle the periods so that they are easier to see.

1. Please get back on the bus

2. Kindly wait for the driver

3. Oh, no, it's a bear

4. Oh, dear, he's coming this way

5. Hey, don't go near the bear

6. Go back to your seats now

7. Please move as quickly as possible

8. Keep the windows closed

Score: _____   Total Possible: 8

Proofread

Read the report below. Using proper proofreading marks, correct the incorrect punctuation marks at the ends of each of nine sentences.

Example: Here I go. Please come with me!

Everywhere we go, signs use huge letters to shout at us. Get your tickets here. Don't ride bikes on the sidewalk. Don't litter. Wait for the crossing light. I feel like I'm in the Army and the drill sergeant is yelling, "Forward, march."

I think signs in small print look more like polite requests. Check coats here! Have exact change ready! It's like the teacher saying, "Pass your papers to the front of the room!"

Of course, when I get home and walk into the kitchen, my sister often greets me with, "Wash your hands." She should use a sign with very small letters.

Practice

Write one exclamation, one request, and two commands. Punctuate each correctly.

_____

_____

_____

_____

_____

Tips for Your Own Writing: Proofreading ....

Choose a piece of your writing that includes dialogue. Look for exclamations that you wrote. Did you remember to use some exclamation points to indicate strong feeling? Do not overuse them. If you use exclamation points too often, they will lose their impact, just like the boy who cried "Wolf!" too often.

 *A*re you using all this important information in your own writing?

131

64 Review: Sentences

A. There are fourteen statements and seven questions in the following report. Use proper proofreading marks to add end punctuation that shows which sentences are statements and which are questions. Circle periods so they are easier to see.

The word *library* comes from an old Latin word that means "book" Did you ever wonder why people started building large rooms just for books Well, remember that books weren't always as common or as inexpensive as they are today After all, early books were written by hand, weren't they Even today it's convenient to be able to read all kinds of books that you don't have in your own house

Libraries are changing, though What will you find in a library besides books Most public libraries carry records, tapes, CDs, and videos Is your public library that well-equipped Some aren't, of course, but they will be someday

Most libraries now have computers Why are they in there with books Well, a computer is another source of information Don't you agree that a computer should be in a building thats name means "book" Libraries are places to go for books and many other sources of information as well

Along with computers, books, CDs, tapes, videos, and all of the other materials in a library, there are people Some of those people work there Do you know which person to ask for help Librarians are often very well-informed and can help you with a lot of projects The other people there are readers like you Libraries make it easy for people to study and learn

Score: _____   **Total Possible: 21**

B. In the blanks below, identify the type of sentence by writing *E* for exclamation, *C* for command, or *R* for request. After each letter, show the end punctuation you would use.

Annie and Charlie started across the bridge that ran above the train tracks.

Annie was scared to death of that bridge, and she knew Charlie didn't like it, either.

He even sounded nervous.

"Walk faster, Annie_____"
$\underset{1}{}$

Annie held on to the railing of the bridge.

"Please don't hurry me, Charlie_____"
$\underset{2}{}$

Annie was watching every step she took and couldn't look at anything but

her feet. She thought "Oh, help_____ We are so high up_____"
$\underset{3}{}$ $\underset{4}{}$

Then Annie realized her brother was standing still. She followed Charlie's

eyes and saw a small boy who had slipped on the bridge just ahead of them.

"His feet are over the edge and he looks stuck_____ Let's help him,
$\underset{5}{}$

Charlie!"

She knew the boy had to be frightened. Charlie started to run toward the

boy. "Come on, Annie_____" Annie came.
$\underset{6}{}$

Charlie and Annie pulled the boy up. He was shaking. As he stood up, he

gave them a weak smile.

"Whew_____ Thanks, thanks, thanks_____"
$\underset{7}{}$ $\underset{8}{}$

Score: _____   **Total Possible: 16**

REVIEW SCORE: _____   **REVIEW TOTAL: 37**

133

65 Grammar: Understanding Sentences I

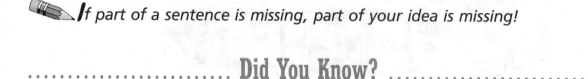 *If part of a sentence is missing, part of your idea is missing!*

.... **Did You Know?** ....

A *sentence* is a group of words that expresses a complete thought.

Summer is one of the four seasons.

Every sentence has two parts: a *subject*—the part that tells who or what the sentence is about—and a *predicate*—the part that tells something about the subject.

SUBJECT   PREDICATE
Summer / is one of the four seasons.

A writer uses sentences to share thoughts and ideas with readers. Be sure your sentences have every word that is necessary to get your ideas across to your readers.

Incorrect: A cool way to spend the summer.
Correct: Swimming every day is a cool way to spend
                the summer.
Incorrect: The girl at the swimming pool.
Correct: The girl at the swimming pool taught me
                how to dive.

Show What You Know
Underline the subject of each sentence below.

Laurie always wanted to be a scientist and search for fossils. She studied

with a famous geologist and his friends. In Nebraska they found dinosaur bones

buried under tons of ash. A museum named Ashfall was built. It is popular and is

visited by many people every year. Visitors can see dinosaur bones as they were

found.

Score: _____   **Total Possible: 6**

Practice

Use the words below to write complete sentences.

1. barked loudly

_____

2. the house

_____

3. in the summer

_____

4. the best time of year

_____

Revise

Unscramble the following sentences by writing them in the correct order on the lines. Then, circle the subject and underline the predicate in each sentence. Use capital letters correctly.

Planned Sanchez Mrs. the trip.   The visited kids park the.   Played they baseball.
They picnic had a.   Good a time had everybody.   Tired happy they but were.

1. _____

2. _____

3. _____

4. _____

5. _____

6. _____

Tips for Your Own Writing: Revising ·······························

When you finish a piece of writing, get in the habit of reading it aloud to yourself. You will be amazed at how many incomplete sentences and other mistakes you will be able to fix before anyone else ever reads your work.

 Check your sentences for both parts—a subject and a predicate.

66 Grammar: Understanding Sentences II

✏️ *Sometimes you want to put more than one idea into a sentence.*

Did You Know?

One way to combine ideas into one sentence is to join the two ideas with words such as *and, but,* or *or.*

Philip is a geologist, **but** he is a college teacher, too.

He searched for fossils in Wyoming, **and** he found interesting ones.

He invites students to work with him, **or** he works alone.

Show What You Know

Match the sentences in Column 1 with the sentences in Column 2. Combine the sentences using *and, but,* or *or,* and write them on the lines below.

Column 1

1. The road was long.

2. We ate all day in the car.

3. My dad couldn't find the road.

4. Dad said to relax.

5. I could go to sleep.

6. We finally reached Isle Royale.

Column 2

A. Believe me, it was worth the trouble!

B. We played every game we knew.

C. I could entertain my twin brothers.

D. I felt responsible.

E. I lost the map.

F. The drive seemed even longer.

1. _____

2. _____

3. _____

4. _____

5. _____

6. _____

Score: _____   **Total Possible: 6**

Practice

Write two sentences using the pattern of the nonsense sentence below. Write in real words for the nonsense words.

That glurb janded plurpily, but this glurb jands with delight.

1. _____

_____

2. _____

_____

Revise

Combine the sentences in the paragraph below into compound sentences using *and*, *but*, or *or*.

A mosaic may be only bits of colored glass and glue. It forms a picture. Old mosaics are beautiful. So are modern ones. You can make mosaics with beads. They won't be as bright as ones made from glass. Make a mosaic with colored paper. Make one with bits of plastic. Try it. You might discover you enjoy it.

_____

_____

_____

_____

_____

_____

Tips for Your Own Writing: Revising ....

Look at something you have written recently. Did you use any compound sentences? If so, look at the sentences you joined together. Are their ideas related? Combine sentences *only* when the ideas in the sentences are closely related.

Combining sentences takes some experimenting, but it's worth the effort!

Lesson

67 Grammar: Combining Sentences I

*A*void short, choppy sentences. They can take your reader's attention away from the ideas you want to share.

.... **Did You Know?** ....

Combining sentence parts when you revise your writing can make a sentence smooth and can cut out extra words as well.

Babe is a video I really like. *Pinocchio* is good, too. *Matilda* is one of my favorites.
Babe, Pinocchio, and *Matilda* are three of my favorite videos *or* I really like *Babe, Pinocchio,* and *Matilda.*

Show What You Know

You do not need all the words in the following sentences to say what you want to say. Rewrite each group of sentences on the line to make one well-combined sentence.

1. I loved *James and the Giant Peach* by Roald Dahl. I also loved *Matilda* by Dahl.

_____

2. *Oink* was illustrated by Arthur Geisert. Geisert illustrated *Haystack,* too.

_____

3. *Jumanji* is a really weird story. *Bad Day at Riverbend* is strange, too.

_____

4. *The Book of Hot Lists for Kids* gave me some great ideas for things to do. *The Kids' Summer Handbook* taught me some things, too.

_____

_____

5. Books make my weekends fun. CDs also give me some fun things to do.

_____

Score: _____   **Total Possible: 5**

138

Practice

Picture some people who are important to you. List their names and write a few words that tell why they are important.

_____

_____

_____

_____

Now choose three of the people on your list who are important to you for the same or a similar reason. Write one sentence about something the people have in common.

_____

_____

Revise

Read the paragraph. Circle the sentences that can be combined. Rewrite them on the lines below.

Steven Kellogg is a well-known children's author. He was born in 1941. He has six stepchildren. He has seven grandchildren. He lives in a small town in Connecticut. His wife Arlene and his dog live there, too. His dog has very long legs. His dog has a big head, too. Steven often includes animals in his stories. Pinkerton is one of his animal characters. Alfonse is another. Pinkerton is the Great Dane. Alfonse is the tadpole.

_____

_____

_____

_____

Tips for Your Own Writing: Revising ....

Combining sentences can help make your writing concise and understandable. But just because two sentences have the same subject or object does not mean they should always be combined.

 *R*emember, strong writing uses no extra words.

68 Grammar: Combining Sentences II

Sometimes writers avoid having too many short sentences by combining verbs.

.... **Did You Know?** ....

If you are saying two things about the same person or place, you can often combine these parts into one sentence. Do this by using more than one verb in a sentence.

Our class **planted** a garden. We **weeded** the garden, too.

Our class **planted and weeded** the garden.

We **found** a video about crops the Inca planted. We **watched** the video.

We **found and watched** a video about crops the Inca planted.

Show What You Know

Combine each pair of sentences into one sentence that has two verbs. Write the new sentence on the line.

1. Nancy Ward thought about her Cherokee people. She worried about them.

_____

2. Nancy talked to the leaders. She begged them to listen to her.

_____

3. She led her people. She showed them a way to survive.

_____

4. Nancy also talked to the white people. She showed them how they could have peace.

_____

_____

Score: _____   Total Possible: 4

Practice

List the names of three real or fictional people who interest you. After each name, jot down two or three strong, active verbs you might use to tell about that person.

_____

_____

_____

Next, write two sentences about one of the people on your list. In each sentence, tell one thing the person did. Keep the sentences simple.

_____

_____

Now combine your sentences into one sentence by combining the verbs.

_____

Revise

Circle the sentences that can be combined. Rewrite them on the lines below.

When our basketball players were introduced, the fans stood up. They cheered the team. The cheering was the loudest for Michael. But the game got off to a bad start. The other team blocked Michael's shots. They made him pass to his teammates. But Michael broke free. He grabbed the ball. He raced down the court. He jammed the ball into the basket. The fans yelled. They screamed. They stomped their feet.

_____

_____

_____

_____

Tips for Your Own Writing: Revising ....

You can make a compound sentence by combining the verbs in sentences _only_ if there is a close connection between the ideas, and the same subject is doing the action.

 Combine sentences to improve your writing.

69 Grammar: Combining Sentences III

Strengthen your writing by cutting out extra words. Make every word count.

.... **Did You Know?** ....

You can improve a piece of writing by using one exact word in place of a whole sentence.

> The parrot has beautiful feathers. They are very **colorful.**
>
> The parrot has beautiful, **colorful** feathers.

> Bats eat mosquitoes and other insects. Bats are **useful** creatures.
>
> **Useful** bats eat mosquitoes and other insects *or* Bats are **useful** because they eat mosquitoes and other insects.

Show What You Know

Combine the sentences in each pair. Write a new sentence by adding a single word from one sentence to the other.

1. My aunt doesn't like this winter weather. It's cold almost every day.

_____

2. She often wears unusual winter clothes. She wears colorful winter clothes.

_____

3. On really cold days, she wears a fluffy jacket. The jacket is purple.

_____

4. She also wears a cap with a pom-pom on top. The cap is made of wool.

_____

5. She says she likes her winter clothes. They are warm.

_____

Score: _____   Total Possible: 5

Practice

Read the pairs of sentences. Combine each pair into one sentence. Write the new sentences on the lines.

1. Those long-legged birds are storks. They are strange-looking.

2. No one can say anything good about mosquitoes. Mosquitoes are pesky insects.

3. The wind is blowing hard, with a roar. It is frightening.

4. We are taking a walk on a path. The path is long and winding.

_____

_____

_____

_____

Revise

Combine each set of sentences into one sentence. Look for different ways to combine the information and choose the best one.

1. Rachel Carson was a biologist. She studied marine life. She was also a science writer.

2. She warned people about air pollution. Pollution is dangerous.

3. She thought that the use of pesticides was destructive. She thought it was hazardous.

4. Carson discovered that pesticides were poisonous. She found they killed many fish.

1. _____

2. _____

3. _____

4. _____

Tips for Your Own Writing: Revising ....

Choose a piece of your own writing. Try to put related ideas together. Combine the descriptive words into one sentence if they describe the same person, place, or thing.

_W_eave the ideas together by combining sentences.

70 Grammar: Combining Sentences IV

A phrase can help make writing clear and strong.

······················· **Did You Know?** ··························

You can combine sentences by using a phrase in place of a wordy sentence. A *phrase* is a group of related words that does not have a subject or verb.

My friend taught me step dancing. She grew up in Ireland.

My friend **from Ireland** taught me step dancing.

That man enjoys watching the dancers. He uses a cane.

That man **with the cane** enjoys watching the dancers.

··

Show What You Know

Change one sentence into a phrase and place it in the other sentence. Write the new sentence on the line.

1. We watched our neighbor walk by. She led a beautiful dog.

_____

2. Our neighbor seems friendly. Her house is that brick one.

_____

3. The Newfoundland puppy is hers, too! It has a floppy ear.

_____

4. She and the dog are going on a hike. She wants to reach Carter Lake.

_____

5. She walks the dog every day. The dog wears a leash.

_____

Score: _____   Total Possible: 5

Proofread

Circle the sentence that shows one correct way to combine the pair of sentences.

1. I have read all those books. That is my collection.

I have a collection of books that I don't read.

I have read all those books in my collection.

2. We have collected many old records. We give them to my uncle.

My uncle has collected many old records.

We have collected many old records for my uncle.

3. Susan has collected many stamps. She takes them from old envelopes.

Susan has collected many stamps from old envelopes.

Susan takes old envelopes for her stamp collection.

Practice

Read the pairs of sentences. Combine each pair by making one sentence a phrase and placing it in the other sentence.

1. Charlie found a granola bar. The granola bars are in the cupboard.

2. Oranges are Kelly's favorite fruit. She likes Florida oranges best.

3. Melanie wanted an unusual snack. She wanted carrot sticks and peanut butter.

4. Jake loves fresh watermelon. He has a garden full of watermelon vines.

_____

_____

_____

_____

Tips for Your Own Writing: Proofreading ....

Using phrases to revise your sentences can help make your writing smoother and more concise. But do not pack a sentence with too many phrases.

 A phrase uses only a few words, so it can help condense writing.

71 Grammar: Combining Sentences V

Sometimes you just want to put two sentences together. That may be a good way to make a connection.

.... **Did You Know?** ....

You can combine two sentences with these words: *and, but,* and *or*. The two parts of the combined sentence are separated by a comma.

> Many people drive to work, **but** people in cities often use public transportation.
> Cars pollute the air, **and** gas for a car may be expensive.
> You can choose to fly long distances, **or** you can drive for several days.

Show What You Know

Combine these pairs of sentences using *and, but,* or *or*. Write the new sentence on the line. Be sure to add a comma.

1. Trains have crossed the United States since the 1860s. They have moved millions of people.

_____

_____

2. Today many people still love to ride the train. Many others think it is too slow.

_____

_____

3. Many families think driving is the easiest for them. It can be tiring.

_____

_____

4. Many people with babies choose to drive. They can fly faster.

_____

_____

Score: _____   **Total Possible: 4**

Practice

Think of a topic you might write about. Write four sentences. If possible, combine some sentences into compound sentences.

_____

_____

_____

_____

_____

Revise

Read the paragraph below. Circle sentences that can be combined and rewrite them on the lines below.

Computers were once rare in homes. Now they are found in many homes. Families use computers for simple tasks such as writing letters. They use them for more complex tasks such as banking. Children use computers to play games. They use them to do homework. In the future, computers will be needed more. Every family will own a computer.

_____

_____

_____

_____

_____

Tips for Your Own Writing: Revising ....

If you combine two or more simple sentences using _and, or,_ or _but,_ remember to place a comma before the word that joins the sentences. Do not combine too many sentences with _and_'s. This will only make a long, boring sentence.

Combining two short sentences into one sentence can help your readers better understand your ideas.

Lesson
72 Review: Understanding and Combining Sentences

A. Use each group of words to write a complete sentence on the lines.

1. fourth-grade students

_____

2. like many subjects

_____

3. science

_____

Score: _____   **Total Possible: 3**

B. Write two short sentences using all the words below. Then combine your sentences using _or, and,_ or _but._

closet is feet the length twelve the of width its only inches is thirty

_____

_____

Score: _____   **Total Possible: 3**

C. Combine each pair of sentences.

1. People in Chicago ride buses. Many of them ride subways.

_____

2. Workers in San Francisco take cars. Others take the BART trains.

_____

3. Older students often drive. Working people often drive.

_____

Score: _____   **Total Possible: 3**

148

D. Combine these pairs of sentences by using both verbs in one sentence.

1. The drums thundered loudly. They echoed through the hall.

_____

2. A horn tooted. Then it stopped suddenly.

_____

Score: _____   Total Possible: 2

E. Use an adjective from one sentence to help you combine sentences.

1. Our guest speaker was very tall. He was thin, too.

_____

2. It was easy to hear his clear voice. It was loud, too.

_____

3. His speech was about vacationing in Virginia. It was fascinating.

_____

Score: _____   Total Possible: 3

F. Use a phrase to help you combine these pairs of sentences.

1. We set out for our trip. We went to the zoo.

_____

2. We were told to stay together. There were three of us.

_____

Score: _____   Total Possible: 2

G. Make one sentence by combining this pair of sentences.

Today I wrote a poem. I was pleased with the results.

_____

Score: _____   Total Possible: 1

REVIEW SCORE: _____   REVIEW TOTAL: 17

Writer's Handbook

Getting Started with the Writing Process

 Writing is easy when you follow the four steps of The Writing Process!

························ **Did You Know?** ························

1. **Selecting,** or choosing, a subject is the first step in the writing process. Let's say you want to write about your dog, Buster. First, write *Buster* and draw a circle around it, like this: (Buster)

   Now put six spokes on your circle.

2. Next you need to **collect** your ideas. Do this by putting a word or words at the end of each spoke that tell something about Buster. Draw a circle around each set of these new words. The more ideas you collect, the easier it will be to write your story.

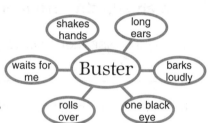

3. Now you are ready to **connect,** or group, all your ideas that tell about the same thing. *Long ears* and *one black eye* describe how Buster looks. Put those ideas together. *Barks loudly and waits for me* tell about things Buster does. Connect those things next. Now connect the tricks that Buster knows. As other ideas come to you, add more spokes and put them in new circles. This will help you shape and organize your writing.

4. Your next step will be **drafting** your thoughts into paragraphs or a report. Start writing about the ideas you have connected. Write about only one group of ideas at a time.

5. Now you should **revise** your writing. Delete unnecessary information and correct errors in mechanics, usage, and grammar. Share your corrected copy with a friend. Ask your friend to suggest other improvements.

6. After you have made all the changes you feel are necessary, you are ready to write your final copy. Be sure to **proofread** it.

Tips for Your Own Writing: ·····································

- **Select** a subject.
- **Collect** your ideas.
- **Connect** all your ideas that tell about the same thing.
- **Draft** your ideas into paragraphs.
- **Revise,** revise, and revise again!
- **Proofread** your final copy.

Clustering ideas in circles helps you think of more ideas. It also helps you organize the ideas.

Writer's Handbook

Getting Ideas

 You are the best source for writing ideas!

·························· **Did You Know?** ··························

The best ideas for writing come from **your** experiences, opinions, and imagination. Ask yourself what you like and care about. List those things. Next, ask yourself what things interest you and what you would like to know more about. Make a list of those things. You now have two lists of ideas!

Look at your two lists and circle the idea that is most interesting to you. Put that idea in a circle on a new sheet of paper. Think about that idea. Draw spokes around the circle and put ideas or details describing your idea at the ends of the spokes and circle them. Select the ideas or details you want to use. It is not necessary to use all of them. Now connect, or group, those ideas that tell about the same thing.

You are ready for your first draft. Write by using the details in the circles. Write quickly and do not revise yet. Experiment if you wish, but remember to be yourself. When you are finished, revise and then proofread. You are the expert!

Tips for Your Own Writing: ···

- Make a list of things that are important to you, and circle your favorite topic from the list.
- Write all your thoughts about that circled topic.
- Select which ideas you want to use.
- Connect the ideas.

 Your best ideas come from inside you.

Each sentence in a paragraph supports one idea.

. . . . **Did You Know?** . . . .

The **beginning** of your paragraph introduces your main idea. You can use one fact, statement, topic, or belief to introduce your main idea or topic. If you stick to your topic, it helps control your writing. A good paragraph is about only one idea and is supported by examples, reasons, or descriptions.

The **middle,** or the body, of the paragraph is where you expand on the main idea by using explanations, descriptions, or details to support it. You arrange those specific details or explanations in some type of logical or effective order. If you are describing the inside of your house, you might describe one room at a time. That would be using spatial order, or space. Sometimes you use chronological order, which means you explain what happened in the same order that it happened. You can also expand your main idea by selecting the details according to their order of importance.

The **closing** of your paragraph is the ending. It comes after the details and explanations in the body. The closing sentence usually reminds the reader what the topic is about. It also makes your paragraph complete.

Tips for Your Own Writing: . . . .

- Put only one idea in a paragraph.
- Write specific details about your topic.
- Arrange the details in a logical or effective order.
- Indent when you start a new paragraph.

 Well-written paragraphs focus on one idea.

Writer's Handbook
Staying on Topic

 Topics should stick like glue!

···················· **Did You Know?** ····························

Each paragraph deals with only one idea. Watch out for sentences that wander from the main idea. Get rid of them. They confuse readers. Read the paragraph below. It has a good introduction. Why did the writer include the sentences shown in orange?

> The day that I broke my arm started out like most days. I struggled out of bed and ate breakfast. Then I looked at the kitchen clock. It was the new clock we gave Mom for Mother's Day. I had only three minutes to get to the bus stop! I grabbed my book bag and flew out the door. I wish I had seen our dog standing outside the door. We got our dog at the animal shelter. I tripped over her and landed on the cement steps. The rest of the story is too painful to tell!

Each sentence in orange has something to do with the sentence just before it. One sentence tells more about the clock. The other tells more about the dog. However, these two sentences have nothing to do with the topic of the paragraph. They do not tell how the writer broke his arm. Take these two sentences out of the paragraph. What kind of an ending sentence does the paragraph have? Does it make the writing seem complete? Although it doesn't tell what happened next, it does tell you why the writer decided not to go on with the story.

Tips for Your Own Writing: ·································

- Read each sentence in your writing and ask, "Does this sentence belong in this paragraph? Does it tell more about the main idea of the paragraph?"
- You may find that the sentences you take out belong in another paragraph.

 Good writers stick to their topic.

Writer's Handbook

5 Proofreading Checklist

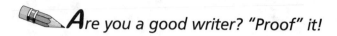

Are you a good writer? "Proof" it!

. . . . **Did You Know?** . . . .

To get mistakes out of your writing, proofread! You can use the proofreading marks on the inside back cover of this book.

Look for one or two mistakes at a time. First, read your writing out loud, word for word. That makes it easier to spot any missing or extra words. Next, check to see if any words need to have capital letters. Remember, each new sentence should begin with a capital, and all names begin with a capital. Maybe you used a capital letter and you shouldn't have. Now see if each sentence has an end mark. Are all words spelled correctly? Look at the words that give you trouble. Ask another student to proof your paper for you. Your friend may see something you missed. Here is how one writer marked the mistakes in her writing:

Do you remember your first day in forth grade? I do. my family had just

moved to northville. I didn't have any friends yet When I got to school, a boy was

waiting for me at the front door. He knew my my name! I was so surprised! He

said his name was jeremy. He would show me my homeroom. I was alredy happier!

Tips for Your Own Writing: . . . .

Can your writing pass this test?
• Did I spell all words correctly?
• Do any sentences have missing or extra words?
• Did I start all sentences and proper nouns with capital letters?
• Do all sentences end with a period, question mark, or exclamation point?
• Did I indent each paragraph?
• Can I tell what each paragraph is about?

The reward for good proofreading is no mistakes!

6 Writer's Handbook
Narrative-Descriptive Story

 Narration combines with description to unfold an appealing story.

Did You Know?

A narrative is a story, either true or imagined. Its purpose is to tell about an event or series of events. Narration usually includes a great deal of description. The plan of a narrative is developed through a **beginning,** a **middle,** and an **end.** The **beginning** of a story usually introduces the people or characters, and the place and time period (setting). The **middle** of the story usually shows the characters doing something (generally facing a problem) when a conflict (the main problem) arises. The **end** of the story shows how the characters deal with or solve the conflict. Remember, every story does not have a happy ending.

Description helps the reader picture a person, place, or thing. It deals with the appearance or nature of a person, place, or thing. Select the details of your description to paint a picture with words so that the reader can not only see, but also smell, touch, hear, or taste what you are describing. All details should be concrete and clear, showing color, sound, and motion. Use description throughout the story to paint clear pictures that make your readers feel as if they are there inside your story.

Tips for Your Own Writing:

- Think of a problem your characters can solve.
- Know your characters. Imagine what they like and dislike. What personality traits make them different and interesting?
- Plan a beginning to your story where you introduce the characters and setting.
- Plan a middle by deciding on the main problem the characters will face and how they will deal with it.
- Plan an end by deciding how the conflict or problem will be dealt with or resolved.

 Before you begin, think about a problem you want your characters to solve.

Writer's Handbook
Expository—Planning the Report

 *W*riting an expository report requires planning and learning about a topic.

································· **Did You Know?** ·····························

Expository writing is used when you write a report. It is used to tell what a thing is, how it works, its history, and how its parts relate to each other. Following the first two steps of the writing process makes planning a report easier.

1. **Selecting**—Your teacher might assign a particular topic for your report. It is best to choose a subject that is interesting to you. Ask yourself what you would really like to know about that topic. Make a list of questions you would like to answer. Go to the library and look through books on the general topic. For instance, if the general topic is fish, you might decide to narrow your topic to a certain kind of fish, like barracuda or angelfish.

2. **Collecting**—

   a. **Gather** interesting facts and details about your subject. Look through encyclopedias, books, and magazines to get background information. On-line computer services, videotapes, and slides are also good sources of information. Write to different organizations to obtain free material. If the topic is fish, visit an aquarium, zoo, or your local pet store.

   b. **Take notes** about important facts and details. To help you with this, you might want to go back to the list of questions that you wrote in step 1. Write each question at the top of a different note card. When you find a fact or detail that helps answer the question, write it in your own words on the note card. Be sure to write the source of your information.

Sample note card:

What do barracuda look like?
• long body
• sharp set of fangs and jutting lower jaw
• great barracuda may grow to more than 10 ft in length
Evans, T.S. *All About Barracuda*. Columbus: McGraw-Hill, 1996

   c. **Organize** your information by choosing one of your note cards to be the main focus of your report. Arrange the rest of your note cards with your focus in mind. Use the information on the main note card to write the first sentence of your report.

Tips for Your Own Writing: ································

- Make sure there is enough information about your topic.
- Write each question that you want answered at the top of a note card.
- Write facts and details about each question in your own words.

 *P*roper planning means an organized report.

Writer's Handbook

8 Expository–Writing the Report

 Writing a report is not difficult when you follow the writing process.

Did You Know?

If you followed the steps for proper planning, the writing of your report should not be difficult. Now follow the next two steps of the writing process. Remember, expository writing is used to tell what a thing is, how it works, its history, and how its parts relate to each other.

Connecting your facts and details involves the writing of your first draft. Arrange your note cards in an order that links the answers to one question with the answers of another. Play around with your note cards until you come up with an order that pleases you. Then, write your draft, writing not only what is on your note cards but what you remember as well. You do not need to copy the questions at the top of each card. As you write, you may think of another way to look at your subject.

Now look at your opening paragraph. It should interest the reader. It should also contain the main idea of your report. If it doesn't, rewrite it.

After you have written your report, write a closing paragraph. Make sure you summarize the main points to leave your readers with a good idea of what your whole report is about. After you have written the first draft, read it aloud to make sure it flows smoothly. Check each paragraph to see if the ideas are arranged in the best possible order. Remember to use your own words, not those of the books you read, and present your facts as clearly as possible. Add charts or illustrations if they will make the report more interesting.

Before asking another person to read the report and suggest changes, check your spelling and punctuation. Revise and edit the report as many times as you feel it needs it. Now it is time for the final stage of the writing process: **proofreading.**

Ask a partner to proofread your report to check for spelling, usage, capitalization, and punctuation. Copy your report, making any changes that are needed. Write a title page, following the guidelines given by your parent or teacher.

Tips for Your Own Writing:

- Write a first draft, connecting information from your note cards and your memory.
- Write an opening paragraph and a closing paragraph.
- Read your report and revise and correct wherever necessary.
- Have another person suggest changes to your report.
- Correct your report by taking a last look at it and writing your final copy and a title page.

 The best report tells what <u>you</u> think about the information you gathered.

Writer's Handbook

Writing a Persuasive Composition

Prove it!

. . . . Did You Know? . . . .

Persuasive writing tries to convince the reader to believe what the writer believes or to do what the writer wants the reader to do. To begin your writing, complete this statement, "I want to convince you that . . . ." You may finish the statement by writing, "I want to convince you that we should visit Gettysburg on our vacation." Consider who will be your reader. How can you make that reader agree with you? You need reasons that would be convincing for that reader. Reasons may be either facts or opinions. Each fact or opinion goes into a separate sentence. A fact can be proven; an opinion cannot be proven. Words like *should*, *dislike*, *delightful*, and *believe* indicate an opinion is being expressed.

Fact: Gettysburg is an important historical place.

Opinion: In my judgment, seeing a place where history happened makes it easier to learn about our past.

Where do you find facts? You find them in dictionaries, encyclopedias, and almanacs. You can find facts and opinions in newspapers, magazines, textbooks, and interviews. Make sure you check your evidence to see if it supports your position. Name the persons you refer to who agree with your position. Write all the information on note cards.

It is time to look at your facts and opinions. Are your reasons convincing? If your facts are accurate and they are supported by the opinions of experts and reliable sources, it is more likely your readers will agree with you.

Conclude your paper by stating your persuasive argument again as strongly as you can. Revise and proofread your paper as often as you need to. Have a classmate proofread it also. Then write your final copy.

Tips for Your Own Writing:. . . . .

- Is your position clearly presented?
- Have you given your reader appropriate reasons for agreeing with you?
- Do all of your reasons support your position?
- Do you conclude with a clear summary of your position and your reasons for it?

Persuasive writing gives <u>your</u> opinion.

Writer's Handbook
Word Lists

....

IRREGULAR VERBS: Below is a partial list of some common irregular verbs.

PRESENT Today I...	PAST Yesterday I...	PAST PARTICIPLE I have...
★be	★was/were	★been
begin	began	begun
come	came	come
eat	ate	eaten
fall	fell	fallen
give	gave	given
go	went	gone
learn	learned	learned
leave	left	left
let	let	let
ring	rang	rung
set	set	set/setting
sing	sang	sung
sit	sat	sat/sitting
take	took	taken
teach	taught	taught

★conjugation of *to be*:	**Singular** I **am** you **are** he, she, *or* it **is**	**Plural** we **are** you **are** they **are**

VIVID VERBS

amble	giggle	plop	slam	thump
blare	glaze	propel	snicker	wail
budge	laugh	saunter	stroll	whack
chuckle	migrate	scramble	stuff	whip

PREPOSITIONS: Below is a partial list of some common prepositions.

about	because of	during	inside	outside
above	before	except	instead of	over
across	behind	for	into	since
after	below	from	like	through
against	beneath	from between	near	to
along	beside	in	off	toward
among	between	in addition to	on	under
around	by	in front of	on top of	up

Writer's Handbook

Postal State and Possession Abbreviations

Use these abbreviations on envelopes to be read by postal workers. In other writing, spell out the names of the states.

States

Alabama . . . . .AL
Alaska . . . . .AK
Arizona . . . . .AZ
Arkansas . . . . .AR
California . . . . .CA
Colorado . . . . .CO
Connecticut .CT
Delaware . . . . .DE
Florida . . . . .FL
Georgia . . . . .GA
Hawaii . . . . .HI
Idaho . . . . .ID
Illinois IL
Indiana . . . . .IN
Iowa . . . . .IA
Kansas . . . . .KS
Kentucky . . . . .KY
Louisiana . . . . .LA
Maine . . . . .ME
Maryland . . . . .MD
Massachusetts . . . . .MA
Michigan . . . . .MI
Minnesota . . . . .MN
Mississippi . . . . .MS
Missouri . . . . .MO
Montana . . . . .MT
Nebraska . . . . .NE
Nevada . . . . .NV
New Hampshire . . . . .NH

New Jersey . . . . .NJ
New Mexico .NM
New York . . . . .NY
North Carolina . . . . .NC
North Dakota . . . . .ND
Ohio . . . . .OH
Oklahoma . . . . .OK
Oregon . . . . .OR
Pennsylvania . . . . .PA
Rhode Island . . . . .RI
South Carolina . . . . .SC
South Dakota . . . . .SD
Tennessee . . . . .TN
Texas . . . . .TX
Utah . . . . .UT
Vermont . . . . .VT
Virginia . . . . .VA
Washington .WA
West Virginia . . . . .WV
Wisconsin . . . . .WI
Wyoming . . . . .WY

District of Columbia . . . . .DC

U.S. Possessions

American Samoa . . . . .AS
Guam . . . . .GU
Puerto Rico .PR
Virgin Islands VI

SPECTRUM

Language Arts

Grade 4
Answer Key

Lesson 1

Lesson 1 Capitalization: People and Pets

CApiTal lettERS can call attention to your writing. Good writers know how to put them in the right places!

.... **Did You Know?** ....

The word *I* is always capitalized.
> I think it's important to take good care of pets.

The names of people always begin with a capital letter. A pet's name should also be capitalized.
> My cousin Jason adopted a dog from the animal shelter.
> The dog is only about ten inches long, but Jason named her Terminator.

....

Show What You Know

Read the sentences below. Circle each word that should begin with a capital letter.

I saw a puppy that would make a great pet. His ears stand up like wolves' ears do, so (I) think we should name him (wolf.) My older sister (colleen) is learning to be a veterinarian, and she will help me learn about taking care of a large dog. Since (wolf) is a malamute, we visited a man who raises these great dogs. A dog named (iditarod) followed us around. The man, whose name is Jake, explained that (iditarod) is named for a dogsled race in Alaska. Malamutes are working dogs. We would have to give (wolf) a lot of exercise, even in very cold weather, and keep him brushed, because malamutes have thick fur. When grown, they can weigh about 85 pounds. (jake) said that we would have to buy a lot of dog food. We're thinking about that.

Score: _____ Total Possible: 8

6

Proofread

Here is part of a report about four famous musicians. The paragraph has five mistakes in capitalization. Draw three lines under each letter that should be capitalized.

Example: Harry connick, jr., is the musician i like best.

Wynton Marsalis is a famous African-American trumpeter who appears in a series of television programs for students. His brothers, branford and delfeayo, are also musicians, and all three brothers play classical music and jazz. The father of these musicians is ellis marsalis, a well-known jazz pianist. The public library has collections of music by the Marsalis family, and i like to listen to their CDs.

Practice

Write four sentences about the kind of music that you like. Name someone who plays or sings that kind of music. Use the pronoun *I* and the names of some people in your sentences. Watch out for the capital letters!

1. _____

Review the sentences to be sure your child has:
- used the pronoun *I* at least once.
2. _____
- used proper names more than once.
3. _____
- correctly capitalized the pronoun *I*.
- correctly capitalized all proper names.
- used periods and capitals correctly to set off sentences.
4. _____

Tips for Your Own Writing: Proofreading

Choose a piece of your own writing and look it over carefully for names and for the pronoun *I*. Check to see that you capitalized each of these words correctly. If you are not sure about some of the words, ask a friend whether you used capital letters correctly.

Hope this lesson about capital letters grabbed your attention!

7

Lesson 2

Lesson 2 Capitalization: Places

From Sacramento, California, to Augusta, Maine, the rules for capitalization are always the same!

.... **Did You Know?** ....

Some place-names refer to any one of a group of places, such as streets, cities, countries, continents, islands, oceans, and deserts. These names do not need to be capitalized.
> There are many mountains and oceans in the world.

Other place-names refer to a specific place. These names should be capitalized.
> The Rocky Mountains are in North America.
> The Hawaiian Islands have a warm climate.

....

Show What You Know

Read the following paragraph. Circle the seven place-names that should be capitalized. Then write them correctly on the lines below. You may need to use a United States map to help Teresa solve "The Best State" mystery.

On a dusty attic wall, Teresa discovered a faded map. "The Best State" it said on the map. "What's the best state?" Teresa wondered. She read the small print carefully. There were many names on the map. She saw (helena) and (billings.) She found (flathead lake,) (clark fork river,) and some other rivers and lakes. She found (bighorn mountain) and then another mountain. To the right of "The Best State" were the words (north dakota,) and at the top, the word (canada.) After some investigation, Teresa figured out "The Best State" was Montana.

1. Helena
2. Billings
3. Flathead Lake
4. Clark Fork River
5. Bighorn Mountain
6. North Dakota
7. Canada

Score: _____ Total Possible: 7

8

Proofread

Six place-names should have been capitalized in the following report on marsupials. Use the proper proofreading marks to correct the errors.

Example: We walked from frontierland to space mountain at disney world.

Almost everyone knows that kangaroos and koalas live in australia, which is a continent south of the equator. Kangaroos and koalas are marsupials. Marsupials also live in tasmania, which is an Australian island, and in New guinea and other nearby islands. There is one marsupial that lives in north America, though. It's the opossum. You can see opossums even in northern states, such as wisconsin and michigan.

Practice

Write directions to help someone who lives far away find the place where you live. Name the part of the country in which you live, the state, a town or city, street names, and any lake, river, mountain, or hill that will help your visitor find you. Watch out for the capital letters!

Review sentences to be sure your child has:
- written directions in a reasonable sequence.
- identified regions, states, and cities correctly.
- named streets and local landmarks.
- capitalized all proper place-names.
- not capitalized generic names, such as a "big *hill*" or the "*bridge* over the river."

Tips for Your Own Writing: Proofreading

Choose one of your papers. Select one that names places. Scan your writing for place-names. Ask yourself whether each of these words is correctly capitalized.

In England, when something is just right, people may say, "That's capital!" Now you can say, "That's capital," about your capitals!

9

Lesson 3

Lesson
3 Capitalization: Dates, Holidays, Groups

You can make a date with a capital letter!

.... Did You Know? ....

The names of specific days, months, and holidays begin with a capital letter.

I believe that **M**ay will always be my favorite month.
I love the way our city celebrates **M**emorial **D**ay!
It's best when a holiday comes on a **M**onday.

The names of specific organizations and events should also be capitalized.

The **G**irl **S**couts and **B**oy **S**couts march in the parade every year.
That weekend our town holds the exciting **L**incolnville **M**usic **F**estival.

....

Show What You Know
Read the newspaper report below. Circle the words that should be capitalized.

Atlanta, Georgia, welcomed ten thousand athletes from all over the world on (july) 19, 1996. World-class athletes competed in the (summer olympic games). The people of Atlanta worked with the (international olympic committee) to plan a special schedule of events. It was the 100th anniversary of the modern (olympic games).

Score: _____   Total Possible: 9

10

Proofread
The story below has eleven mistakes in the use of capital letters. Use the proper proofreading mark for each to correct the errors.

Example: We always celebrate thanksgiving on a thursday.

People in countries all over the world celebrate the beginning of the new year, but not always on the same day. The Chinese New year falls somewhere between january 10 and february 19. The Jewish new year celebration, rosh hashanah, usually begins in september and lasts two days. Muslims celebrate the year's beginning on muharram, sometime during May. In ancient Egypt, the new year began in mid-june when the Nile River reached its peak.

Practice
Write four sentences to advertise the event in the picture. What day and month will it take place? What organization will sponsor it? What name will you give to the event? Watch out for the capital letters!

1. _____ Review sentences to be sure your child has:
   • written four mechanically correct sentences.
2. _____ • included the following information:
   place
3. _____ day and month
   event (various situations are possible)
4. _____ sponsoring organization
   • capitalized the names of days, months, organizations, holidays, and events.

Tips for Your Own Writing: Proofreading ....
The next time you write a letter, look it over carefully for names of days, months, organizations, events, and holidays. Check to see that you capitalized each of these words correctly.

Capital letters are head and shoulders above the rest!

11

Lesson 4

Lesson
4 Capitalization: Titles of Written Works

Many important words are not capitalized except in titles. They need to jump out at the reader.

.... Did You Know? ....

The important words in the titles of books, stories, poems, songs, movies, and plays should always begin with capital letters. The important words are all words except conjunctions (and, but, or), articles (a, an, the), and prepositions (on, in, at, of, by).

Have you read *Ring of Bright Water*? It's a book about otters.
The old song "There's a Hole in the Bucket" is fun to sing.
We always watch *Where in the World Is Carmen Sandiego?*

Capitalize an article, conjunction, or preposition if it is the first or last word in a title.

I saw the play *The Wizard of Oz.*
"At the Seaside" is a poem by Robert Louis Stevenson.
Josh read *And to Think That I Saw It on Mulberry Street* to his brother.

....

Show What You Know
Read each sentence. Circle the capitalization mistake in each title.

1. Artist Marilyn Hafner drew funny pictures for the poem "(an) Only Child" by Mary Ann Hoberman.
2. *Tales of (a) Fourth Grade Nothing* is my favorite book by Judy Blume.
3. Did you ever read the book *Chicken Soup (with) Rice* by Maurice Sendak?
4. One of Lettie's favorite books is *The (gold) Cadillac* by Mildred Taylor.
5. Stephen's choir sang "Swing (low,) Sweet Chariot" at the winter concert.
6. A good book about stars is *The Sky Is Full (of) Stars* by Franklyn Branley.
7. Casey gave the book *Why (in) the World?* to her dad for his birthday.
8. Our class went to see the play *The Man Who Loved to (laugh).*

Score: _____   Total Possible: 8

12

Proofread
Following is the table of contents for a creative writing book by students at Adams School. Find one capitalization mistake in each title. Use the proper proofreading marks to correct the errors.

Example: My favorite book is *Bridge to terabithia* by Katherine Paterson.

Title	Page
When I Grow Up, Just Watch me Go!	4
Trevor And His Too Tall Hat	5
Somebody Stepped on my Homework!	7
the Day Dad Bit the Dog	10
A Bike! I Need a Bike now!	11

Practice
Imagine that you have written a book about endangered species. Write three titles for your book. Use at least one article, conjunction, or preposition in each title.

1. _____ Review titles to be sure your child has:
   • written titles that connect to the assigned topic.
2. _____ • used capitals for all words except conjunctions, articles, and short prepositions.
3. _____ • capitalized all initial and final words.

Tips for Your Own Writing: Revising ....
Choose one of your book reviews. Check your title and scan for titles of other works. Be sure you have followed the rules for capitalization.

Always remember to "cap" your written work with a title!

13

Lesson 5

Lesson
5 Capitalization: People's Titles

Capitalizing titles of respect can be tricky, but a few suggestions here will help you.

.... Did You Know? ....

Titles, such as *Mr., Mrs., Miss, Ms.,* **and** *Dr.,* **are often included with a person's name. When used as part of someone's name, titles and their abbreviations are always capitalized.**

Dr. Mary Faber talked to our class about first aid.
Mr. Sherman is the new gym teacher.

A word that just shows relationship should not be capitalized. Words such as *my, your, his, her, its, our,* **or** *their* **come before a word that just shows relationship.**

My **g**randfather seems to do everything really well.

However, if a word that shows relationship is used in place of a name, or with a name, it should be capitalized.

"**G**randfather," I said, "you certainly are a better fisherman than I am."
"Well," he answered, "**A**unt Minnow catches more fish than any of us."

....

Show What You Know
Read the paragraph below. Circle the seven words that should be capitalized.

Celia Sandoz grew up in western Nebraska. Her grandfather was Jules Sandoz, a very early settler in the region. Celia's father was also named Jules. "Oh, (father)," Celia often asked, "why did (grandfather) and (grandmother) settle in this very dry land?" Celia had always heard stories about (grandfather) Jules's family, who had a very difficult life. Celia's aunt, Mari Sandoz, became a famous writer. Once, (aunt) Mari wrote a book called *Winter Thunder.* It was about Celia's adventure during a rare blizzard in Nebraska. The famous (ms) Sandoz also wrote a biography of her father. Travelers today can see the home of (mr) Jules Sandoz.

Score: _____ Total Possible: 7

14

Score: _____ Total Possible: 7

Proofread
The following journal entry might be kept by a boy who lives on a space station. The entry has eight mistakes in capitalization. Use the proper proofreading mark to correct each error.

Example: My mom and m̲rs. Flowerpot were planning a trip into space.

Well, m̲other and I decided today to plant flowers. d̲r. Wilson insisted they wouldn't grow in this artificial air, but m̲r. Clement, a scientist, said they would. We took a vote. Both f̲ather and a̲unt Ina told us to go ahead. I wish g̲randfather Amos were here. He knows so much. To use our scarce water for seeds that might not grow would be a terrible waste, even though m̲rs. Jordan and u̲ncle Matthew have agreed to share their water rations.

Practice
Write four sentences. Use at least one of these words or abbreviations in each sentence: grandfather, grandmother, uncle, aunt, father, mother, Mrs., Miss, Ms., Mr., Dr.

1. _____ Review sentences to be sure your child has:
2. _____ • used at least one of the required terms in each sentence.
3. _____ • correctly capitalized titles.
4. _____ • correctly capitalized words that show relationship.

Tips for Your Own Writing: Proofreading ....
Choose a piece of your own writing and look it over carefully for names and titles. Check to see that you capitalized words that show relationship when they are used as names. If you aren't sure about some of the words, ask a friend whether you used capital letters correctly.

A name or title never takes off its "cap-ital" letter!

15

Lesson 6

Lesson
6 Capitalization: Friendly Letters

The best way to keep in touch with friends and family members when you or they move away is by writing great letters.

.... Did You Know? ....

A friendly letter has five parts. Capital letters are needed in all these parts.

1. **Heading:** Capitalize the name of the month and the names of the city, state, and street in the return address.
2. **Greeting:** Capitalize the name of the person to whom you are writing.
3. **Body:** Use capital letters correctly in every sentence you write.
4. **Closing:** Begin the first word with a capital letter.
5. **Signature:** Capitalize your name.

....

Show What You Know
Circle the twelve words that should be capitalized in the letter below.

Heading {
4224 (north) (cass) (street)
(omaha), (nebraska) 68102
(january) 3, 2000
}

(dear) (leonard), ◄— Greeting

Yesterday Jerome and I borrowed (uncle) Darren's old snowshoes and hiked along the river. I guess we got carried away. By the time we got home, we were a mess! And we were tired! I felt like I'd been walking bowlegged for about 48 hours! Mom laughed, and (dad) said using snowshoes is supposed to make getting around easier. Ha! The only bad part is that you can't do stuff with us anymore. Write and tell us what you do to have fun. } Body

Closing ———► (your) favorite cousin,
Signature ———► (mike)

Score: _____ Total Possible: 12

16

Proofread
Find the nine mistakes in capitalization in the letter below. Use the proper proofreading mark to correct each error.

Example: For a joke, i̲ wrote "your mystery pen pal" to close my letter to m̲om.

18 w̲est Maine a̲venue
Fort w̲isdom, m̲ontana 59711
j̲uly 4, 2000

d̲ear Marta,

I just want you to know i̲'ll see you next Sunday. When I asked when we'd get there, d̲ad said probably by lunchtime. I'm bringing my camera to take pictures of your new pony. Did you think of a name for him yet? I can hardly wait to see the two of you!

g̲oodbye for now,

Annalise

Practice
Write the body of a letter to a member of your family on the lines below. Tell him or her about your summer vacation. Check your capitalization. Rewrite it on another piece of paper, adding the other four parts of a friendly letter.

Review sentences to be sure your child has:
• used capital letters correctly.
• written a clear and friendly message.

Tips for Your Own Writing: Proofreading ....
Choose a piece of your personal writing or an entry in your journal. Use the information in that piece of writing to write a friendly letter to a real or imaginary person.

Whoever gets the next letter you write is really going to be impressed!

17

Lesson 7

Lesson 7 Capitalization: Business Letters

A business letter is more formal than a friendly letter. It should be clear and brief, including only necessary information.

.... Did You Know? ....

The form of a business letter is like that of a friendly letter in many ways, but business letters have six parts. Capital letters are needed in all these parts.

1. **Heading:** Capitalize the name of the street, city, state, and month.
2. **Inside Address:** Capitalize the name of the company or person to whom you are writing and the names of the street, city, and state.
3. **Greeting:** Capitalize the first word and words like *Sir* and *Madam* or the name of the person to whom you are writing.
4. **Body:** Use capital letters correctly in every sentence you write.
5. **Closing:** Begin the first word with a capital letter.
6. **Signature:** Capitalize your name. Write your full name.

Show What You Know

Circle the twenty-one words that should be capitalized in the business letter below.

Heading: 1412 (north) (iowa) (boulevard) / (chicago), (illinois) 60640 / (april) 20, 2000

(kidware) (hardware) / 1820 (east) (denver) (avenue) — **Inside Address** / (chicago), (illinois) 60602

(dear) (sir) or (madam) ← **Greeting**

Please send me a (kidware) (hardware) catalog for personal computers. | **Body**

Closing → (yours) truly,

Signature → (latoya) (swift)

Print Name → Latoya Swift

18 Score: _____ Total Possible: 21

Proofread

Find nine mistakes in capitalization in the letter below. Use the proper proofreading mark to correct the errors.

Example: Mr. wipple's video store is on wiggle street.

> 432 eleventh Avenue South
> Kansas city, Missouri 64101
> july 13, 2000
>
> Games and More Games
> 10011 East california street
> Omaha, nebraska 68100
>
> dear mr. Duffy:
>
> Thank you for sending me a new set of directions for my game. I'm going to make myself an extra copy in case I ever misplace the directions again. I think your company is efficient because you answered my letter immediately.
>
> yours truly,
>
> *Andrew Flood*
>
> Andrew Flood

Practice

On another piece of paper, write a business letter to a city's chamber of commerce asking for information on any activities or places to see that might be of interest to people your age.

Tips for Your Own Writing: Proofreading ....

Reread your letter. Use proofreading marks to correct capitalization. You could send your letter and see what kind of information you receive.

A well-written letter tells the reader that you mean business!

19

Lesson 8

Lesson 8 Review: Capitalization

A. There are eight mistakes in capitalization in the sentences below. Use the proper proofreading mark to correct them.

1. Ten-year-old rita leno comes to school on a horse named patches.
2. She wrote to her friend Brian, "anna and i are learning dances at our pueblo."
3. "My friend joel and i," answered brian, "will come to see you dance."

Score: _____ Total Possible: 8

B. Use the proper proofreading mark to correct eight place-names in the paragraph below.

Kathleen's family visited canada and parts of the united states last year. She says the best parts of chicago are michigan avenue and lake michigan. They went shopping on oak street. Later they saw grizzlies in glacier national park in the rocky mountains.

Score: _____ Total Possible: 15

C. Use the proper proofreading mark to correct nine mistakes in capitalization in the paragraph below.

People from all over the World came to the olympic games. Some visitors arrived just after independence day. Our high school named its new football team the olympians. The Team can't begin practice until september.

Score: _____ Total Possible: 9

D. Use the proper proofreading mark to correct the capitalization in nine words in the titles below.

Book: *birds of North america* **Song:** "this land is your land"
Story: "Her seven Brothers" **Movie:** *Homeward bound II*

Score: _____ Total Possible: 9

E. Angela's letter to her grandparents has twelve mistakes in capitalization. Use proofreading marks to correct each mistake.

> 1237 Kelley street
> Dubuque, iowa 52001
> September 15, 2000
>
> dear grandmother and grandfather,
>
> Thanks again for coming to help us out. That was a nasty spill Mom took on my skateboard in the memorial day parade. i hope her cast will be off so that she can drive us to see you on the fourth of july.
>
> love,
>
> *angela*

Score: _____ Total Possible: 12

F. Correct nine mistakes in the inside address and body of the business letter below. Then write the letter correctly on another piece of paper. Add your address, the date, and a proper greeting and closing. Sign your name.

> **Inside Address:**
>
> Ms. Jessica Kline
> 5 cash Street
> San antonio, texas 78227
>
> **Body:**
>
> I saw an ad for Geo videotapes in your magazine. I'm interested in buying the Tape about the denali national park in alaska. Could you send my Father and me information about it?

Score: _____ Total Possible: 9

REVIEW SCORE: _____ REVIEW TOTAL: 62

20   **21**

Lesson 9

Lesson 9 Punctuation: Periods

✏️ *Think about it! What if there were no periods? Reading would suddenly be a lot more difficult.*

.... **Did You Know?** ....

A period should follow a sentence that makes a statement or gives a direction.
> I don't like cold weather, unless there's snow.
> First, turn on the computer.

Titles of respect, such as *Mister* and *Doctor*, are abbreviated when they are followed by a person's name. A period should follow the abbreviation.
> Dr. Jonas Salk developed a vaccine for polio.
> Mr. and Mrs. Casey is James's uncle and aunt.

Initials are also followed by periods.
> John F. Kennedy was the thirty-fifth president.
> My friend's name is Katherine Colleen, but she uses her initials, K. C.

If an abbreviation appears at the end of a sentence, you need only one period.

....

Show What You Know

Read the paragraph below. Add periods where they are needed. Circle them so they are easier to see.

Have you decided how you will sign your name when you are famous? Many well-known writers and artists use their first and last names⊙ For example, Tasha Tudor is the author and illustrator of books for children⊙ On the other hand, a photographer whose pictures are in a book about Ms⊙ Tudor uses one name and one initial⊙ He is Richard W⊙ Brown⊙ A well-known writer of children's books, R⊙J⊙ Stine, uses just initials and his last name. The amazing Dr⊙ Seuss doesn't use his real name at all, just a title and a made-up name⊙

Score: _____   Total Possible: 10

22

Proofread

The report below has seven mistakes in the use of periods. Use the proper proofreading mark to show where each period should be used.

Example: M⊙ Greenthumb owns the garden store⊙

Three all-time favorite movies for children are *The Little Mermaid, The Wizard of Oz,* and *Peter Pan⊙* Each of these films is based on a book⊙ Hans Christian Andersen wrote *The Little Mermaid.* L⊙ Frank Baum wrote a series of books about Dorothy and her visits to Oz⊙ James M⊙ Barrie first told the story of Peter Pan, Wendy, and the dog Nana⊙

Practice

Write a story that you think would make a great movie or television show. Include at least one character with a title, such as Dr., Mr., Mrs., or Ms. Include a character who uses his or her initials. Be sure your sentences are correctly punctuated.

Review sentences to be sure your child has:

• used punctuation correctly.

• included titles of respect and has correctly punctuated each.

_____

_____

_____

_____

Tips for Your Own Writing: Revising ....

Choose a piece of your own writing and look it over carefully for the use of periods. Be sure you used a period at the end of each sentence and after every initial and abbreviation.

✏️ *Use periods correctly to make your writing clear to your reader.*

23

Lesson 10

Lesson 10 Punctuation: Abbreviations

✏️ *Mrs. Brief moved to Pine Ave. on Thurs., Jan. 3. There was a mix-up with the movers; her furniture didn't arrive until Fri., Jan. 4.*

.... **Did You Know?** ....

The names of some months of the year may be abbreviated in an informal note or where there is little space. A period should follow each abbreviation. May, June, and July are not abbreviated.
> Call me after **Apr.** 3, please. I'll see you on **Dec.** 27.
> I'm free anytime after **May** 12.

The names of the days of the week may be abbreviated in an informal note or where there is little space. A period should follow each abbreviation.
> Make your appointment for **Mon.** or **Thurs.**

....

Show What You Know

Read the diary entries below. Add periods where they are needed. Circle them so they are easier to see.

Dear Diary,

This is the last Mon⊙ in Feb⊙, and I'm going to write to you every day this week except Wed⊙ because I have to go to swimming class and band and won't have time. I got you last Tues⊙ as a tenth birthday present. I'm glad to have you here.

Dear Diary,

I didn't write any more during Feb⊙ I had poison ivy. I've stopped scratching, and now I'm back to you. I'll be deep-sea fishing during Mar⊙ and Apr⊙ and most of May. Then I'm going on vacation for all of June and July to my aunt's ranch in Colorado. Yea!

Score: _____   Total Possible: 7

24

Proofread

This photographer's list of appointments has five mistakes in punctuation. Use the proper proofreading mark to show where each period should be used.

Example: I have a haircut appointment on Wed⊙ Sept⊙ 10, at 3 o'clock.

Superman	Tues⊙	May 8	6 P.M.
Princess Jasmine	Fri⊙	Jan. 12	3 P.M.
Aladdin	Mon.	Feb⊙ 3	4 P.M.
Minnie Mouse	Fri⊙	Apr⊙ 9	10 A.M.

Practice

Create a calendar that begins on Monday and ends on Friday. Use abbreviations for the days of the week. The calendar can be used to keep track of your activities. On the lines below write the months of the year and their abbreviations.

Check to be sure your child has used the calendar format,

shown five-day weeks, Monday through Friday, shown

one month, and used appropriate abbreviations.

January—Jan.; February—Feb.; March—Mar.; April—Apr.; May; June; July; August—Aug.;

September—Sept.; October—Oct.; November—Nov.; December—Dec.

Tips for Your Own Writing: Proofreading ....

Choose a piece of your own writing in which you used abbreviations. Be sure you used abbreviations only in informal writing or in charts, calendars, and other places where you have little space. Check your use of periods.

✏️ *A period at the end of an abbreviation tells your readers that you've stopped short of writing the whole word.*

25

Lesson 11

11 Punctuation: Question Marks, Exclamation Points

Little punctuation marks can make a big difference in your writing! Do you know how to use them correctly?

.... **Did You Know?** ....

A sentence that asks a question ends with a question mark.
What's your favorite kind of weather?
Why are you watching that pointless television show?

A sentence that expresses a strong feeling, such as surprise, disgust, or great pleasure, ends with an exclamation point.
Don't say that again!
What a terrible plan!

An exclamation point also follows a single word that expresses strong feeling.
Amazing! Beautiful!

....

Show What You Know
Read the paragraph below. Circle the periods that are correct. Draw a line through the ones that are incorrect and write the correct punctuation mark above each.

Do you enjoy learning about animals? You can do it in your own neighborhood. Watch that house finch, the small bird with a bright red cap and neck. Do you hear his pretty, clear song? That tiny bird makes so much noise!

Is there a cat in your neighborhood? Watch quietly as it stalks a bug or butterfly. Now close your eyes. Can you imagine a lion or cougar stalking a small animal? Amazing! The small cat and the large one make the same moves.

Do you want to learn more? Your librarian may be able to help you find books published by the National Geographic Society. You can also watch National Geographic programs on television. What a great way to learn new things!

Score: _____   Total Possible: 15

26

Proofread
Three sentences in the report below are not punctuated correctly. Use the proper proofreading marks to add two question marks and one exclamation point.

Example: How do you like my new shoes?

How did people live in America long ago? About two thousand years ago, a group of farmers experimented with new kinds of seeds. Do you like corn on the cob, peanuts, tomatoes, and beans? All of these were grown in the parts of North America that we call Mexico, Arizona, and Colorado. How wonderful that these farmers gave us such important foods!

Practice
Write two questions about animals. Then write the answers to the questions in complete sentences. In your answers, include at least one sentence or word that expresses strong feeling. Punctuate your questions and answers carefully. You might want to exchange questions with a friend and share what you know about animals.

1. Review sentences to be sure your child has:
   • written clear, meaningful questions.
   • punctuated questions properly.
2. • written accurate, informative answers.
   • written answers in correct sentence form.
   • included at least one exclamatory sentence correctly punctuated.

Tips for Your Own Writing: Revising ....
Choose a piece of your own writing and look carefully at the kinds of sentences you used. You may be able to make the writing more interesting by including a few questions and perhaps even an exclamation.

If you use the proper punctuation signals, you will always be heading in the "write" direction!

27

Lesson 12

12 Punctuation: End Marks

Every sentence ends with some type of punctuation, doesn't it? It's up to the writer to know which type is correct.

.... **Did You Know?** ....

A period follows a sentence that makes a statement or gives a direction.
You are probably anxious to get started.
Turn on your computer.

A question mark follows a sentence that asks a question.
Why did you choose this program?

An exclamation point follows a sentence or phrase that expresses surprise or any strong feeling.
No way would I ever buy that software!

....

Show What You Know
Read the following paragraphs. Add the correct punctuation where it is needed. Circle the periods.

In order to build a kite, you must first decide on the type of kite you want. Would you prefer a two-stick kite, a box kite, or a flexible kite? The two-stick kite is probably the simplest.

The materials for a two-stick kite are inexpensive and easy to locate. Find two straight, lightweight, strong sticks of approximately the same length. You will need twine to lash the sticks together in the form of a t. You also will need a paper cover to catch the wind. Would you like your kite to be very simple? Then newspaper makes a good cover.

In addition to these materials, you will need a tube of glue and a ball of strong, light string to make a flying line. Choose a bright ribbon for the tail, and you are ready to put your kite together. Then go fly your kite.

Score: _____   Total Possible: 12

28

Proofread
Six of the following sentences have incorrect end marks. Use proper proofreading marks to delete the incorrect punctuation marks and add the correct ones.

Example: A giant sequoia is huge!

Many redwood trees and giant sequoia trees are more than two thousand years old. One bristlecone pine tree is believed to be almost six thousand years old. Now, that's old! But can trees be hurt? Yes, they can, and you will want to prevent that. Never injure a tree by cutting it, putting nails into it, or breaking its branches. Take care of trees near you. Be sure they get enough water. Remove dead and dying branches. Call a professional tree doctor if your tree is not doing well.

Practice
Write four sentences about the tree in the picture. Write at least one question and one sentence that ends with an exclamation point.

1. Review sentences to be sure your child has:
   • written complete sentences.
2. • made each sentence relevant to the picture.
   • shown an understanding of the relationship
3. between child and tree.
   • used at least one question and one exclamatory sentence.
4. • punctuated all sentences correctly.

Tips for Your Own Writing: Proofreading ....
Choose a piece of your own writing and look it over carefully for the use of end punctuation. If you find mistakes, copy the writing, correcting mistakes.

Do you feel sure about how to use end punctuation? Good!

29

Lesson 13

Lesson 13 Punctuation: Sentences

✏️ *Who do you know who talks without stopping? Maybe you do! When you write without stopping, though, you aren't helping your readers.*

·············· Did You Know? ··············

Some writers put sentences together that do not belong together. Using end punctuation and capital letters correctly will help you avoid this.

Incorrect punctuation: Mr. Aono is Jodi's father, he is an actor in Chicago.
Correct punctuation: Mr. Aono is Jodi's father. He is an actor in Chicago.
Incorrect punctuation: We watched the skaters in the park, aren't they good.
Correct punctuation: We watched the skaters in the park. Aren't they good?

Show What You Know

Rewrite the following paragraphs. Use correct end punctuation and capital letters to correct sentences.

There is only one place in the United States where four states meet, the four states are Colorado, Utah, New Mexico, and Arizona they meet at a place called Four Corners.

At Four Corners, you can see mountains and deserts, you can also visit parks and campgrounds, it is one of the most beautiful regions in the United States.

There is only one place in the United States where four states meet. The four states are Colorado, Utah, New Mexico, and Arizona. They meet at a place called Four Corners.

At Four Corners, you can see mountains and deserts. You can also visit parks and campgrounds. It is one of the most beautiful regions in the United States.

Score: _____ Total Possible: 8

30

Proofread

Use proper proofreading marks to show where four end marks and two capital letters should be used to correct the sentences.

Example: We went to a Chicago Bulls game they won!

Megan finally had the camera she had asked for it was a little heavier than her old one. She watched the dancers fly past her. She had never been to a polka party before would she be able to get any good pictures Everyone danced so fast Megan just knew she would end up with blurred pictures.

Practice

Write four sentences about a place you would like to visit. It may be a real place or an imaginary one. Make your sentences interesting by using questions and exclamatory sentences as well as statements. When you have written your sentences, read them very carefully to be sure you do not have two or more sentences joined together.

1. Review sentences to be sure your child has:
   • written four correct sentences.
2. • described a place.
3. • used a variety of sentence structures.
4. • used correct end punctuation.

Tips for Your Own Writing: Revising ·············

Choose a piece of your own writing and look it over carefully for incorrect sentences. Rewrite any incorrect sentences that you find. Be sure you use correct end punctuation in your sentences.

✏️ *A period can help you stop a sentence from running on and on and on!*

31

Lesson 14

Lesson 14 Punctuation: Sentence Fragments

✏️ *As a good writer, you know where to put end punctuation. Do you know there may be times when you need to take out some punctuation?*

·············· Did You Know? ··············

Some writers break sentences into parts, leaving one part that is not a complete sentence. These pieces of sentences are called sentence fragments. Using end punctuation and capital letters carefully will help you avoid sentence fragments.

Sentence and fragment: Please stay with me. Until the work is done.
Corrected sentence: Please stay with me until the work is done.
Sentence and fragment: We planned to go on a picnic. After it stopped raining.
Corrected sentence: We planned to go on a picnic after it stopped raining.

Show What You Know

Read the following paragraph. Underline the four sentence fragments.

For a long time, people believed that they had to eat a lot of meat. In order to be healthy. They ate meat. Whenever they could. Today we eat more whole-grain foods. Like bread, cereal, rice, and pasta. Fruits and vegetables are also important. For a healthy diet.

Score: _____ Total Possible: 4

32

Proofread

Find three sentence fragments in the paragraph below. Correct the sentence fragments by using proper proofreading marks for end punctuation and capitalization.

Example: I love to eat candy Whenever I can.

Wendell and his sister Jessica like games Although they like different kinds. Wendell spends most of his time throwing a ball around. He can move so fast in his wheelchair That his sister can't keep up with him. Jessica is always looking for someone to play Scrabble with her. She doesn't often ask her brother Because he can't spell very well. Sometimes they get together and have a swimming race.

Practice

Read the sentence fragments in the box below. Then write four sentences. Use one fragment in each sentence. End punctuation can help make your sentences clear and correct.

after the game	wondering what happened
not a competitor	no way to know

1. Review sentences to see that your child has:
2. • used each fragment in a clear sentence.
3. • used correct end punctuation.
4. • used correct capitalization.

Tips for Your Own Writing: Revising ·············

Choose a piece of your own writing and look it over carefully for sentence fragments. Then make corrections. Use end punctuation and capital letters correctly to help you make complete sentences.

✏️ *Did you see the sign on the good writers' clubhouse door? It read: No Fragments Allowed!*

33

168 Answer Key

Lesson 15

Lesson

15 Review: Punctuation

A. Use proper proofreading marks to add eight periods to the following paragraph.

There's always something interesting going on in my neighborhood.Early this morning, Ms.Bonnie Blair challenged me to a race around her Olympic-sized skating rink.I took a few swings in the batting cage of Mr.Cal Ripkin, Jr.Mr.David Robinson recently built a new basketball court.Last week, he invited Mr.Michael Jordan over to shoot some hoops.

Score: _____ Total Possible: 8

B. Use proper proofreading marks to show where seven periods should be placed in this paragraph.

Keith is the busiest friend I know. On Sat.he had dinner with the President. Tues.morning he recorded a CD with the Atomic Artichokes. He'll be on a world tour from Nov.to Feb.He plans to finish his new book in early Apr.Keith knows he'll be tired out by Sept.he's planning to relax for one hour every Fri.morning!

Score: _____ Total Possible: 7

C. Add seven question marks and three exclamation points to the sentences in the following paragraph.

What a happy story that is!Didn't Jeannie always want to be a teacher?Why was that a problem?Didn't she have arthritis when she was a kid?Of course she did!But didn't she finish college anyway?Yes, and didn't she become a teacher? She made it, so hurrah for Jeannie!Do you think her students will understand how hard she worked?Couldn't we tell them?

Score: _____ Total Possible: 10

D. Add three periods, one question mark, and two exclamation points where they are needed.

In the eighteenth century, lead was discovered in southwestern Wisconsin. Miners from Cornwall, a place in Great Britain, came to work in the mines.Why did the Cornish people come here?They were miners whose mines had closed. What a great opportunity!Later on, the Wisconsin mines closed, too.How awful!

Score: _____ Total Possible: 6

E. Use the proper proofreading marks to correct three sentence fragments.

1. Last week we saw a Winnebago storyteller.she used signs to tell her story.
2. What do you mean, she used signs?you can't tell stories with signs.
3. This woman did.it was just beautiful.

Score: _____ Total Possible: 7

F. Rewrite the following sentences to correct sentence fragments.

1. The traffic in any large city is terrible. Because there are so many cars.
2. Why don't people ride the bus? When they need to go downtown.
3. Someday there will be different forms of transportation. Because the air is getting so polluted.

1. _____ The traffic in any large city is terrible because there are so many cars.

2. _____ Why don't people ride the bus when they need to go downtown?

3. _____ Someday there will be different forms of transportation because the air is getting so polluted.

Score: _____ Total Possible: 3

REVIEW SCORE: _____ REVIEW TOTAL: 41

34

35

Lesson 16

Lesson

16 Punctuation: Commas in Series and Introductions

Commas help make a sentence clear.

Did You Know?

Words in a series should be separated by commas.
The five planets nearest the sun are Mercury, Venus, Earth, Mars, and Jupiter.
Mars, Earth, and Jupiter have satellites.

An introductory word is separated by a comma from the rest of the sentence.
Yes, those are some facts about the planets.
No, Mercury and Venus don't have satellites.
Well, let's find more information about planets.

Show What You Know

Read the report below. Add commas between the words in a series and after introductory words.

Some modern structures are best known for their great size. The tallest dams in the United States are in Colorado,Arizona,Idaho,and Nevada. The dams in the United States that hold the most water are in Arizona,Montana,and South Dakota. The United States also has three of the world's longest bridges. They are in New York,California,and Michigan.

Yes,there were also huge structures in the ancient world. Among these were statues,gardens,sphinxes,and temples. No,not all of these are still standing, but you still can see the Egyptian pyramids. All of these structures were the results of work by ancient artists,architects,engineers,and laborers.

Score: _____ Total Possible: 15

Proofread

Six sentences in the following paragraph contain mistakes in the use of commas. Use a caret to add commas where they are needed.

Example: I have my towel,swimsuit,and sunscreen.

Last year Lauren Brody's family tried a different kind of Labor Day celebration. Like many Americans, they usually celebrate with family trips,picnics, and swimming parties. Last year they traveled to Michigan to take a long walk across the Mackinac Bridge. On Labor Day, the bridge is closed to cars, buses, vans, and other vehicles. Walkers,runners,and wheelchair racers line up to cross the bridge, which is more than 3,800 feet long. The Brodys who planned to do the walk were Lauren, Michael,Mother,Dad,and Grandpa. The day was warm, sunny,and breezy. Yes,they all finished the walk and liked the new way to celebrate.

Practice

On another piece of paper, list three of your favorite hobbies or sports. Then use your list to help you write three sentences with words in a series. Begin at least one sentence with the word *well, yes, or no*. Use commas correctly.

Review sentences to be sure your child has:

• written his or her list of hobbies or sports.

• created clear sentences using correctly punctuated series.

• used an introductory word followed by a comma in at least one sentence.

Tips for Your Own Writing: Revising

Choose a paragraph from a piece of your own writing that you could improve by using names of places, words, or activities in a series. Rewrite the paragraph, using commas to make your series clear for your reader.

Well, now you know ways to use commas in lists, after introductory words, and in a series of ideas!

36

37

Lesson 17

Lesson

17 Punctuation: Commas in Dates, Addresses, and Direct Address

Wendy the warrior writer says, "Use commas to divide and conquer your sentences."

.... Did You Know? ....

A comma in a date separates the year from other words in the sentence.
On July 4, 1976, the U.S. celebrated its 200th birthday.

A comma in an address separates the name of a state from the rest of the sentence.
The movie was filmed in Cheyenne, Wyoming.

When a person is addressed by name, that person's name is separated from the rest of the sentence by a comma.
William, that movie was so boring I fell asleep.

Show What You Know

Read the letter below. Add commas where they are necessary.

72809 East Saddle Road
Omaha, Nebraska 68102
October 5, 2000

Dear Andrew and Jennifer,

Andrew, you have to come next month to ride with us in the parade. Afterward, we can go to Council Bluffs, Iowa, for a picnic. Jennifer, you wanted to see Arbor Lodge. That's in Nebraska City, Nebraska, and not far away. We can also go there if you come.

Your friend,
Jerry

Score: _____   Total Possible: 8

38

Proofread

Use a caret to add seven commas in the letter below.

Example: Grandpa, I understand you're coming for a visit on July 11, 1999.

712 Albert Avenue
Kansas City, Missouri 67153
June 6, 2000

Dear Grandma,

Mom, Dad, and I have moved around a lot, haven't we? The first time I remember moving was August 5, 1993, when we moved into a huge house in Chicago, Illinois. I didn't start third grade until after we moved on September 3, 1998. That move was to Kansas City, Missouri, which is my favorite place so far. I guess that's all for now, Grandma.

Love,
Angela

Practice

Write a funny story about these travelers. Use direct address, at least one date, and the name of one or two cities and states.

Review the story to be sure that your child has:

• based their story on the art.

• included at least one city and state.

• included at least one date.

Tips for Your Own Writing: Proofreading ....

The next time you write a letter, check your use of commas. Use proofreading marks to show changes that you need to make.

Isn't a comma a convenient little mark?

39

Lesson 18

Lesson

18 Punctuation: Commas in Dialogue

When writers include people in stories and reports, they often use dialogue to help readers "hear" these people. A comma separates the speaker's words from what is said.

.... Did You Know? ....

Dialogue is conversation between two or more persons. Dialogue is always separated from the rest of a sentence by a comma. Notice that the comma is always before the quotation marks.
"I'd like to make a box with three sides," Latisha said.
"Then use this pattern, cut it out, and fold it into a box," Jorge told her.

The words that someone says are always separated from the rest of the sentence by a comma.
"I'm sure you all know how to tie a knot," the mathematician told us.

Show What You Know

Read the dialogue below. Add commas to separate each speaker's words from the rest of the sentence.

When Arthur and his friend Albert get together, they often end up having a duel with weird facts that they have read. "It's a fact that picky eaters grow up to be an inch shorter than less fussy eaters," Arthur read while reaching for chips.

"Less fussy doesn't mean eating all the time," mumbled Albert.

"If you eat lots of sugar, you might have low intelligence," Arthur continued.

"You'll eat four tons of potatoes in your life," volunteered Albert.

"You'll drink two thousand gallons of milk in your lifetime, too," said Arthur.

"Don't eat pasta for lunch. It can make you sleepy," Albert mentioned.

"Yeah, but sleeping helps you grow," responded Arthur.

Score: _____   Total Possible: 7

40

Proofread

Use a caret (^) to add five commas to these sentences.

Example: "Please read us a book," begged the students.

"This is a great mystery story," Miss Lacy said.

"Tell us what it's about," Judith requested.

"Well, all I can tell you is that there is a treasure hidden somewhere here in Minneapolis," the teacher told them.

"People have looked for it for years," Laura explained.

"The clues to find the treasure map are in chapter five," Miss Lacy told the class as she held up the book with the bright cover.

Practice

Write a dialogue at least four sentences long for the girls in the picture.

Review sentences to be sure your child has:

• used the activities shown in the illustration.

• changed the wording to fit into a dialogue.

• used commas correctly.

• written dialogue that is interesting to peer readers.

Tips for Your Own Writing: Revising ....

Choose a story you have written that could have dialogue added. Rewrite the story, adding dialogue. Use a comma to separate the speaker's words from other parts of each sentence.

"I can't imagine a story without dialogue," said Gertie Grammar. Peter Punctuation agreed, "It would surely be boring!"

41

170   Answer Key

Lesson 19

Lesson 19 Punctuation: Commas and Sentences

You can often combine two sentences, but be on the alert for two sentences that shouldn't be punctuated as one.

Did You Know?

Two or more sentences written as though they were one sentence are hard to read. To correct this kind of problem, use a comma before the word *and* or *but* to separate the two short sentences.

Incorrect punctuation: I need a world map there's one in here.

Correct punctuation: I need a world map**,** and there's one in here.

A comma alone is not strong enough to join two sentences. It must be used with the word *and* or *but*.

Incorrect Sentence: I needed a book on iguanas, they were all checked out.

Correct Sentence: I needed a book on iguanas**,** but they were all checked out.

Show What You Know

Read the report below. Add five commas to correct the sentences.

North America is an interesting continent‚and it has great variety. There are many types of landforms, such as mountains, deserts, and prairies. Many kinds of animals live here‚but there are not as many as there used to be. There are still many wide-open spaces in North America‚but there are crowded cities, too. The United States and Mexico are part of North America. Canada is also in North America, and it is the biggest of the three countries. Farming is important in these countries‚but more people work in industry. Central America is a part of North America‚and it is made up of seven countries. In addition, there are many islands in the Caribbean that are considered to be part of North America.

Score: _____ Total Possible: 5

42

Proofread

Use a caret (^) to show where five commas should be added to correct the sentences in the paragraph below.

Example: One of my favorite sports is basketball‚but I also like football.

Basketball has become one of America's most popular sports‚and it can be played outside or indoors. Basketball became an Olympic Game in 1936‚but it was invented in 1891. Behind the basket is a backboard‚and this is usually made of a special type of glass. A team player's name is sometimes printed on his jersey‚and so is his number. A basketball is filled with air‚but it cannot weigh more than 22 ounces.

Practice

Match a sentence in Part I with a sentence in Part II to create a new sentence. Use commas and the words *and* or *but* to combine the sentences.

Part I
A hippopotamus is the third-largest land animal.
A hippopotamus has a good sense of smell.
The word *hippopotamus* means "river horse."

Part II
The animal is more like a hog than a horse.
Its vision is only fair.
Only the elephant and rhinoceros are larger.

1. A hippopotamus is the third-largest land animal, and only the elephant and rhinoceros are larger.

2. A hippopotamus has a good sense of smell, but its vision is only fair.

3. The word *hippopotamus* means "river horse," but the animal is more like a hog than a horse.

Tips for Your Own Writing: Proofreading

Choose a piece of your own writing. If you have used any incorrect sentences, rewrite them. You might add commas and words like *and* or *but*.

Commas can help you keep your words from running into each other!

43

Lesson 20

Lesson 20 Review: Commas

A. Use the proper proofreading mark to add six commas to the sentences below.

1. Well‚anyone who wants to learn about birds should begin with a good book.
2. Yes‚Chris bought one last week.
3. She told us that she has seen finches‚woodpeckers‚blackbirds‚and sparrows in her yard.
4. No‚she hasn't seen a large bird yet, but she hopes that she will.

Score: _____ Total Possible: 6

B. Use the proper proofreading mark to add three missing commas in this E-mail letter.

Sharon‚in my last note I told you about the visit to the Raven House in Fargo‚ North Dakota. Let me know if you want to see the pictures I took. The photographs were taken January 1‚2000.

Score: _____ Total Possible: 3

C. Read the paragraph below. Use the proper proofreading mark to add three commas where they are needed in three sentences.

The meanings of some words will surprise you‚and you can learn a lot about words you use all the time. An example is the word *margarine*. Until about a hundred years ago, there was nothing like the margarine we eat today. People used butter or lard on their bread and for cooking. Good lard was pearly white‚ and people began to call it "margarita." *Margarita* is the Latin word for "pearls." In 1854 a scientist named it *oleomargarine*‚but this word was too long. Soon people were calling it margarine.

Score: _____ Total Possible: 3

D. Read the following quotations carefully. Use the proper proofreading mark to add eight commas where they are needed.

"Once a lion fell asleep in the woods‚" I told my sister Emma. "A little mouse came along and crawled up on him" I said in a scary voice.

"The lion's going to get that mouse!" Emma exclaimed.

"When the lion felt those feet on him, he woke up and roared‚" I went on. "I'll bet you'd get out of this trouble if you were the mouse," I said to Em.

"That mouse isn't as smart as I‚" she reminded me.

So I went on. "The mouse told the lion he would help him someday‚" I said, smiling at my sister.

"I guess he is pretty smart," she said.

"The lion thought that was pretty funny, so he didn't hurt the mouse‚" I said.

"I can't imagine a mouse helping a lion‚" said Emma.

"We're both glad he got away, though‚" I said, and Emma nodded.

Score: _____ Total Possible: 8

E. Use the proper proofreading mark to add fourteen commas where they are needed in the book review.

On July 20‚1969‚Vivian and Gil Staender flew to the Brooks Range of Alaska. They were flown north from an area near Fairbanks‚Alaska‚in a small plane‚but the pilot of the plane who took them returned right away to the south. They planned to stay for a year in this Arctic spot. Yes‚it took courage‚but the Staenders had planned well. After the plane left them, Gil spoke. "It certainly is quiet here‚" he said. Everything was new. "Viv‚listen‚" Gil would often say. They were soon able to hear the sounds of moose‚bears‚wolves‚hawks‚and falcons.

Score: _____ Total Possible: 14

REVIEW SCORE: _____ REVIEW TOTAL: 34

44

45

Lesson 21 — Punctuation: Quotation Marks and Commas in Dialogue I

Quotation marks that point out a speaker's exact words help readers make sense of a piece of writing.

Did You Know?

A quotation begins and ends with quotation marks.
"Somebody cut down all the milkweed," Dr. Alvin complained.
"I don't like that. The monarch butterflies won't come," said Kwok.

When a comma separates the quotation from the rest of the sentence, the comma comes before the closing quotation mark.
"Well, let's plant more milkweed," suggested Alicia.

Show What You Know

Read the dialogue below. Add quotation marks before and after each speaker's words.

Cathal and his sister Colleen were searching a book of names for babies. "I'm glad we get to name the twins," said Colleen.

"Me, too," agreed Cathal.

"Here's a great name," cried Colleen as she held up the book. "We could call the girl Melissa."

"I want to call the boy Collin," Cathal said.

"OK, then we'll call the girl Constance," his sister stated firmly.

"We'll all have the same initials," warned their dad.

Score: _____ **Total Possible: 14**

46

Proofread

Use proper proofreading marks to add eight quotation marks where they are needed.

Example: "Monarch butterflies feed on milkweed," said Alicia.

1. "It took more than thirty minutes for that storm to pass," Joe said nervously.

2. "This is our home, so we are used to these storms," Agnes told him.

3. "Look, the moon is rising now," Grandmother pointed out.

4. "That means there will be no more storms for a while," Agnes stated quietly.

5. "Parts of the Southwest where you live, Joe, have few storms, but they can be strong ones, too," Grandmother warned.

6. "When you live here in the mountains, you get used to severe weather," Agnes added.

Practice

Write four statements about the weather where you live. Then write a dialogue between you and a visitor from a place that has different weather. Use quotation marks and commas to show the exact words of both speakers.

Review the dialogue to be sure your child has:
- written statements that are weather-related.
- produced reasonable and accurate dialogue.
- used quotation marks and commas correctly.

Tips for Your Own Writing: Revising

You can often make a written report stronger and more interesting by adding quotations. Find a piece of your own work that could be improved by adding quotations or dialogue. Rewrite the piece. Use commas and quotation marks carefully.

A story without dialogue is like a day without playtime!

47

Lesson 22 — Punctuation: Quotation Marks and Commas in Dialogue II

Quotation marks and commas help your reader keep tabs on who's saying what to whom.

Did You Know?

A quotation can be divided into parts. In a divided quotation, use a comma to separate both parts of the quotation from the rest of the sentence.

Undivided: "Geese can travel all day without stopping until evening," the scientist told us.
Divided: "Geese can travel all day," the scientist told us, "without stopping until evening."
Undivided: "We often hear them coming, and they head directly for our cornfield," the farmer said.
Divided: "We often hear them coming," the farmer said, "and they head directly for our cornfield."

Show What You Know

Read the paragraphs below. Add quotation marks and commas where they are needed.

"We're here because we know we need clean water," the group leader began, "and we're worried that it's becoming polluted."

"My dad says they used to drink water from the creek," a girl from a ranch told us, "but I certainly wouldn't do that today!"

"We get all of our drinking water from a well behind the house," a boy from a small town said, "and some days I think it smells funny. I'm afraid it won't be good much longer."

"Some days," a city kid announced, "our tap water is sort of gray."

"Well," the leader agreed, "it looks like we all need some help."

Score: _____ **Total Possible: 30**

48

Proofread

Use proper proofreading marks to add five commas and nine quotation marks to the dialogue below.

Example: "Spiders have eight legs," said Ms. Web, "and they spin silk."

"It has wings, six legs, and a light body," Miss Brave Bird said, "so it's a butterfly." She looked right at me. "Is that right?" she asked.

"Well, sure," I answered, "that's what butterflies look like." For some reason, a few kids were giggling.

"Listen to this sentence then," she said, "and see if you agree with it, too."

"If it has wings, six legs, and a light body," she repeated, "it's a moth."

"I'd better look it up," I told her. Miss Brave Bird smiled.

Practice

Rewrite these quotations as divided quotations.

1. "A lepidopterist studies insects, including butterflies and moths," I told Mother.
2. "I know butterflies are out in the day, but I don't know about moths," she said.
3. "Butterflies fold their wings vertically, and moths fold theirs horizontally," I added.

1. "A lepidopterist studies insects," I told Mother, "including butterflies and moths."

2. "I know butterflies are out in the day," she said, "but I don't know about moths."

3. "Butterflies fold their wings vertically," I added, "and moths fold theirs horizontally."

Tips for Your Own Writing: Proofreading

Choose a story you have written using quotation marks. Have you used quotations that might sound better if you rewrote them as divided quotations? If so, revise your work.

Divided quotations and undivided quotations in the same story will give your sentences some variety and keep your writing from being dull.

49

Lesson 23

Lesson
23 Punctuation: Quotation Marks in Titles

Quotation marks are used for more than quotations.

.... Did You Know? ....

Quotation marks are used to set off the titles of reports, short stories, and poems.

The class put together a report on caring for the environment. They called it "Take Care of That!" They had read Mitsumasa Anno's story, "The King's Flower," about respecting little things. They also read a poem called "Song of the Pop-Bottlers" by Morris Bishop.

....

Show What You Know
Add quotation marks around titles of reports, poems, and stories in the paragraphs below.

Do you like to read stories? Stories come from all over the world. "Abiyoyo" is about magic and comes from South Africa. "Remaking the World" is a story told by the Brule Sioux. "The Fox and the Grapes" is a fable from Greece.

Perhaps you love poems. People seem to write poems about anything, even sometimes about weird things. Aileen Fisher wrote "Noses" after looking into her mirror. "Things To Do If You Are a Subway" is a poem by Bobbi Katz. "Rudolph Is Tired of the City" is a poem by Gwendolyn Brooks.

If you ever write a report about the kinds of things you like to read, you'd have to think of a title. Titles should get the reader's attention. Here are two titles—"Mixed-up People with Mixed-up Tales" and "Reading I Liked"—that could be used for a report. Which one would attract your attention?

Score: _____   Total Possible: 16

50

Proofread
Use proper proofreading marks to add ten missing quotation marks to the titles below.

Example: When I was very young, my favorite nursery rhyme was "Little Boy Blue."

1. "Narcissa" is a poem by Gwendolyn Brooks.

2. Rudyard Kipling's "The Way Through the Woods" is a serious poem.

3. My two favorite poems are "Silver" and "Bones" by Walter De La Mare.

4. "Small Star and Mud Pony" is an old Pawnee tale.

5. Did you read the story "The Thirteen Clocks" by James Thurber?

6. "Gotcha" is a very interesting report on new books.

Practice
Think of four people or animals you know who would be good subjects for a funny poem or story. Write one sentence about each one. Then write a great title you might use if you decide to write the story or poem.

Review to be sure that your child has:

• named four persons or animals and written an
  informative sentence about each.

• created a title for each poem or story.

• written the titles with proper spelling, capitalization, and punctuation.

• written titles that are intriguing and/or original.

Tips for Your Own Writing: Proofreading ....
Choose a report, short story, or poem you have written. Use proofreading marks to show where quotation marks should be placed.

Have you read the new report "A Thousand and One Uses for Quotation Marks"?

51

Lesson 24

Lesson
24 Punctuation: Book and Movie Titles

Do you write with a pen or on a computer? It will make a difference when you write some kinds of titles.

.... Did You Know? ....

There are special rules for writing titles of books and movies.

When the name of a book or movie is published, or is printed on a computer, the title is shown in italic type like this: *Babe.*

How to Make a Mummy Talk
Where in the World Is Carmen Sandiego?

When the name of a book or movie is written by hand, the title is underlined.

How to Make a Mummy Talk

....

Show What You Know
Circle the titles of books and movies in the story.

For her tenth birthday, Rosa Garcia's mother bought her a book about a ten-year-old girl who was also named Rosa. Rosa de Jong lived in Holland during World War II, more than fifty years ago. The name of the book about her life is Dancing on the Bridge of Avignon. Then Rosa Garcia found a paperback book about a boy who had also lived during World War II. Yankele lived in Poland. That book's title is Along the Tracks. Rosa thought both books were sad but very interesting, so she and her mother watched an old movie about the war. The movie's title is Mrs. Miniver and it helped Rosa see the war through an Englishwoman's eyes. Together, Rosa and her mother read another book about two kids escaping from the war. The title is She Flew No Flags. It was harder to read, but Rosa thought it was exciting and romantic and not as sad.

Score: _____   Total Possible: 4

52

Proofread
Underline the titles of two books and two movies below.

Example: They have made the book The Hunchback of Notre Dame into a movie.

Two books I'd like to read are:

1. Strange Journey Back by Paul McCusker

2. Stranger in the Mirror by Allen Say

Two videos I'd like to see are:

1. Strangers in Good Company

2. D2: The Mighty Ducks

Practice
Make a list of two favorite books and two movies you enjoyed. Write a sentence describing each one. Perhaps you can share your list with a friend.

Review the list to be sure your child has:

• listed genuine titles.

• correctly underlined titles.

Tips for Your Own Writing: Proofreading ....
Choose a report you wrote on a book or movie. Are all titles written correctly?

When you're typing on a computer, remember to use italic type for titles of books and movies. When you write, underline them!

53

Answer Key **173**

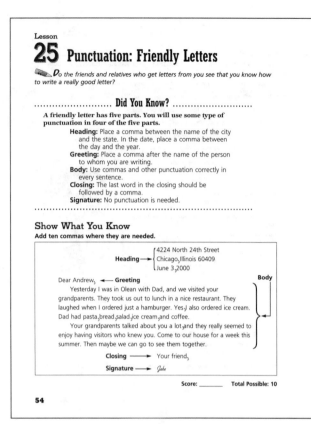

25 Punctuation: Friendly Letters

Do the friends and relatives who get letters from you see that you know how to write a really good letter?

.... **Did You Know?** ....

A friendly letter has five parts. You will use some type of punctuation in four of the five parts.

Heading: Place a comma between the name of the city and the state. In the date, place a comma between the day and the year.

Greeting: Place a comma after the name of the person to whom you are writing.

Body: Use commas and other punctuation correctly in every sentence.

Closing: The last word in the closing should be followed by a comma.

Signature: No punctuation is needed.

Show What You Know

Add ten commas where they are needed.

Heading → 4224 North 24th Street
Chicago, Illinois 60409
June 3, 2000

Dear Andrew, ← **Greeting**

Body

Yesterday I was in Olean with Dad, and we visited your grandparents. They took us out to lunch in a nice restaurant. They laughed when I ordered just a hamburger. Yes, I also ordered ice cream. Dad had pasta, bread, salad, ice cream, and coffee.

Your grandparents talked about you a lot, and they really seemed to enjoy having visitors who knew you. Come to our house for a week this summer. Then maybe we can go to see them together.

Closing ————→ Your friend,

Signature ————→ *Jake*

Score: _____ Total Possible: 10

54

Proofread

Find the punctuation errors in the letter below. Use proper proofreading marks to add four commas and a period.

Example: Gina, can you meet me in Denver, Colorado, on May 16?

18 Western Boulevard
Butte, Montana 59701
October 16, 2000

Dear Grandmother,

Remember when you read <u>Jumanji</u> to us? Well, now it's a movie. If you see it, let me know if you liked it. I loved it.

You should come here next summer. We'd have a lot of fun.

Love,

Susan

Practice

Write the body of a letter to a friend or relative who lives in another town. Tell about something that made you think of him or her. Copy the letter onto another piece of paper, adding the other four parts.

Review the letter to be sure your child has:

• included all five parts of a friendly letter.

• used commas and periods correctly, including in the body of the letter.

• written a clear and friendly message.

Tips for Your Own Writing: Proofreading ....

Look at the letter you just wrote. Check to see that you used commas appropriately in the heading, the greeting, and the closing of your letter.

Punctuation helps you make your point!

55

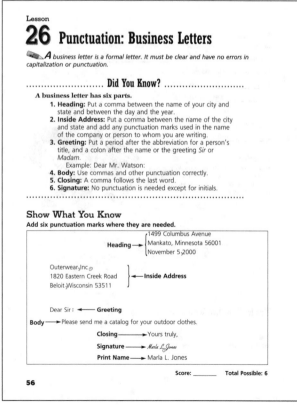

26 Punctuation: Business Letters

A business letter is a formal letter. It must be clear and have no errors in capitalization or punctuation.

.... **Did You Know?** ....

A business letter has six parts.

1. Heading: Put a comma between the name of your city and state and between the day and the year.

2. Inside Address: Put a comma between the name of the city and state and add any punctuation marks used in the name of the company or person to whom you are writing.

3. Greeting: Put a period after the abbreviation for a person's title, and a colon after the name or the greeting *Sir* or *Madam*.
Example: Dear Mr. Watson:

4. Body: Use commas and other punctuation correctly.

5. Closing: A comma follows the last word.

6. Signature: No punctuation is needed except for initials.

Show What You Know

Add six punctuation marks where they are needed.

Heading → 1499 Columbus Avenue
Mankato, Minnesota 56001
November 5, 2000

Outerwear, Inc.
1820 Eastern Creek Road → **Inside Address**
Beloit, Wisconsin 53511

Dear Sir : ← **Greeting**

Body → Please send me a catalog for your outdoor clothes.

Closing ————→ Yours truly,

Signature ————→ *Marla L. Jones*

Print Name ————→ Marla L. Jones

Score: _____ Total Possible: 6

56

Proofread

Find five punctuation mistakes in the letter below. Use proper proofreading marks to show corrections.

Example: We live in Grand Rapids, Michigan.

1929 May Boulevard
Kansas City, Kansas 66106
October 1, 2000

Games for You
12 Rush Street
Grand Junction, Colorado 81501

Dear Ms. Green:

Thank you for sending your catalog. I want to order Item 6682, the game "Let Me Help." A check from my father is enclosed.

Yours truly,

Joey Waters

Practice

Write the body of a business letter to the President of the United States. Tell the President what you like best about the nation. Copy the letter onto another piece of paper, using the correct form for a business letter.

Review the letter to make sure your child has:

• addressed his or her letter correctly.

• written a clear message.

• used correct business letter form.

• used correct business letter punctuation.

Tips for Your Own Writing: Proofreading ....

When you write a business letter, check your punctuation carefully. Did you use commas in the heading, the inside address, and the closing? Did you use a colon in the greeting?

People won't take your letters seriously if the letters have lots of mistakes.

57

Lesson 27

Lesson
27 Review: Quotation Marks

A. Use proper proofreading marks to show where eight quotation marks should be placed in the following sentences.

1. "Everybody likes watching basketball on TV," Aki said.

2. "I think you're wrong," Jessica told her.

3. Carl said, "Jessica is right, because I'd rather play than watch."

4. "Well, we're watching it now, anyway," Aki told them.

Score: _____ Total Possible: 8

B. Use proper proofreading marks to show where to add five commas and ten quotation marks in the following sentences.

"Winds can reach 65 miles an hour during a storm here," a ranger told us as we set up camp.

"A tent won't be any protection in that kind of storm," Angela said.

"We'll turn on our radio several times a day," Mr. Simon promised her. He said, "That should warn us in plenty of time if a storm is coming."

The ranger added, "Then you will all come to the cabins if the weather gets bad."

Score: _____ Total Possible: 15

C. Use proper proofreading marks to show where to add ten quotation marks.

Yaeko wrote a report called "Something to Do This Weekend." He listed two poems and two stories he thought his friends would enjoy.

Stories
"Blue Moose" by Manus Pinkwater
"The Case of the Stolen Yacht" by Walter Myers

Poems
"The Bat" by Theodore Roethke
"Explanations" by Aliki Barnstone

Score: _____ Total Possible: 10

58

D. Underline fourteen titles in the sentences below.

1. If you liked <u>Morning Girl</u> by Michael Dorris, you will love his newer book, which is called <u>Guests</u>.

2. You'll find mystery stories by Walter Dean Myers in <u>Smiffy Blue, Ace Crime Detective</u>.

3. Shel Silverstein wrote and illustrated a book of poems called <u>A Light in the Attic</u>.

4. If you liked J.K. Rowling's book <u>Harry Potter and the Sorcerer's Stone</u>, you can find other books by the same writer.

5. Gail Carson Levine's book, <u>Ella Enchanted</u>, offers a twist on the Cinderella story. Is it as good as her other book, <u>The Princess Test</u>?

6. Do you read science fiction? Try <u>The Arkadians</u> by Lloyd Alexander.

7. Carol Fenner's book, <u>Yolonda's Genius</u>, is about an African-American girl.

8. If you read aloud to younger kids, try <u>Twist with a Burger, Jitter with a Bug</u> by Linda Lowery and <u>A Drop of Rain</u> by Wong Herber Yee.

9. Lois Lowry has written many popular books. <u>Number the Stars</u> and <u>The Giver</u> both won Newbery awards.

10. Try <u>The St. Patrick's Day Shamrock Mystery</u> by Marion M. Markham if you want something easy and fun to read.

Score: _____ Total Possible: 14

E. Write a one-sentence movie review for two of your favorite movies. Underline each movie's name.

Sample reviews are given.

1. The movie *Flipper* will make a dolphin lover out of you. _____

2. *Babe* is a great movie for all ages. _____

Score: _____ Total Possible: 2

REVIEW SCORE: _____ REVIEW TOTAL: 49

59

Lesson 28

Lesson
28 Usage: Verbs—Came/Come, Rang/Rung, Sang/Sung

Today we sing. Yesterday we sang. We sang a song we had sung before. Verb forms tell you when something has happened.

.... **Did You Know?** ....

Some verbs have two forms that you can use to tell about past actions. Notice how the spelling of these verbs changes when the verb has a helping word with it. Three of the most common helping words are *have, has,* and *had.*

I **came** home late yesterday.
Have you ever **come** too late for something important?

I was late because the school bell **rang** early.
It **had rung** early in the morning, too.

My cousins **sang** a great song.
They **had sung** it before, but I hadn't heard it.

....

Show What You Know
In each space below, write one word from the pair of words at the top of the paragraph.

came, come

Summer has __come__ , and the goat herders are moving their flocks. In
        1
earlier years, when summer __came__ early, they moved the animals sooner.
                          2

rang, rung

Many years ago, one goat often wore a bell. The flock would follow the
bell. If the bell had __rung__ from far off, the herder knew something was
                     3
wrong. A bell that __rang__ nearby signaled that the flock was near.
                   4

sang, sung

Cowhands are herders, too. There are stories about cowboys who sing to
their herds to keep the animals calm. Many of the songs these herders
__sang__ are well known today. Perhaps you have __sung__ them in school.
  5   6

Score: _____ Total Possible: 6

60

Proofread
Read the sentences. If an underlined word is not used correctly, draw a delete mark through the word and write the correct word above it. There are four mistakes.

Example: She had ~~sing~~ very nicely. (sung)

All of Megan's friends had <u>come</u> to a party to help her celebrate getting
well again. Megan's grandmother <u>come</u> late from work, but she was glad to see (came)
                                     2
everybody.

At the party they ate and ate and ate, and then they <u>sang</u> songs. Everything
                                                         3
that they had <u>sang</u> was new to Grandma. "I bet you learned all of those songs (sung)
               4
from your CDs," she said.

Just as the party was getting really fun, the doorbell <u>rung</u>. Terri's Dad had (rang)
                                                          5
<u>come</u> to take her home. Soon, the doorbell had <u>rang</u> for every guest, and only (rung)
  6   7
Megan and her family were left.

Practice
Write a story, a poem (some of the words in this lesson rhyme), or sentences. Use each of these verbs at least once: *sang, sung, rang, rung, came, come.*

Review the writing to make sure your child has:
• used the given verbs correctly.
• written and punctuated sentences correctly.

Tips for Your Own Writing: Proofreading ....
Choose a piece of your own writing and look for verbs used in this lesson and for other verbs that have several forms. Did you use helping words such as *has* or *had* with forms such as *rung* and *sung*?

Have you (sang, sung) a song to celebrate finishing this lesson?

61

Lesson 29

Lesson 29 Usage: Verbs–Took/Taken, Gave/Given, Ate/Eaten

In the right place at the right time—the right verb form will get you there.

Did You Know?

Some verbs have one spelling when they tell about the past without a helping word and another spelling when they follow a helping word. Some helping words are verbs such as *have, has, had, was,* and *were.*

> We each **took** an apple for the horses to eat.
> We **have taken** apples with us every time we have gone to the farm.
> Eva, though, **has taken** a box of sugar cubes before.
>
> Eva **gave** her favorite horse some sugar cubes.
> She **has given** all the best treats to that lucky horse!
>
> The horses came to the fence and **ate** the apples.
> When all the apples **were eaten,** we went for a ride.

Show What You Know

In each space below, write the correct word from the pair of words in parentheses at the end of each sentence.

1. Public television has __given__ viewers many nature programs. (gave, given)

2. If you have __taken__ advantage of these programs, you probably know a lot about animals in distant places. (took, taken)

3. One nature program __gave__ exciting facts about lions and hyenas. (gave, given)

4. Viewers learned that these animals often __ate__ the same foods. (ate, eaten)

5. After the lions have __eaten__, they are ready to sleep. (ate, eaten)

6. Students who __took__ time to watch these programs found them interesting. (took, taken)

Score: _____   Total Possible: 6

62

Proofread

Look at the word in bold type in each sentence. If a word is used incorrectly, draw a delete mark through it. Then write the correct form of the word above it. There are five mistakes.

Example: The horse had ~~ate~~ *eaten* all the hay.

1. "Who **given** *gave* us the directions to get here?" Michael asked.

2. "Well, I was **gave** *given* the wrong ones," complained Jennifer.

3. "Yes," agreed Karl. "If I had **took** *taken* those directions, I'd be lost."

4. "I **took** them," said Colin. "And I got here!"

5. "Well, you're so late that we have already **ate** *eaten*. Ask Mom for more sandwiches if you're hungry," Maggie told them.

6. "I've **ate** *eaten*, so I'm not hungry," Michael replied.

Practice

Write a paragraph of at least four sentences about the picture. Use at least one of the words *gave, given, ate, eaten, took,* and *taken* in each sentence.

_____ Review sentences to make sure your child has:

_____ • punctuated sentences correctly.

_____ • written sentences relevant to the picture.

_____ • used at least four of the given words.

_____

_____

Tips for Your Own Writing: Proofreading

Read aloud a piece of your writing. Do all of your verb forms sound right? Check to see that you used the correct verb form.

Have you (took, taken) care to use verbs correctly? You have been (gave, given) rules in this lesson.

63

Lesson 30

Lesson 30 Usage: Verbs–Began/Begun, Fell/Fallen, Went/Gone

Writers with good timing learn the verb forms that tell when in time the action takes place.

Did You Know?

Began, begun, fell, fallen, went, and *gone* are among the words that need special attention. One in each pair of these words needs a helping verb. Some helping verbs are *have, has, had, was,* and *were.*

> Marilyn **began** to enjoy poetry.
> She **had begun** reading poems a year ago.
>
> Marilyn says a book of poetry **fell** in front of her.
> Do you think she would read math all the time if a math book **had fallen** at her feet?
>
> Anyway, she **went** right to the poetry section.
> She liked the poems so much that she **has gone** to that section often.

Show What You Know

If the underlined word is used correctly, write C in the space. If it is used incorrectly, write the correct form of the word.

1. It was October, and leaves <u>began</u> to fall. __C__

2. That meant the cranes had <u>began</u> traveling south. __begun__

3. Along the Platte River, cottonwood leaves <u>fell</u> into yellow piles. __C__

4. Soon, visitors arrived, kicking through leaves that had <u>fell</u>. __fallen__

5. As the cranes <u>began</u> to arrive, more visitors came to watch them. __C__

6. Scientists <u>went</u> to the river, too. __C__

7. They stayed until the last cranes had <u>went</u> south. __gone__

Score: _____   Total Possible: 7

64

Proofread

Read the story below. If the word in bold type is used incorrectly, draw a delete mark through it. Then write the correct word above it. There are five mistakes.

Example: They ~~gone~~ *went* to the store.

Bryan watched all day, but no snow **fell**. First, he had ~~went~~ *gone* to the kitchen, then he **went** to the window in the front room. Still, no snow had ~~fell~~ *fallen*. Finally, Bryan ~~gone~~ *went* to the basement to get his toboggan. He found it in the corner, covered with dust. He filled a pail with some warm, soapy water and ~~begun~~ *began* to wash the toboggan. "Well," he said, "if it ever does snow, I'll be ready." Bryan put the toboggan back in the corner and **went** upstairs. Passing the kitchen door, he looked out. Snow had ~~began~~ *begun* falling!

Practice

Choose one pair of words: *began, begun; fell, fallen;* or *went, gone.* Write a story in which you use that pair of words at least one time.

_____ Review the story to make sure your child has:

_____ • written a story with a beginning, middle, and end.

_____ • used each word of the selected pair at least one time.

_____ • used each word correctly.

_____ • written properly organized sentences.

_____ • shown creative thought in the organization of the story.

Tips for Your Own Writing: Proofreading

Next time you write about something that happened in the past, check carefully for verbs that change their spellings when they are used with helping words. Remember, a dictionary can help you find the correct spellings for these verbs.

Did you ever fall into the trap of mixing up the words fell and fallen?

65

Lesson 31

Lesson 31 Review: Verbs

A. Write in the blank the word that correctly completes each sentence.

1. Scientists have __come__ to the ocean to study the dolphins. (came, come)
2. Last year many __came__ from far away. (came, come)
3. At the oceanarium, trainers have __rung__ bells to have dolphins do tricks. (rang, rung)
4. In the ocean, no bells __rang__ as the beautiful animals circled gracefully. (rang, rung)
5. Those who listened said the dolphins __sang__. (sang, sung)
6. They have always whistled or __sung__ to talk to one another. (sang, sung)

Score: _____ Total Possible: 6

B. Write in the blank the word that completes each of the six sentences.

(took, taken)

A diver __took__₁ a camera underwater. He has __taken__₂ a tank with enough air to keep him safe for an hour.

(gave, given)

He knows these dolphins and has __given__₃ them names. He says they __gave__₄ one another names long ago.

(ate, eaten)

The dolphins __ate__₅ as they swam together. When dolphins have __eaten__₆ the food in one area, they will move away.

Score: _____ Total Possible: 6

C. Write in the blank the word that correctly completes each of the six sentences.

1. People's interest in dolphins __began__ long ago. (began, begun)
2. Scientists had __begun__ studying the intelligent animals. (began, begun)
3. They noticed that the number of dolphins had __fallen__ in some areas. (fell, fallen)
4. Why the number __fell__ was not known. (fell, fallen)
5. Sometimes the dolphins simply __went__ away. (went, gone)
6. Where, and why, had they __gone__? (went, gone)

Score: _____ Total Possible: 6

D. Write in the blanks the ten words that correctly complete each sentence.

The audience had known the program would be good because the students had __given__ ₁(gave, given) concerts before. Students holding handbells had __rung__ ₂(rang, rung) the bells in perfect order. Then the chorus had __sung__ ₃(sang, sung) winter songs. As the audience __went__ ₄(went, gone) home, they said they were glad they had __come__ ₅(came, come).

Most of those who __came__ ₆(came, come) were friends and families of the students. They knew the children worked hard every time they __gave__ ₇(gave, given) a concert. They __rang__ ₈(rang, rung) their handbells at long practices and __sang__ ₉(sang, sung) hard songs over and over to get them right. The students had __gone__ ₁₀(went, gone) to a lot of work for this concert.

Score: _____ Total Possible: 10

REVIEW SCORE: _____ REVIEW TOTAL: 28

66 67

Lesson 32

Lesson 32 Usage: Verbs—Sit/Set

Sometimes people spell words the way they hear them pronounced. Say the words sit and set until you can hear the difference.

.... **Did You Know?** ....

Sit means "to take a seat." *Sitting* and *sat* are other forms of *sit*. *Sitting* shows an action that is going on. *Sat* shows an action that happened in the past.

> Do you **sit** in the same seat on the bus every day?
> I **sat** there yesterday.
> I **have sat** there every time I have taken the bus.
> Are you **sitting** there now?

Set means "to put something in a place." *Set* has one other form: *setting*.

> Please **set** the pizza on the table.
> I **have set** the plates on the table already.
> You should be **setting** the glasses on the counter.

Show What You Know

Write *sit, sat, sitting, set,* or *setting* in each space in the following paragraphs.

Do you know the story of Jack Sprat who __sat__₁ down at the table and asked for lean meat? His wife, who was __sitting__₂ across from him, said she would eat the fatty parts. They were the kind of people who always ate the same food and __sat__₃ in the same place. Maybe they would have had more fun if they had __sat__₄ at a different table and eaten different food.

Then there's the story of Dr. Foster who went to Gloucester when it was raining. He __set__₅ his foot down in a big puddle. The story says Dr. Foster wouldn't go to Gloucester anymore. What if he had __set__₆ his foot in a dry spot? I don't think that __setting__₇ your foot in one puddle should make you dislike a whole town. Of course, the story says that the puddle was "up to his middle." I guess he really had __set__₈ his foot in a puddle!

Score: _____ Total Possible: 8

Proofread

Draw delete marks through the five words in bold type that are not correct. Write the correct form above each word.

Example: He has ~~sit~~ *set* the table for dinner.

The crystals in the geology museum were **set** out in rows on a table. "No two crystals are exactly alike," said a guide who was ~~sitting~~ *setting* labels next to the crystals. He pointed to the label of a green crystal as he ~~sat~~ *set* it down. The label said "Beryl Crystal." A white crystal with needlelike edges had been **set** inside a closed glass box. "This is like asbestos," the guide said as he ~~sat~~ *set* its label down next to it. "Its needles are soft."

A boy who was ~~setting~~ *sitting* at the table said he owned a crystal with hard needles. "It's gray, not silvery like this one," he said. He **sat** there a long time, examining every crystal. Some museum visitors were invited to ~~set~~ *sit* on the floor to listen to a lecture on crystals.

Practice

Write four sentences. Use *sit, sat,* and *set* at least one time each.

1. Review sentences to make sure your child has:
   • used correct sentence structure.
2. • used the assigned words correctly.
3. • included the words *sit, sat,* and *set* at least once.
4.

Tips for Your Own Writing: Proofreading

Next time you write about someone *sitting* or *setting*, stop and ask yourself, "Is this person taking a seat or putting something in place?" This test will help you choose the right word.

Don't just sit there! Learn the difference between sit *and* set.

68 69

Answer Key **177**

Lesson 33

Lesson

33 Usage: Can/May, Of/Have

✏️ *When their meanings or sounds are similar, words sometimes get mixed up.*

.... **Did You Know?** ....

Can means "to be able to."
> **Can** you ice skate? (Are you able to ice skate?)
> **I could** skate better if I had my own skates. (I would be able to skate better if I had my own skates.)

May means "to be allowed to."
> Your mother says you **may** go skating with the class. (You are allowed to go.)

The meanings of the words *of* and *have* are not alike at all, but they can be mixed up because they sometimes sound alike. Read these sentences aloud:
> I **could have** gone skating.
> I thought **of** going yesterday.

Think how most people would say the first sentence: I could've gone skating. When you hear the sentence, it is easy to hear *could of*. When you write, make sure you use the correct spelling: *could've*.

....

Show What You Know

Write *may* or *can* in each space in the sentences.

I'll climb the mountain if you think I ___can___ make it to the top! The ranger said we ___may___ have permission to camp overnight. ___Can___ you play a guitar? We want music at our campfire. I'm glad my parents said I ___may___ come to this camp again.

Write *of* or *-'ve* in each space in the sentences.

We would ___'ve___ skated better if it weren't so cold. We all learned a lot ___of___ new skating moves, though. We all should ___'ve___ brought our own skates. Then we might ___'ve___ stayed longer, too.

Score: _____   Total Possible: 8

70

Proofread

Draw delete marks through any incorrect words in bold type. Write the correct form above each incorrect word. There are four mistakes.

Example: You ~~can~~ have some cookies. *(may)*

A tornado **can** do great damage. Ask neighbors if you ~~can~~ go into their *(may)* basements in case of a tornado. During the storms last summer, more people should ~~of~~ taken shelter. Earlier warning would also ~~of~~ helped people avoid *('ve)* *(have)* injury. Have you heard **of** any tornadoes in your part of the country? Ask if sometime you ~~can~~ visit a weather center and talk about storms. *(may)*

Practice

Write a sentence using *can* and a sentence using *may*. Then, write three more sentences using *should've* or *might've*, and *heard of.*

1. _____
   Check sentences to make sure your child has:
2. _____
   • used each term correctly.
   • written sentences that make sense.
   • used correct spelling and punctuation.
3. _____
4. _____
5. _____

Tips for Your Own Writing: Proofreading ....

Using *of* in place of *have* or *-'ve* is a common error in writing. Next time you write, remember that *have* or *-'ve* follows helping words such as *might, could, would,* or *should*.

✏️ *Should've, would've, could've—don't let* of *get in the way of correct writing.*

71

═══════════════════════════════════════

Lesson 34

Lesson

34 Usage: Verbs—Let/Leave

✏️ *Don't let these words mix you up; if you know what they mean, you can leave confusion behind.*

.... **Did You Know?** ....

Let means "to allow" or "to permit."
> Will your parents **let** you come to the concert with me?

Leave means "to go away from" or "to allow something or someone to remain as is." *Left* is the form of the word *leave* used when speaking or writing in the past tense.
> When you **leave** the room, don't **leave** the door open.
> I hope you **left** those papers the way they were.

Leave and *let* have the same meaning in just one case. Either word can be used.
> Please **leave** me alone.   Please **let** me alone.

....

Show What You Know

Write *let, leave,* or *left* in each sentence below.

1. The librarian ___let___ us use a tape recorder to listen to Shel Silverstein's funny poems.
2. We didn't ___leave___ a single book of his poems on the shelf.
3. My friend Harold should have ___left___ his other tapes at home!
4. He kept taking my tape—he wouldn't ___let/leave___ me alone.
5. Knowing how to use the library catalog will ___let___ you find other books of poems.
6. Don't ___leave___ the library without *A Drop of Rain* to read to a younger brother, sister, or friend.

Score: _____   Total Possible: 6

72

Proofread

Five of the words in bold type are used incorrectly. Draw a delete mark through each incorrect word and write the correct word above it.

Example: Please ~~leave~~ us go to the movies. *(let)*

The Feldman family **left** for vacation in South Dakota the day school ended.
"~~Leave~~ me ride in the front, please," Morley said. *(Let)*
"We may ~~let~~ you at home," teased his father. They had planned to ~~let~~ their *(leave)* *(leave)* dog Poppy behind. At the last minute, Sarah decided she couldn't ~~let~~ without *(leave)* Poppy. Dad **let** the dog climb into the back of the car. Then Morley started teasing Poppy.
"~~Leave~~ him sit still," said Sarah. While driving across Iowa, Sarah said to her *(Let)* family, "Now, everybody, **let** me alone so that I can read all about South Dakota."

Practice

Write a story in which you use the words *let* and *leave* at least twice. Use the picture for story ideas.

Review the story to make sure your child has:
• used the picture as a starting point for his or her story.
• used words in the assigned pair at least twice.
• used the assigned words correctly.

Tips for Your Own Writing: Proofreading ....

See if you can find a piece of your writing in which you used *let* and *leave*. To test whether you chose the right word, substitute *permit* for *let*, and *go away from* or *allow someone or something to remain* for *leave*. If the sentence still makes sense, you will know that your word choice was correct.

✏️ *Let us leave no stone unturned when looking for mixed-up words.*

73

Lesson 35

Lesson 35 Review: Verbs

A. Write *set, sat,* or *sitting* in each blank to correctly complete each of the five sentences below.

Chairs had been ___set___ up for Joseph's party guests. The guests
___sat___ in a circle around a huge birthday cake. They ___set___ the
birthday gifts they had brought on a big rock nearby. Quickly, Joseph reached
out, grabbed the cake, and ___set___ it on the ground. The elephant paid no
attention to the guests who were ___sitting___ there, waiting to celebrate his
birthday.

Score: _____   **Total Possible: 5**

B. Write the word *can* or *may* to complete each of the six sentences below.

You ___may___ use this pool only if a lifeguard is present. Members
___may___ bring one guest. If you ___can___ swim, you ___may___ may use
the deep end of the pool. Good swimmers ___may___ sign up to pass
Intermediate Tests. Swimming ___can___ be fun or dangerous. Be careful!

Score: _____   **Total Possible: 6**

C. Write *of* or *-'ve* in the blanks to correctly complete each of the five sentences below.

My friends couldn't find enough ___of___ the books they wanted to read
yesterday. They all wanted to read *Guests*, but should ___'ve___ checked first
to see that there were enough copies of the book in the library. Some of them
could ___'ve___ read *Morning Girl*. Then they might ___'ve___ shared their
ideas about the two stories. It seems that many ___of___ my friends like the
same kinds of books.

Score: _____   **Total Possible: 5**

74

D. Write the word *let, leave,* or *left* to complete each of the following eight sentences.

"Please ___leave/let___ me alone—I need to think," said Kevin. Our parents had
___left___ us at the zoo by mistake. We were supposed to go at 3:00, but we
didn't ___leave___ the big cat house on time. "I wish the zookeeper would
___let___ me feed the tigers," Kevin said. The tigers wouldn't ___leave___ the
door where the zookeeper was preparing to feed them.

"We should go now," I said. "Mom and Dad might ___leave___ us here."

"They would never ___let___ us stay here!" Kevin said, laughing. Our
parents found us where they had ___left___ us—at the ice cream stand.

Score: _____   **Total Possible: 8**

E. Complete each of the eight following sentences with one of the following: *sit, set, of, -'ve, let, leave, can,* or *may*.

1. ___Can___ you play an instrument?
2. My grandmother wouldn't ___let___ me touch her new piano.
3. I knew I could ___'ve___ played it because I had taken piano lessons.
4. But Grandma said, "You ___may___ not play this piano."
5. "She's afraid I might break it or ___set___ something on the keys," I said to myself.
6. "I'll show you how to play it before you ___leave___ today," Grandma said.
7. Later she said, "___Sit___ here beside me." Then she pushed a button.
8. The piano began to play by itself! Now I knew why she treated it as if it were made ___of___ gold.

Score: _____   **Total Possible: 8**

REVIEW SCORE: _____   **REVIEW TOTAL: 32**

75

Lesson 36

Lesson 36 Usage: Adjectives That Compare

One way to compare things is to use different forms of an adjective. Use one form of an adjective to compare two things. Use another form to compare three or more things.

.... Did You Know? ....

Most adjectives can be compared by adding *-er* to compare two things, and *-est* to compare more than two.

Hyenas are **fast** runners. Gazelles are **faster** than hyenas. Cheetahs are the **fastest** of all.
A hippopotamus is a very **large** mammal, but an elephant is **larger**. The **largest** of all is the whale.

Some adjectives are compared by placing the word *more* or *most* in front of the adjective.

Deer are **frequent** visitors to our camp, but black bears are **more frequent** than the deer. The **most frequent** visitors are raccoons.

To compare some adjectives, change the word completely.

Our back porch is a **good** place to watch deer.
The park at the edge of town is **better** than the porch.
The **best** of all places is the beach on Summer Lake.

The mosquitoes are **bad** this year.
Some people say they were **worse** two years ago.
Everyone agrees the **worst** year was 1990.

Show What You Know
Write the correct form for each adjective shown in parentheses.

1. This path is ___safer___ than that one. (safe)
2. This is the ___best___ view in the park. (good)
3. Would you be ___more comfortable___ on a raft than in a canoe? (comfortable)
4. Upsetting the canoe was the ___scariest___ accident I ever had! (scary)
5. Ms. Jason was ___more helpful___ than I was. (helpful)

Score: _____   **Total Possible: 5**

76

Proofread
Draw delete marks through the four incorrect adjectives. Write the correct form above each incorrect word.

Example: That classroom is the ~~smaller~~ *smallest* one in the building.

My aunt's garden was ~~more pretty~~ *prettier* than the one at home. "I'm taking ~~gooder~~ *better* care of the roses this year than I did last year," she said. Just then, my cousin brought in the ~~redder~~ *reddest* rose we had ever seen. "I may enter the best rose competition at the fair," said my aunt.

"Choosing the winner will be the ~~easy~~ *easiest* decision in the world for the judges," I said.

Practice
Write a sentence using a comparative form of each word in parentheses.

1. (tall) _____

2. (silly) _____

3. (wise) _____

4. (dangerous) _____

5. (good) _____

Review sentences to make sure your child has:
• used each word correctly.   • constructed sentences properly.
• spelled each word correctly.

Tips for Your Own Writing: Revising ....
Choose a piece of writing in which you compared things. Rewrite your description, using as many adjectives that compare as possible. Remember to add *-er* or *more* when comparing two things, and *-est* or *most* when comparing more than two.

Be sure to check spellings when you add endings to words in a comparison.

77

Lesson 37

Lesson

37 Usage: Adjectives and Adverbs

Adjectives and adverbs are easy to mix up. Here are some ways to keep them straight.

.... Did You Know? ....

Adjectives describe nouns or pronouns. Adjectives can come just before a noun, or they can come after a verb.
>The men sang a **loud** song about buffalo.
>Those huge buffalo were **loud**.

Adverbs usually tell how, when, or where something happens.
>The buffalo called **loudly** to one another.

Some adjectives and adverbs are very much alike. Writers and speakers must think carefully to use the correct form. Many adverbs end with -ly.
>The beaver was **quiet**.
>The deer moved **quietly** through the trees.

....

Show What You Know

Choose the correct word from the pair of words in parentheses and write it in each space in the sentences below.

This was the ___final___ picnic of the year. We ___finally___ found a
⟨1 (final, finally)⟩   ⟨2 (final, finally)⟩
nice place to eat. A deer appeared, moving ___slowly___ All of us sat
                                       ⟨3 (slow, slowly)⟩
___quietly___ and watched it.
⟨4 (quiet, quietly)⟩
"There aren't many deer left here," Grandfather said ___sadly___
                                             ⟨5 (sad, sadly)⟩
We were ___quiet___ as we listened to him.
     ⟨6 (quiet, quietly)⟩
"Well, we at least saw this one," Mother reminded us ___gently___
                                              ⟨7 (gentle, gently)⟩

Score: _____ Total Possible: 7

78

Proofread

Draw delete marks through the five incorrect words in the following sentences. Write the correct form above the incorrect word.

>   loud
>**Example:** The crowd was too ~~loudly~~.

>   carefully
>"Drive ~~careful~~," the officer warned everyone. "Animals crossing the road
>   slowly
>move ~~slow~~."

>   suddenly
>A bear appeared next to the car very ~~sudden~~. It swung its head back and
>   quickly
>forth angrily. "Roll the window up ~~quick~~!" James shouted.
>   silently
>Suddenly the bear moved away. It walked ~~silent~~ into the trees.

Practice

Choose four of these words and write a sentence using each: *slow, slowly, soft, softly, wild, wildly*. Write something about the picture.

1. Review sentences to make sure your child has:
   • used words correctly.
2. • capitalized and punctuated sentences correctly.
   • used the illustration as a focus for the sentences.
3. _____
4. _____

Tips for Your Own Writing: Proofreading ....

Look over a story you wrote in which you used dialogue. Adding adjectives and adverbs may make the dialogue more interesting and vivid for your reader.

Try not to write sentences like "Sing soft" or "Do that quicker."

79

....

Lesson 38

Lesson

38 Usage: Your/You're, Its/It's

If two words sound exactly alike, how can you tell which spelling to use? Here are some facts to help you.

.... Did You Know? ....

Your is a pronoun that shows possession. It always comes before the name of something or someone.
>We saw **your** cousin at the show yesterday.
>Was she wearing **your** hat?

You're is a contraction. It is the shortened form of the two words "you are." The apostrophe means that the letter *a* is missing from *are*.
>**You're** going to the show tomorrow, aren't you?
>I'll bet **you're** going to be early, as usual!

Its is a pronoun that shows possession. It always comes before the name of something.
>**Its** mane was huge and made the lion look scary.

It's is a contraction. It is the shortened form of the two words "it is." The apostrophe means that the letter *i* is missing from *is*.
>**It's** very clear that the lion is dangerous.

....

Show What You Know

Write *your*, *you're*, *its*, or *it's* in each space in the following report.

If ___you're___ a computer user, you know that when a problem arises with
   ⟨1⟩
___your___ computer it is called a "bug." ___It's___ a term that was first used
 ⟨2⟩   ⟨3⟩
more than fifty years ago when a computer malfunctioned. The programmer
found a dead moth in ___its___ interior. ___Its___ presence there was
                    ⟨4⟩   ⟨5⟩
probably not the cause of the problem. If you have a problem with a computer,
___you're___ not going to be able to blame moths. ___It's___ probably not
 ⟨6⟩   ⟨7⟩
___your___ fault, either.
 ⟨8⟩

Score: _____ Total Possible: 8

80

Proofread

Read the sentences below. Draw a delete mark through each incorrectly used word, and write the correct word above it. There are eight mistakes.

>   Your
>**Example:** ~~You're~~ dog was barking.
>Your   its
>"~~You're~~ turn has come," the fox leader told Alla. She heard ~~it's~~ voice but
>could not see the beautiful red animal.
>It's cool in the forest. That is why Alla and her brother Karsh had moved
>   its
>into ~~it's~~ shade.
>You're
>"~~Your~~ next," the leader's voice reminded them. Together, they crept slowly
>   its
>out of the forest, stopping at ~~it's~~ edge.
>You're
>"~~Your~~ almost there," the voice whispered. Quietly, Karsh and Alla walked
>toward a baby fox and its proud mother.
>   it's
>"Oh, ~~its~~ just beautiful," Alla sighed.
>Your
>"~~You're~~ new baby is a treasure to behold," Karsh told the fox leader.

Practice

Use *its*, *it's*, *your*, and *you're* in a story of your own. Use the picture for ideas or write from your own imagination.

Review the story to see that your child has:
• created a sequential story.
• used the picture or another clear focus for the story.
• used the four words correctly.
• written correct sentences with appropriate capitalization and punctuation.

Tips for Your Own Writing: Proofreading ....

Choose a report you have written and check it carefully for the four words you studied in this lesson. Remember, *your* and *its* show possession and always come before the name of someone or something. Use *you're* for "you are" and *it's* for "it is."

You're going to find it's easy to use these words correctly—with practice.

81

Lesson 39

Lesson
39 Usage: There/Their/They're, Here/Hear

Words that sound alike but are spelled differently and have different meanings are called homophones.

.... **Did You Know?** ....

There may mean "in that place," or it may be used to introduce a sentence before a word such as *was*, *were*, *is*, or *are*. The word *here* is in the word *there*, which may help you remember.

> We found the treasure chest right over **there**.
> **There** were pieces of gold in the chest.

Their means "belonging to them."

> The pirates said the chest was **their** property.

They're means "they are."

> **They're** not going to like it if we take their treasure.

Here may mean "in this place," or it may be used to introduce a sentence.

> Let's leave the treasure **here**.
> **Here** is the map that we used.

Hear means "to listen." The word *ear* is in *hear*, which may help you remember.

> Didn't you **hear** the pirates' warning?

....

Show What You Know

Read the sentences below. Write *their*, *there*, or *they're* in each space.

Many people work hard to develop ___their___ muscles. ___There___ are
                                       1   2
some muscles that you can control. ___They're___ called voluntary muscles.
                                        3
___There___ are also involuntary muscles, which you cannot control.
    4

Write *here* or *hear* in each space.

___Here___ is a fact you may not know. You have about 700 muscles.
   5
Would you like to ___hear___ more information about your muscles?
                       6

Score: _____   Total Possible: 6

82

Proofread

Draw delete marks through the four incorrect words in the poem below. Write the correct word above each incorrect word.

Example: ~~Hear~~ are the papers you lost. (*Here*)

Now, ~~here~~ this tale of two travelers in space. (*hear*)

~~They're~~ trip through the universe became a bad race. (*Their*)

"Here is the goal," one said to his friend,

"But ~~their~~ is a quick way to get to the end." (*there*)

~~There~~ still on the way and may never be found. (*They're*)

They found the "quick way" was the *long* way around!

Practice

Write four sentences about the travelers in the poem. Use *there*, *their*, *they're*, *hear*, and *here* at least once each.

1. _____ Review sentences to make sure your child has:

   • used the assigned words at least one time.

2. _____ • related the sentences to the poem on the page.

   • used correct sentence structure, capitalization,

3. _____ and punctuation.

4. _____

Tips for Your Own Writing: Proofreading ....

Choose a piece of your writing and check it carefully for mistakes in the use of the three homophones *there*, *they're*, and *their*. You may want to trade writing with a friend and check each other's work. Remember, *they're* tells *who*; *their* tells *whose*; and *there* tells *where*.

There, they're, their, now! That wasn't hard, was it?

83

Lesson 40

Lesson
40 Review: Adjectives, Adverbs, Homophones

A. Write the word in the blank that correctly completes each of the five sentences below.

Lupe won the medal for the ___best___ vegetable garden in the
                              1(better, best)
neighborhood. Joel's garden was voted the ___worst___ of all. Donna's
                                            2(baddest, worst)
watermelons were the ___sweetest___ on the block. Mr. Stern's corn was
                       3(sweeter, sweetest)
good, but Mr. Castle's was ___better___. Mrs. Meloy's zucchinis were
                             4(better, best)
___bigger___ than anyone else's.
5(bigger, biggest)

Score: _____   Total Possible: 5

B. Write the word that completes each of the five sentences below.

1. Some plants will grow ___easily___ in sandy soil. (easy, easily)

2. Other plants even grow ___rapidly___ in plain water. (rapid, rapidly)

3. Marina sings to her plants, but not ___loudly___, though. (loud, loudly)

4. She says singing makes them grow more ___quickly___. (quicker, quickly)

5. "Just sing ___softly___, please," her mother teases her. (soft, softly)

Score: _____   Total Possible: 5

C. Write *its*, *it's*, *your*, or *you're* to correctly complete each of the five sentences below.

___It's___ not enough just to like gardens. ___Your___ garden will be a
   1   2
success only if you know how to grow plants. Writer and illustrator Tasha Tudor
wrote about a garden ___you're___ sure to like. ___Its___ bright colors are
                         3   4
exciting. ___Your___ idea of gardens will grow if you read Tudor's book.
            5

Score: _____   Total Possible: 5

84

D. Write *their*, *there*, *they're*, *your*, or *you're* to complete each of the six sentences below.

Long ago ___there___ were gardens to help win a war. During World
            1
War II, the government asked people to grow vegetables in ___their___
                                                             2
gardens. If you had a garden, you shared ___your___ vegetables.
                                            3
Everyone agreed, "___You're___ able to grow a garden if you have a yard!"
                      4
Some people even planted ___their___ tiny gardens in window boxes.
                            5
"___They're___ being creative," their neighbors admitted.
    6

Score: _____   Total Possible: 6

E. Write fourteen words to correctly complete the sentences below.

Long ago, ___there___ was an unusual garden ___here___.
             1(there, their, they're)   2(here, hear)
___Its___ bed was built on the side of a hill, where ___there___ was
   3(Its, It's)   4(there, they're, their)
very little room. Small bells rang ___softly___ to keep birds away, and people
                                     5(soft, softly)
could ___hear___ the music. The garden had the ___tallest___
         6(here, hear)   7(tallest, most tall)
sunflowers and the ___tiniest___ tulips anyone had ever seen. ___Its___
                      8(tiniest, tinier)   9(Its, It's)
success was assured because all the neighbors did ___their___ best
                                                     10(there, their, they're)
to help. ___Here___ the flowers grew ___brighter___ than in the next
            11(Here, Hear)   12(brighter, brightest)
town. Today people still like to ___hear___ about beautiful gardens because
                                    13(here, hear)
___there___ are not many of them anymore.
14(there, their, they're)

Score: _____   Total Possible: 14

REVIEW SCORE: _____   REVIEW TOTAL: 35

85

Answer Key 181

Lesson 41

Lesson
41 Usage: Plural Nouns
There's more than one way to write words that refer to more than one thing.

.... **Did You Know?** ....

A singular noun refers to one person, place, or thing.
A **blackbird** lives near the pond.

A plural noun refers to more than one person, place, or thing. Most plurals are formed by adding *-s.*
Those **blackbirds** are beautiful.
The farmer has three **donkeys.**

If a word ends with *ch, x, s, ss,* or *sh,* add *-es* to form the plural.
Red **foxes** are quick and quiet.
Aren't **walruses** ugly?

When a word ends with a consonant and the letter *y,* change the *y* to *i* and add *-es* to form the plural.
Six **ponies** are spotted, but one pony is not.

For some words that end with the letter *f,* change the *f* to *v* and add *-es.*
Those **calves** are twins. One **calf** is brown.

Words that end in *o* are tricky. Some form the plural by adding *-s.* Others add *-es* to form the plural. Look up in a dictionary the words you need to know. Then, memorize them.
That **burro** is small, but **burros** are very strong.
Dad asked if I wanted a baked **potato** or mashed **potatoes.**

....

Show What You Know
On the lines below, write the correct plural ending of each underlined word.

Cut two orange __s__ in half. Then slice two peach __es__ or tomato __es__. Cut two hard-boiled egg __s__ in half and put everything on dish __es__. Add a few sandwich __es__ and some chips if you are really hungry.

86

Score: _____ Total Possible: 6

Proofread
Draw delete marks through the seven incorrect plurals in the sentences below. Write the correct word above each incorrect word.

Example: We put all the books onto three ~~shelfs.~~ *shelves*

1. The science museum is an interesting place, with tiny ~~flys~~ *flies* in a large glass case.
2. Pretty ~~boxs~~ *boxes* hold valuable things, like rare watches and golden ~~rings.~~ *rings.*
3. Laser demonstrations were shown to large ~~groupes~~ *groups* every half hour.
4. ~~Modeles~~ *Models* of animals were exhibited in various areas.
5. On the museum bookstore shelves are ~~studys~~ *studies* of leaves, echoes, and ~~elfs.~~ *elves.*

Practice
Write five sentences about detectives. Use the plurals of these words: *penny, box, key, knife, hero, radio.*

1. ___ Review sentences to make sure your child has:
   • written five sentences.
2. ___ • used all six plurals.
   • written sentences that relate to the topic.
3. ___ • used correct sentence structure, following conventions for capitalization and punctuation.
4. ___
5. ___

Tips for Your Own Writing: Proofreading
Next time you write, pay close attention to the plural nouns that you use. Memorize the rules for forming plural nouns so that you can automatically recognize mistakes.

Hang on to that dictionary for the words that end in o!

87

Lesson 42

Lesson
42 Usage: Irregular Plural Nouns
For help with some plurals, make the dictionary your friend!

.... **Did You Know?** ....

Plural forms for some nouns follow no pattern.
The **geese** flew south. One **goose** was left behind.

Some singular and plural nouns are the same.
That **deer** has a white tail. Many **deer** live in the city.

A few plurals are formed by adding *-en.*
Babe was a blue **ox.** Two **oxen** pulled wagons.

Sometimes abbreviations written with capital letters are used as words. To form their plurals, add a lowercase *-s.*
The store had all the **TVs** tuned in to the ball game.

To form the plural of some hyphenated words, add *-s* to the first part of the word.
Marty had two **sisters**-in-law.

Some plurals can be formed in more than one way.
The plural of **fish** is **fish** or **fishes.**

Some singular and plural nouns both end in *-s.*
Please bring six **scissors** to the table.
Will you please hand me a pair of **scissors?**

....

Show What You Know
Write the correct plural form above the singular word in parentheses.

1. Presidents are also called (commander-in-chief). *commanders-in-chief*
2. The backyard was filled with (goose). *geese*
3. For supper we ate the twelve (fish) Grandmother caught. *fish/fishes*
4. You can get any type of music on (CD). *CDs*
5. Are (ox) really as strong as they look? *oxen*
6. All of the servers wore blue shirts and (pants). *pants*

Score: _____ Total Possible: 6

88

Proofread
In the sentences below, there are four mistakes in the spelling of a plural. Draw a delete mark through each incorrect word and write the correct word above it.

Example: There are many ~~gooses~~ *geese* in the pond behind my house.

José's grandfather raises ~~oxes~~ *oxen* on his farm. José and his ~~brother-in-laws~~ *brothers-in-law* help take care of the crops and the farm animals. They sometimes see ~~deers~~ *deer* in the fields, and they enjoy the songs of many species of birds.

Sometimes the men like to roll up the legs of their jeans and go fishing. They caught eight fish last weekend. José's sisters prefer watching movies to fishing. They can watch movies on the six ~~TVies~~ *TVs* in their house.

Practice
Write four sentences about a problem in the picture. Use at least three plural words.

1. ___ Review sentences to make sure your child has:
   • written four complete sentences about the picture.
2. ___ • used at least three plurals correctly.
   • applied past lessons in capitalization, punctuation, and spelling.
3. ___
4. ___

Tips for Your Own Writing: Proofreading
You may not have a lot of these irregular plurals in your own writing. However, proofreading a piece of your own writing will help you catch any spelling mistakes you have made when writing any kind of plural noun. Make corrections if you find mistakes.

"Oh, give me a home where the buffalo/buffaloes/buffalos roam." Which one should it be?

89

Lesson 43

Lesson
43 Usage: Possessives

Nouns have a form that shows ownership or possession.

.... **Did You Know?** ....

The possessive of a singular noun is formed by adding an apostrophe and -*s*.

Elena**'s** hat   Cass**'s** jeans

The possessive of a plural noun that ends in *s* is formed by adding only an apostrophe.

the teams**'** caps   the players**'** awards

The possessive of a plural noun that does not end in *s* is formed by adding an apostrophe and -*s*.

children**'s** clothing   men**'s** jackets

The possessive of a hyphenated noun is formed by adding an apostrophe and -*s* to the last word.

his brother-in-law**'s** warm-up jacket

....

Show What You Know
Write the correct possessive form above each underlined word.

Liz thought it would be cool to visit the past. She thought her
great-grandmother's
great-grandmothers quilt was beautiful. She wondered how hard the women
    1   women's
                                   family's
work was if they had to take time to make quilts. Did a farm familys day begin
                                           2
           children's
early? Were the children' chores hard? Would she ever know her ancestors'
           4
stories?

Score: _____ **Total Possible: 4**

90

Proofread
Use proper proofreading marks to show where an apostrophe or -'s is needed in four words in the paragraph below.

Example: That is my dad**'s** car.

Two artists**'** paintings hang in the museum. The paintings are by Berthe Morisot and her brother-in-law Edouard Manet. The woman**'s** picture is of a mother with two children. One child**'s** clothes are dark. Her brother-in-law**'s** work shows a garden.

Practice
Use the following words in a story about or a description of a picture you have seen or about an imaginary picture you would like to paint.

bears'   horse's   hero's   children's

Review the story to make sure your child has:

- written a sequential story or a description.
- correctly used the possessive nouns listed.
- used imagination in creating his or her story.
- used correct sentence structure, capitalization, and punctuation.

_____

_____

_____

Tips for Your Own Writing: Proofreading ....
Look at a story you have written and see where using possessives might improve the story. If so, make the changes. Remember, the rules for forming the possessives of singular and plural nouns are different. Read the old and the new versions. Keep the better piece of writing.

Whose is it? The apostrophe will tell you where to look!

91

Lesson 44

Lesson
44 Usage: Plurals and Possessives

Most plurals end with s. Most possessives end with s. There's an important difference between plurals and possessives, though.

.... **Did You Know?** ....

The plural of most nouns is formed by adding -*s* or -*es* to the singular.

boy–boy**s**   day–day**s**   store–store**s**   brush–brush**es**

The plural of many other nouns is formed by changing the last letters of the singular form and adding -*s*.

knife–kni**ves**   grocery–groce**ries**   lady–lad**ies**

The possessive of most nouns is formed by adding an apostrophe and -*s*.

man**'s**   girl**'s**   shop**'s**   Mrs. Sands**'s**

The possessive of plural nouns that end in *s* is formed by adding only an apostrophe.

teachers**'**   artists**'**   shoppers**'**   waiters**'**

Show What You Know
If the underlined word is plural, write *Pl* **above it. If it is singular and possessive, write** *SP.* **If it is plural and possessive, write** *PP.*

        Pl   SP
Many shops at the mall sell kids' shoes. A lady's jewelry store attracts many
Pl   PP
customers around Mother's Day. A sign on another store is for gentlemen's
   4   5
                        PP   Pl
hairstyles, but that shop is not very busy. Teens' clothes are a big seller. Clerks in
                            6   7
these stores can help you put together outfits.
  SP
George's two brothers work in a sporting goods store at the mall. George is
  8   PP
always eager to visit his brothers' store.
                  9
                           PP
In the music store, customers' orders are filled quickly because of the large
                           10
SP   SP
stock. Elena's favorite store is the music store. I share my friend's love of music,
    11   12
too.

Score: _____ **Total Possible: 12**

92

Proofread
Each of the five sentences contains one mistake in the writing of a possessive or a plural noun. Draw delete marks through the incorrect plurals and write the correct words above them. Use proper proofreading marks (ᵥ) to show where apostrophes are needed.

Example: I know where those boy's ~~watchs~~ watches are hidden.

1. Who borrowed Miss Mark**'s** copy of the big dictionary?
2. Borrower**'s** rules are on the chart in front of the desk.
3. Please read them before you take books off the ~~shelfs~~ shelves.
4. The jackets that library helpers wear are from the women**'s** and men's departments in the store at the mall.
5. Will you help in the library? We need volunteers to unpack ~~boxs~~ boxes of books.

Practice
Write four sentences about a shopping trip you have taken. Use at least two plurals and two possessives in your sentences.

1. Review sentences to make sure your child has:
   - used plurals and possessives accurately.
2. - written clear sentences.
   - used structure, grammar, and mechanics correctly.
3. _____
4. _____

Tips for Your Own Writing: Proofreading ....
Next time you write, use possessives to add detail to your descriptions or dialogue. Before you write, review the differences between plurals and possessives.

The position of an apostrophe tells you how many owners a thing has.

93

Lesson 45

Lesson 45 Usage: Contractions

When you speak, you may pronounce two words as if they were one. For example, instead of saying, "I have not been there," you might say, "I haven't been there." Read on to find out how to make contractions in your writing.

Did You Know?

A contraction is a shorter way to say and to spell two words. When you write, you use an apostrophe to show where you have left out a letter.

The computer store **was not** open that evening.
The computer store **wasn't** open that evening.

You are learning to use your computer.
You're learning to use your computer.

In questions, the order of words may be changed when a contraction is used.

Can you **not** understand why we need a computer?
Can't you understand why we need a computer?

Why **did** she **not** listen during class?
Why **didn't** she listen during class?

Show What You Know

Circle the two words in each sentence that can be combined to form a contraction. Write the contraction on the line at the end of the sentence.

1. The class (had not) visited Shedd Aquarium before. ___hadn't___
2. "(It is) home to thousands of beautiful fish," the guide said. ___It's___
3. "Please (do not) tap on the glass," she added. ___don't___
4. "(That is) very disturbing to the fish." ___That's___
5. At the Shedd, (there is) a giant squid hanging from the ceiling. ___there's___
6. You (can not) see some of the fish because they hide so well. ___can't___
7. (You will) want to go to the main aquarium at feeding time. ___You'll___
8. A diver will get into the tank; (she will) feed the fish. ___she'll___
9. (They are) from many different parts of the world. ___They're___

Score: _____ Total Possible: 18

94

Proofread

Use proper proofreading marks to show where six apostrophes are needed below.

Example: I don't want to go.

Why wasn't the team on the field? The Jayhawks hadn't forfeited a game in years!

"Where's everyone?" the coach asked.

Sam grew impatient; he didn't understand his teammates. "We've waited a long time for this game," he said to himself. "But now they're all late. We'll probably have to forfeit the game."

At last, the team's van arrived. "Sorry we're late," the assistant coach called.

"I'm the only one who is warmed up," Sam thought. "At least Coach can count on me."

Practice

Write four sentences about the picture. Use the contraction for each of the following words at least once: *will not, should not, he will, she is, that is.*

1. Review sentences to make sure your child has:
   • used each pair of words correctly as a
2. contraction.
   • written sentences that relate to the soccer game.
3. • used proper sentence form, spelling, punctuation, and capitalization.
4.

Tips for Your Own Writing: Proofreading

Proofread a piece of your own writing in which you used dialogue. Look for pairs of words that might be written as contractions. Read aloud the dialogue using the contractions. Does it sound better? Dialogue often sounds more natural if contractions are used.

Contractions are usually not used in business letters and other kinds of formal writing.

95

Lesson 46

Lesson 46 Review: Plurals, Possessives, Contractions

A. There are five misspelled plurals in the following paragraph. Draw delete marks through the misspelled words. Write the correct spellings above the words.

Where I live, ~~leafs~~ leaves begin to fall in the ~~monthes~~ months of September and October. The ~~familys~~ families in our neighborhood go to the lake for a fall picnic. One neighbor brings ~~ponys~~ ponies for the kids to ride. Most of us play softball and eat ~~sandwichs~~ sandwiches, corn, and peaches.

Score: _____ Total Possible: 5

B. Four plural words are spelled incorrectly in the following sentences. Draw delete marks through the misspelled plurals and write the correct spellings above them.

The mayor, her sisters, and her ~~brother-in-laws~~ brothers-in-law march in the Memorial Day parade. The event is watched on ~~TVes~~ TVs all over town. On the holiday, people dress in their old shirts and ~~jeanes~~ jeans. Children play in the parks, scaring away ~~deers~~ deer and birds. Along the riverbank, people enjoy the sunshine and try to catch as many fish as they can.

Score: _____ Total Possible: 4

C. There are eight mistakes in the paragraph below. Use proper proofreading marks to show where an apostrophe or an apostrophe and *-s* should be added to a word.

In western Nebraska, the early settlers' families faced hard times. All of the family members had to work from sunrise to sunset. A farmer's land was usually sandy, so the settlers' crops were often poor at first. The children's school was far off. A woman's day was filled with hard work around the home and in the fields. But many people stayed in the state's dry region despite the hardships. They would even invite an uncle or a brother-in-law's family to join them in Nebraska.

Score: _____ Total Possible: 8

96

D. The following report has six mistakes in plurals and possessives. Use proper proofreading marks to correct the mistakes.

A report in our city's newspaper stated that many big store's have bad spelling habits. A photograph showed a mistake. The sign in the story said Mens Shoes instead of Men's Shoes. The writer said these are foolish mistake's. Writer's for ad ~~company's~~ companies should know better.

Score: _____ Total Possible: 6

E. On the line at the end of the sentence, write a contraction for the underlined words.

1. <u>Nothing is</u> more fun than taking pictures. ___Nothing's___
2. "Do cameras <u>not</u> break easily?" ___Don't___
3. "<u>Is it not</u> hard to choose the right film?" ___Isn't___
4. "I <u>would not</u> have any idea how to get good pictures." ___wouldn't___
5. "Let Uncle Ed take pictures; <u>he will</u> get good ones." ___he'll___
6. "You <u>can not</u> expect me to take a photo!" ___can't___
7. These are some excuses, but <u>they are</u> not good ones. ___they're___
8. If <u>you would</u> like to be a photographer, get started now. ___you'd___

Score: _____ Total Possible: 8

REVIEW SCORE: _____ REVIEW TOTAL: 31

97

184 Answer Key

Lesson 47

Lesson 47 Usage: Verb Tense

Verb forms are the clue to the past, present, and future.

.... **Did You Know?** ....

The past tense of a verb tells you that something happened in the past.

The past tense of most verbs is formed by adding *-ed.*
I love to **learn** new songs. I **learned** a funny one yesterday.

The past tense of verbs that end in silent *e* is formed by dropping the *e* and adding *-ed.* If the verb ends with a single consonant, double the consonant and add *-ed.*
The song was about a cowhand who had to **saddle** a horse.
After he had **saddled** it, it refused to move.
The cowhand tried to **plan** ways to make the horse move, but everything he **planned** failed.

The past tense of some verbs is formed by changing the spelling of the verb.
I like to **sing.** I **sang** the saddle song over and over.
I **know** that I **knew** all the words perfectly yesterday.
I **think** I've forgotten them, but I **thought** I had them memorized.

....

Show What You Know

Write the correct past-tense verb above each underlined verb in the paragraph below.

       thought   was
I <u>think</u> television <u>is</u> unhealthy for kids. We <u>sit</u> around too much. How many
     1   2   sat
   played   3
of us <u>play</u> sports every single day? <u>Are</u> most teens in sports? You say that you
skated 4 loved   5 walked
<u>skate</u>? You <u>love</u> hiking? Well, most kids <u>walk</u> very short distances! We all <u>plan</u> to
 6   7   8   9
                   exercised
exercise, right? Next week, be able to say, "I <u>exercise</u> every day!"
                           10

Score: _____ Total Possible: 10

98

Proofread

Draw a delete mark through each of the two verbs in each sentence below. Then write the correct past-tense form above each verb.

        played
Example: Have you ~~play~~ the piano?
          corrected   found   worked
   The careful carpenters ~~correct~~ every mistake they ~~find~~. The scientists ~~work~~
discovered   created
hard and ~~discover~~ a new medicine. Writers ~~create~~ wonderful poems and
composed   searched   solved
~~compose~~ exciting stories. Police officers ~~search~~ patiently and ~~solve~~ many crimes.
made   organized
Teachers ~~make~~ colorful bulletin boards and ~~organize~~ exciting activities. But some
      sat   got
people just ~~sit~~ around and ~~get~~ really lazy!

Practice

Use the past tense of *experiment, boil, write,* and *catch* in four sentences of your own.

1. _____ Review the writing to make sure your child has:
    • used *experimented, wrote, boiled* and *caught*
2. _____ correctly.
    • shown an understanding of sentence
3. _____ construction, grammar, and usage already reviewed or
4. _____ learned earlier.

Tips for Your Own Writing: Proofreading ....
Many stories describe events as though they happened in the past. Next time you write a story, try writing it in the present, and then write it in the past tense. Which account sounds better? Stories written in the present tense sometimes capture an excitement and suspense better than those written in the past tense. However, most stories you read are written in the past tense.

Like magic, you can change present to past by changing the verb tense.

99

Lesson 48

Lesson 48 Usage: Subject-Verb Agreement I

The ending of a verb may change to match the subject of the verb.

.... **Did You Know?** ....

In the present tense of most verbs, the endings change to match the subject. If the subject is a singular noun or the pronoun *he, she,* or *it,* the verb should end in *-s.*
She **walks** with us.   John **walks** for exercise.
It **walks** on its hind legs.   He **walks** with a cane.

If the subject is a plural noun, or the pronoun *I, we, you,* or *they,* you do not add *-s* to the verb.
They **walk** often.   I **walk** every day.
You **walk,** too.   The workers **walk** to the fields.

If the verb ends in *o, ch, sh, ss,* or *x,* add *-es* to the base word for singular nouns, or the pronoun *he, she,* or *it.*
I **fish**   Do you **fish?**   Jason **fishes** every day.

....

Show What You Know

In the spaces below, write the correct forms of the verbs in parentheses.

1. A camel __carries__ heavy burdens. (carry)
2. Camels __live__ in Africa. (live)
3. The camel __looks__ a little like some of its relatives in America. (look)
4. You __know__ what a llama is, don't you? (know)
5. The furry animal __behaves__ a little like a camel. (behave)
6. A llama, though, __does__ not have a hump. (do)
7. A llama __carries__ a burden, just as a camel does. (carry)
8. The animals __carry__ many pounds at a time. (carry)
9. A herder __watches__ the valuable animals. (watch)

Score: _____ Total Possible: 9

100

Proofread

In the sentences below, eight of the underlined verbs have incorrect endings. Draw a delete mark through any verb that is spelled incorrectly. Write the correct verb above it.

        enjoy
Example: We ~~enjoys~~ riding our bikes.
         work
   The cyclists ~~works~~ hard at practice every day. Eliza acts as team leader
         1   rides   2watches
for the track racers. She ~~ride~~ at the rear of the group. She ~~watch~~ for riders who
             3   4
            cycle
are not careful. Team members ~~cycles~~ carefully, even at high speeds. They try not
                5   6
                            tries
to make mistakes that would lose a race. Eliza ~~try~~ to catch every mistake they
        feel   7   knows
make. The riders ~~feels~~ that it is an honor to be on the team. Eliza ~~know~~ that it is
        8   wears   9
an honor to be team leader. She ~~wear~~ her leader's badge proudly.
                   10

Practice

Write a story about the shepherd boy in the picture. Describe how he feels about his work. Use at least three of these verbs, adding correct endings: *watch, play, carry, walk, climb.*

_____ Review the story to make sure your child has:
    • written about the pictured situation.
    • used the required verbs correctly.
    • shown a clear focus in the story.
    • told his or her story using accurate grammar, usage, and mechanics.

_____
_____

Tips for Your Own Writing: Proofreading ....

Choose a piece of your own writing. Check to be sure that verb forms match subjects in your sentences. This kind of review is very important because subjects and verbs that do not agree draw the reader's attention away from your message.

A story should unwind like a ball of yarn; don't let your subjects and verbs get tangled!

101

Lesson
49 Usage: Subject-Verb Agreement II

I practice. You practice. She practices. How do you know which verb form to use?

.... **Did You Know?** ....

When the subject of a sentence is one thing or one person, except *you* or *I*, add an *-s* to the verb.
  Alan seems tired in the early morning.

When the subject of the sentence is made up of two singular persons or things joined by *and*, use a verb that does not end in *-s*.
  Alan and his trainer seem tired when they come in.

When the subject is made up of two words joined by *or* or *nor*, add an *-s* to the verb unless the word closest to the verb is plural.
  Neither **Alan nor his trainer seems** tired.
  Neither **Alan nor his friends waste** time.

Take special care when a helping verb comes before its subject, as it does in many questions.
  Why **do skaters and coaches** work so hard?

Show What You Know

Underline the words that make up the subject of each sentence. In the blank, write the correct form of the verb in parentheses.

Why __do__ readers and television viewers get animal groups mixed up?
1 (do, does)
Often, the viewer and the reader __decide__ that animals are alike or
2 (decide, decides)
different because of their appearance. Both the cassowary and the emu
__belong__ to the group of birds that can't fly. On the other hand, koalas
3 (belongs, belong)
and kangaroos seem different, but they both __fit__ into the same species.
4 (fit, fits)
However, the bear and the koala are different and __raise__ their young in
5 (raise, raises)
different ways.

Score: _____   Total Possible: 15

102

Proofread

Five of the underlined verbs are not correct. Draw a delete mark through each incorrect verb and write the correct form above it.

                          swims
Example: The team ~~swim~~ every day.

                                                    begin
  It is dark as Nora and her mother ~~begins~~ their long train journey. Neither
                      is
her father nor her uncle ~~are~~ with them. Uncle Joshua and his children plan to
                                                          drive
take a plane at a later date. Dad and Nora's brother always ~~drives~~ when they
travel. When boarding the train, either Nora or her mother trips on the step of
                                                              fall
the train. The women, bags, and the carrying case for the cats ~~falls~~ to the
ground. Neither the cats nor people are hurt. The train conductor and all the
            wave
passengers ~~waves~~ as the train moves away. A new home and new friends
promise a new adventure for Nora.

Practice

Write three sentences comparing the two vehicles in the drawing. How are they alike? How are they different?

1. Review the writing to be sure your child has:
   • written three complete sentences.
2. • compared and contrasted two pictured types of vehicles.
   • used subjects and verbs that agree.
3. _____

Tips for Your Own Writing: Proofreading

Choose a paragraph from a piece of your writing. Look for sentences that have more than one subject. Check the verbs. Remember which forms need *-s* and which do not.

A subject and a verb in a sentence must agree with each other. Be sure to match them correctly.

103

Lesson
50 Review: Verbs

A. Write the correct past tense form of the ten underlined verbs in the blank in each sentence.

Yesterday's storm seem __seemed__ to come without warning. Suddenly,
1
the sky turn __turned__ the color of charcoal. Thunder shake __shook__ the
2   3
houses. It rattle __rattled__ the windows. Lightning strike __struck__ the
4   5
biggest tree on the block. Some small children cry __cried__ in fright. When it
6
was over, everyone celebrate __celebrated__. Then some people ask __asked__
7   8
about the storm. No one expect __expected__ it! It had really surprise __surprised__
9   10
them.

Score: _____   Total Possible: 10

B. Use the underlined word in each sentence below to form the correct verb for each blank. Write it in the blank.

1. The swim team is supposed to swim daily, but Andrew __swims__ only weekly.

2. At the meet we want the other team to chase us, but Andrew always __chases__ the other team!

3. "Smile if you lose," the coach said. He even __smiles__ at Andrew.

4. Sometimes we succeed. Sofia __succeeds__ when she swims one on one.

5. Watch the competition. A good coach __watches__ other teams carefully.

6. Our team likes to win, but the team that practices a lot __wins__.

7. Maybe if we practice two hours, we could beat the team that __practices__ one hour.

Score: _____   Total Possible: 7

104

C. Write the correct verb form above each of the fourteen underlined verbs in the paragraphs below. Use the present tense.

                                  promises   comes
  The news arrives. President Harrison ~~promise~~ land to any settler who ~~come~~
1   2
                                seems
to Oklahoma. To Jonas, April 22, 1889, ~~seem~~ like the most important day of
3   wants
his life. The family will have the farm Jonas ~~want~~ to live and work on.
                4
            lines
  Jonas ~~line~~ up with his family and thousands of others. At exactly noon, a
5   rushes   chooses
signal is given and Jonas ~~rush~~ across the line. With his family, he ~~choose~~ a good
6   7
            heads   thinks
section of land. His friend Alfred ~~head~~ to a place where he ~~think~~ a town will
8   9
        hurries   desires
grow. While Jonas ~~hurry~~ to start a farm, Alfred ~~desire~~ to find a place for a town.
10   11
                        lives   asks
  Elias, an Osage boy, ~~live~~ in the region. He ~~ask~~ whether his father could help
12   13
                        knows
Jonas set up the farm. Elias ~~know~~ that the Osage have farmed in that area for
14
hundreds of years.

Score: _____   Total Possible: 14

D. Write the correct verb in each blank.

1. Foxes and wolves __work__ out ways to get along. (works, work)

2. Foxes and wolves __live__ in the same region. (lives, live)

3. __Do__ foxes and wolves fight one another? (Does, Do)

4. Foxes and wolves __hunt__ at different times. (hunts, hunt)

5. However, a fox __eats__ some of the same things as a wolf. (eats, eat)

Score: _____   Total Possible: 5

REVIEW SCORE: _____   REVIEW TOTAL: 36

105

186   Answer Key

Lesson 51

Lesson 52

Lesson 53

Lesson 53 Usage: Double Negatives

No! Never! None! are words that have a negative meaning. How many others can you think of?

.... Did You Know? ....

A negative is a word that means "no." Some common negatives are *no*, *not*, *never*, *nothing*, and *none*.

Fishing is **not** allowed in this part of the lake.
There is **nothing** to do but fish in the other part.

Avoid using two negatives in the same sentence.

Incorrect: Susan would **not never** swim in the lake.
Correct: Susan would **not** swim in the lake.
Susan would **never** swim in the lake.

Remember that part of some contractions are negatives. Do not use another negative when the contraction already has *not* in it.

Incorrect: The city has**n't no** lifeguards at the lake.
Correct: The city has**n't** any lifeguards at the lake.
The city has **no** lifeguards at the lake.

....

Show What You Know

Underline the sentence in each pair that uses negative words correctly.

1. Some writers never use no rhymes in their poems.
   <u>Some writers never use rhymes in their poems.</u>

2. Other writers don't never write without using rhyme.
   <u>Other writers never write without using rhyme.</u>

3. "Warning" by John Ciardi doesn't use no rhyme.
   <u>"Warning" by John Ciardi doesn't use rhyme.</u>

4. <u>Readers might think that Ciardi has no poems that rhyme.</u>
   Readers might think that Ciardi hasn't no poems that rhyme.

5. <u>None of the lines in Carl Sandburg's poem "Arithmetic" rhyme.</u>
   Not none of the lines in Carl Sandburg's poem "Arithmetic" rhyme.

Score: _____ Total Possible: 5

110

Proofread

Draw delete marks through the six double negatives below and write the correction above each one. There is more than one way to correct each sentence.

is never/isn't ever
Example: She isn't never going to leave again.

doesn't ever/does never
When Charlie visits his grandparents, he doesn't never get bored. They have
are no/aren't any
a big backyard filled with birdhouses and feeders. There aren't no cats or dogs in
aren't ever/are never
the yard, so the birds aren't never afraid. Charlie has seen finches and red-
winged blackbirds at the feeders, but hasn't ever seen a grosbeak. His
none/one never
grandparents said grosbeaks were there once, but none never came this
summer.
hadn't ever/had never
Until this year, Charlie's grandparents hadn't never seen any bluebirds in the
yard. But one day when Charlie was not there, one came. Now Charlie is hoping
haven't ever/have never
to see a bird his grandparents haven't never seen.

Practice

Write sentences that answer the following questions about the picture. Use *no*, *not*, *none*, *never*, or any other negative in each sentence.

1. Have you ever seen a bird this large?
2. What would you do if you did see one?
3. Could a bird like this fly? Why or why not?

Review the writing to be sure your child has:

• answered the three questions.

• used a negative in each answer.

• avoided double negatives.

Tips for Your Own Writing: Proofreading

Look for the negatives *no*, *not*, *never*, *none*, and *nothing* in a piece of your writing. Then check for contractions with *not*. They already have a negative, so do not use another negative in the sentence.

Never, never, never put two negatives in the same sentence!

111

....

Lesson 54

Lesson 54 Review: Pronoun Agreement, Double Negatives

A. Circle the correct pronoun in each pair. In three sentences, the pronouns are in the wrong order. Write them in the correct order above the sentences.

Daria and I
Daria and (I, me) took a trip to the Grand Canyon National Park.
Daria and I
Me and Daria were among the three million visitors who come to the park each
year. Other visitors and (we, us) began our sightseeing. (She, Her) and (I, me)
walked along the South Rim of the Grand Canyon with five other visitors.
the others and us
(Them, They) and (I, me) never stopped being amazed by the beautiful views at
Desert View and Hermit's Rest. Our families joined us and the others as we
reached Mather Point. Later, our families and (we, us) boarded a bus for the
They and I
North Rim. (We, Us) marveled at the view from Bright Angel Point and Point
Imperial. I and they will never forget the beauty of the Grand Canyon.

Score: _____ Total Possible: 11

B. Circle the correct pronoun in the parentheses.

King Midas was kind, but many called (he, him) and his helpers foolish.
Midas had a daughter. He loved (she, her) and the rest of his family.

Once Midas helped a poor creature who granted (he, him) a wish. Midas
told the creature that he and his helpers had decided that they wanted
everything he touched to turn to gold.

Just then his daughter and her friends ran into the room. Midas reached out
to greet (she, her) and her friends. His touch turned (she, her) to gold.

The teller of this story has a lesson for all adults and (we, us). The storyteller
might be telling both (they, them) and (I, me) to be content with what we have.

Score: _____ Total Possible: 8

112

C. Complete each sentence by correctly writing a pronoun in each of the five blanks.

Do you know some famous fictional pairs? What about Calvin and Hobbes?
They
___ and Charlie Brown and Snoopy are pairs of characters in cartoon
1
books. Of course, you know Bert and Ernie. Sesame Street was the place where
them   I
you found ___ and Big Bird. My brother and ___ have read
2   3
us
about Paul Bunyan and Babe, another famous pair. The librarian told our mother
and ___ about Mutt and Jeff and Ike and Mike. Oh, I must remind
4
her
___ about Hansel and Gretel.
5

Score: _____ Total Possible: 5

D. Draw delete marks through the five double negatives below and write the corrections above them.

have never/haven't ever
Railroad trains haven't never been through Hazel Green. There are other
no trains ever/trains never
towns where no trains never went. Sometimes there was a bus route, and
were none/weren't any   could never/couldn't ever
sometimes there weren't none. Many people in small towns couldn't never travel
were no/weren't any
far from home. Then, more and more people got cars, and soon there weren't no
places you couldn't go.

Score: _____ Total Possible: 10

REVIEW SCORE: _____ REVIEW TOTAL: 34

113

Lesson 55

Lesson 55 Grammar: Nouns

When we want to name things, we use nouns.

.... **Did You Know?** ....

A **noun** is a word that tells who or what did the action or was acted upon by the verb in the sentence.

> The **scientists** search for the **bones** of **dinosaurs**. They use soft **brushes** to remove the **dirt**.

Nouns can be singular or plural.

> They found a small **bone** next to those large **bones**.

Some nouns, called proper nouns, name a specific person, place, or thing: *Paul Sereno* and *South America*. They are always capitalized. Nouns like *fossils* are common nouns. They are capitalized only at the beginning of sentences.

> **Paul Sereno** found many important **fossils** in **South America**.

Proper nouns may be made up of a group of words.

> The **Museum of Natural History** houses dinosaur bones.

....

Show What You Know

Find the twenty-nine nouns in the following report. Circle each noun you find. Some nouns are made up of more than one word, like *prairie dogs*.

The (Badlands National Park) is in (South Dakota). Its (rocks), (woods), and (hills) were shaped by (wind), (rain), (frost), and (streams). The (hills) are surrounded by (grass). Many (animals) live there. (Visitors) can see (deer), (bison), (antelope), (coyotes), and (prairie dogs). (People) live in the (Badlands), too. (Ranchers) work on this dry (land). (Rangers) patrol the (park). (Men) and (women) run (stores), (hotels), and (restaurants).

Score: _____   Total Possible: 29

114

Practice

Tell a story by writing a noun in each blank.
Sample answers are given.

I visited a __park__ in __California__ last __summer__. I saw many __deer__ there and ran to the __ranger station__ when I heard a __noise__ that seemed too close. Later, __Mom__ and I ate __popcorn__ and watched the amazing __sunset__.

Review the sentences to be sure your child has used nouns that make sense in the paragraph.

Revise

Make the following story clearer by writing a more specific noun above each underlined noun or phrase. Sample answers are given.

      engineers   swamp
The <u>men</u> who were draining the <u>body of water</u> found an <u>animal</u> living there. <u>People</u> came to watch as <u>workers</u> tried to move <u>the animal</u>. <u>The people</u> knew <u>these animals</u> will bite and that they are very strong. By the end of the day, <u>someone</u> had caught <u>the animal</u> and taken it to a <u>park</u> where it would be safe.

(specific nouns above: alligator, Spectators, rangers, the creature, alligator, alligators, a ranger, the alligator, nature preserve)

Review the sentences to be sure your child has used more specific nouns and that they make sense in the paragraph.

Tips for Your Own Writing: Revising ....

Choose a piece of your writing. Look at the nouns you used. Could you make some of them more specific? For example: *shovel* instead of a *tool* or *daisy* instead of a *flower*.

Use precise nouns in your writing to paint a clear word picture.

115

Lesson 56

Lesson 56 Grammar: Pronouns

By using pronouns, a writer can avoid repeating the same nouns and can tie the ideas together in sentences.

.... **Did You Know?** ....

Writers use **pronouns** to avoid using nouns over and over again. A pronoun can refer to a person, a place, or a thing. The words *she*, *her*, and *it* are pronouns.

> Franny raced toward **Franny's** goal. **Franny** knew **the goal** was a mile away.
> Franny raced toward **her** goal. **She** knew **it** was a mile away.

The form of a pronoun changes depending upon how it is used in the sentence. The pronouns *I*, *myself*, *my*, and *me* all refer to the same person.

> I wanted to hike there by **myself**, but **my** parents wouldn't let **me**.

Sometimes pronouns make writing confusing. A reader cannot tell if *his* in the first sentence refers to Carl or Jacob. The second sentence makes it clear.

> Carl told Jacob to bring **his** coat.
> Carl said, "Bring **my** coat, Jacob."

....

Show What You Know

Underline any words that should be changed to pronouns to make the writing smoother and clearer. Write the pronouns above the nouns.

Terri was flying in a hot-air balloon faster than the leader had promised. The wind above the town felt cold. _Terri_ (She) felt uncomfortable and scared. This kind of flying wasn't what the leader had said _flying_ (it) would be, _Terri_ (she) thought. Then another thought came into _Terri's_ (her) mind. The leader hadn't said how _Terri_ (she) could stop flying. Terri remembered a plastic tool in a _jeans_ (her) pocket. Would it help?

Score: _____   Total Possible: 12

116

Practice

In real life, who flies? What flies? Make a list.

Possible answers: *pilots, birds, bats, kites, planes, bugs*

Review the list to be sure your child has made imaginative and informed answers.

Now, write a three-sentence paragraph about a person, place, or thing. Use nouns and pronouns to make the scene very clear to your readers.

Review the writing to be sure your child has:

• used an item from the list.

• used pronouns for clarity.

• written good sentences in a unified paragraph.

Revise

Delete six nouns in this story that are used too frequently, and write a pronoun above each one. Sample answers are given.

                he   his
Joshua felt for the penknife ~~Joshua~~ had put in ~~Joshua's~~ jeans pocket. It would help
 he
when ~~Joshua~~ had to cut branches to sleep on. ~~Joshua~~ (He) did not remember what the ranger had said about bears. Joshua hoped the ranger had said ~~bears~~ (they) were not in this part of the park. ~~Joshua~~ (He) will have to spend the night here.

Review the sentences to be sure your child has replaced the nouns with appropriate pronouns.

Tips for Your Own Writing: Revising ....

From your own writing, choose a paragraph about a person, place, or thing. Are any pronouns you used confusing? Check to be sure that the reader can clearly see to what or whom each pronoun refers.

Use pronouns to improve your writing.

117

Lesson 57

Lesson 57 Grammar: Verbs

Verbs are the hardest workers in a paragraph. With wishy-washy verbs, you'll have a wishy-washy story!

.... **Did You Know?** ....

A <u>verb</u> tells what the person, place, or thing in a sentence is doing, or it links or connects the subject to the rest of the sentence. A verb might tell about being rather than acting. The words *felt and hiked* are verbs.

The boys **felt** tired as they **hiked** on the trail.

Verbs also show whether something happens in the present, the past, or the future. The word *hike* is present tense, *hiked* is past tense, and *will hike* is future tense.

Today I **hike.**   Yesterday I **hiked.**   Tomorrow I **will hike.**

Verbs must match their subjects. In the present tense, the verb *walk* changes when its subject is a third-person singular noun, such as *girl.*

I often **walk** on that trail.
Girls from my school **walk** on it, too.
I know a girl who **walks** on the trail every day.

Some verbs express a state of being. The most common verbs that show being are *am, is, are, was, were,* and *be.*

The cougar **was** huge, and the boys **were** terrified.

Show What You Know

Write a correct verb in each blank. Sample answers are given.

Mountain climbing __is__ (1) a popular sport. People __climb__ (2) mountains for many reasons. Some people __enjoy__ (3) the challenge of trying to reach high and dangerous places. Others __like__ (4) to explore the outdoors and __admire__ (5) the beauty of nature. Whatever the reason, mountaineering __is__ (6) serious business. Every climber __needs__ (7) to work with experienced teachers.

Review the sentences to be sure your child has used verbs that are in the appropriate tense and that make sense.

Score: _____   Total Possible: 7

118

Practice

Imagine standing at the top of the world's highest mountain peak. What would you do? Write three verbs to fill the blanks in this sentence.

Sample answers are given.

At the top of the mountain, I __stood__ (1) __shouted__ (2) and __waved__ (3)

Review the verbs to be sure your child has used verbs that are strong and applicable to the context.

Next, write three sentences that use the verbs you chose. Add details to create interesting sentences.

Review the writing to be sure your child has used verbs and details that create interest.

Check for accurate sentence structure as well.

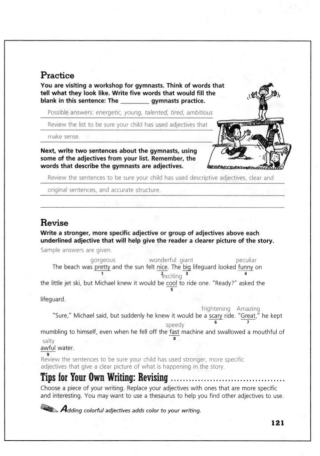

Revise

Write a stronger, more specific verb above each underlined verb.

Sample answers are given.

First, the frightened turtle <u>walked</u>[scrambled] (1) toward the water. Then it seemed to <u>know</u>[realize] (2) it could not <u>go</u>[waddle] (3) as fast as the dogs could <u>move</u>[race] (4). The turtle pulled its head and legs into its shell. The dogs <u>ran</u>[dashed] (5) up and stopped. They <u>barked</u>[whined] (6) and <u>touched</u>[poked] (7) the turtle with their noses. Then they <u>went</u>[wandered] (8) away. The turtle <u>moved</u>[shuffled] (9) again toward the sea.

Review the sentences to be sure your child has used appropriate verbs that are stronger and more specific.

Tips for Your Own Writing: Revising ....

Reread a story or poem you have written. Replace some of the verbs to add action and interest to your story. A word like *walk* could be replaced with *march, tiptoe,* or *prance.* Each verb gives a slightly different meaning to the action and provides a different image.

Vivid verbs add vitality to your writing.

119

Lesson 58

Lesson 58 Grammar: Adjectives

The adjectives you use can bring a story to life for your reader.

.... **Did You Know?** ....

An <u>adjective</u> is a word that describes a noun or pronoun. An adjective is a word that can fit in both these blanks:

The _____ tree is very _____.

In the following sentence, the words *smooth, dark, big,* and *green* are adjectives.

The artist had **smooth, dark** skin and **big, green** eyes.

Adjectives usually come before the words they describe. Sometimes two or more adjectives describe the same word. Adjectives may tell *how many, what kind,* or *which one.*

Adjectives sometimes follow a verb.

The bicycle was **rusty.**

Adjectives should be specific. They should help give the reader a clear picture of whatever is being described.

....

Show What You Know

Circle the twenty-three adjectives in the following paragraph. Do not circle the words *the, an,* and *a.*

The (unexpected) visitors left their (enormous) (wooden) boats and waded through the (rough) (warm) water to the shore. The visitors were (tall) and had (pale) skin. Their (dark) (long) hair was tied back with (red) (blue) and (brown) cord. The men's (bright) clothing covered their bodies. Their (wet) faces showed that they were (tired). The (first) man to touch shore wore a (red) cape and a (blue) hat. He carried a (long) (black) stick, which he pointed at the (surprised) people standing on the (sandy) (white) shore.

Score: _____   Total Possible: 23

120

Practice

You are visiting a workshop for gymnasts. Think of words that tell what they look like. Write five words that would fill the blank in this sentence: The _____ gymnasts practice.

Possible answers: *energetic, young, talented, tired, ambitious*

Review the list to be sure your child has used adjectives that make sense.

Next, write two sentences about the gymnasts, using some of the adjectives from your list. Remember, the words that describe the gymnasts are adjectives.

Review the sentences to be sure your child has used descriptive adjectives, clear and original sentences, and accurate structure.

Revise

Write a stronger, more specific adjective or group of adjectives above each underlined adjective that will help give the reader a clearer picture of the story.

Sample answers are given.

The beach was <u>pretty</u>[gorgeous] (1) and the sun felt <u>nice</u>[wonderful] (2). The <u>big</u>[giant] (3) lifeguard looked <u>funny</u>[peculiar] (4) on the little jet ski, but Michael knew it would be <u>cool</u>[exciting] (5) to ride one. "Ready?" asked the lifeguard.

"Sure," Michael said, but suddenly he knew it would be a <u>scary</u>[frightening] (6) ride. "<u>Great</u>,[Amazing] (7)" he kept mumbling to himself, even when he fell off the <u>fast</u>[speedy] (8) machine and swallowed a mouthful of <u>awful</u>[salty] (9) water.

Review the sentences to be sure your child has used stronger, more specific adjectives that give a clear picture of what is happening in the story.

Tips for Your Own Writing: Revising ....

Choose a piece of your writing. Replace your adjectives with ones that are more specific and interesting. You may want to use a thesaurus to help you find other adjectives to use.

Adding colorful adjectives adds color to your writing.

121

Lesson 59

Lesson
59 Grammar: Adverbs

Adverbs add a little energy to your verbs. Even a strong verb needs help once in a while.

.... Did You Know? ....

An <u>adverb</u> is a word that describes a verb, an adjective, or another adverb. Adverbs tell *how, when, where,* and *how much.*

> The children giggled **wildly** as the clowns ran past.
> (*Wildly* is an adverb that describes the verb *giggled.*)
>
> One large clown sat **very** carefully on a tiny stool. (*Very* is an adverb that describes the adverb *carefully.*)
>
> Another clown carried a **brightly** painted banner. (*Brightly* is an adverb that describes the adjective *painted.*)

Many adverbs end in *-ly: wildly, sadly, quickly, slowly.* However, some common adverbs do not: *almost, not, often, too, very.* Some adverbs are spelled like their matching adjectives: *hard, first, far.*

....

Show What You Know

Find the thirteen adverbs in the following paragraph. Circle each adverb you find. Remember, an adverb will tell *how, when, where,* or *how much.*

The class had studied (seriously) to learn about the (historically) important pier. They had (finally) come to visit it, but it was (too) crowded to see much. People were packed (tightly) in the restaurants. The museum was (completely) filled with visitors. The air-conditioned bookstore felt (only)(slightly) cool (inside) because of the crowds. The lines for the rides were (ridiculously) long. Why was everybody (so) happy? Why were they all (extremely) glad that they had come to this (very) exciting place?

Score: _____   Total Possible: 13

122

Practice
Write an adverb in each blank to complete the story.
Sample answers are given.

Tess, Carol, and Jake __quickly__ got on their bikes
1
and started down the trail. Their aunt had __happily__
2
agreed to meet them __later__ and to take them
3
and their bikes home in her van. Taking the lead, Carol
rode __quietly__. "Do you think we'll make the whole
4
twenty miles?" Tess asked __worriedly__.
5
"Sure!" Jake said __firmly__.
6

Review the sentences to be sure your child has used adverbs that add description to the story.

Revise
Choose a different adverb that sets a different mood and write it above each underlined adverb below. Adverbs you might choose are *eagerly, gently, hesitantly, rapidly, suddenly, softly, unexpectedly,* and *violently.*
Sample answers are given.

           eagerly   hesitantly
A canoe ride! Casey ran <u>fast</u> toward the river. Sheila moved more <u>slowly</u>. She liked to
1
                           suddenly
think about things, and this chance to ride in a canoe had come too <u>fast</u>. The current
      gently   unexpectedly
moved <u>slowly</u> here, so it would be safe, Sheila told herself. Then, <u>surprisingly</u>, rain began
4   5
  softly   violently   rapidly
to fall, <u>a little</u> at first, then <u>hard</u>. The girls turned and ran <u>fast</u> toward the house.
6   7
Review the sentences to be sure your child has used adverbs that give the story a different mood.

Tips for Your Own Writing: Revising ....
Select a piece of writing you have done. Revise it to include adverbs that help your reader know where, when, or how something happened. Remember—do not overuse the word *very.* Choose adverbs like *quickly* or *rapidly* instead.

Tell how. Carefully. *Tell when.* Today. *Tell where.* Outside. *Adverbs add useful details.*

123

Lesson 60

Lesson
60 Grammar: Articles

There are only three articles in the English language. Using the right one is easy if you listen carefully.

.... Did You Know? ....

An <u>article</u> is a kind of adjective. There are only three articles: *the, a, an.*

The is a definite article because it identifies a specific noun.

> Beryl Markham was **the** first person to fly solo across **the** Atlantic Ocean from east to west.

A and *an* are indefinite articles because they refer to any one of a group of nouns.

> **A** small plane and **an** unexpected storm made her flight dangerous.

Use the word *a* before words that begin with a consonant sound. Use *an* before words that begin with a vowel sound.

> Markham had been **a** pilot in Africa for many years.
> A compass is **a** useful tool.
> She had flown in **an** open cockpit plane through all kinds of weather.
> She waited **an** hour before taking off.

....

Show What You Know
Write the correct article *a, an,* or *the* in each sentence.

Elephants from Africa are __the__ ones with large, fanlike ears.
1
Elephants also live on __the__ continent of Asia. __An__ elephant has
2   3
__an__ almost hairless body. It also has __a__ long, flexible trunk.
4   5
Elephants are __the__ largest mammals that live on land. __The__ only
6   7
larger mammals, whales, live in the ocean.

Score: _____   Total Possible: 7

124

Proofread
Proofread the paragraph. Circle seven incorrect articles. Write the correct article above each incorrect one.

    Do you know how a moth is different from (the) butterfly? A butterfly has a
                                   a
knob on (a) antenna. A butterfly is active during (a) daytime. A butterfly has
      an   the
brighter colors than (the) moth. A butterfly folds its wings upward when it rests. A
butterfly has (the) smooth body, and a moth may have (the) hairy one. Although
            a   a
the butterfly is (a) insect that almost everyone likes, many people
         an
don't like the moth.

Practice
Write *a* or *an* in each blank below.

1. __a__ happy trip   4. __an__ hourly schedule

2. __a__ useful guidebook   5. __a__ foreign country

3. __an__ apple   6. __a__ united group

Now write a journal entry or a letter describing your imaginary travels. Use several of the phrases you created above.

Review the writing to be sure that your child has:
• used articles correctly.
• described imaginary travels.

Tips for Your Own Writing: Proofreading ....
Remember that the article *a* is used before words beginning with a consonant sound. The article *an* is used before words beginning with a vowel sound.

The three most commonly used words in English are the, a, and an.

125

Lesson 61

Lesson 61 Review: Parts of Speech

A. Circle the five common nouns below. Write a proper noun to replace each article and common noun.
Sample answers are given.

1. The (president) arrived. — President Clinton
2. The (mayor) is traveling. — Mayor Daley
3. I visited a (museum). — The Museum of Modern Art
4. The (street) is busy and noisy. — California Street
5. The (city) is large and exciting. — Milwaukee

Score: _____ Total Possible: 10

B. Write the correct pronoun in each blank.

Clint's mother just told __him__(1) about the family's vacation plans. Now __he__(2) is excited and is telling all of __us__(3) about this great trip. __They__(4) are going to Disney World, a place Clint and __his__(5) brother have always wanted to see. My sister and __I__(6) told __our__(7) mother that __we__(8) thought a trip to Florida sounded great. __She__(9) agreed but said __it__(10) won't happen soon!

Score: _____ Total Possible: 10

C. Underline seven verbs in the paragraph. Above each underlined verb, write a stronger verb to make the story more exciting.
Sample answers are given.

The storm came (raged). Thunder sounded (boomed). Suddenly, a bolt of lightning hit (struck) the tree in the yard. The tree broke (shattered) into pieces and fell (collapsed). We came (scrambled) up from the basement. The storm moved (rushed) toward the next part of town.

Score: _____ Total Possible: 14

126

D. Make the sentences more interesting by writing an adjective in each blank.
Sample answers are given.

1. The __enormous__ car led a __circus__ parade.
2. The __exciting__ event was well-attended.
3. __Hysterical__ boys and girls wore __wild__ clothes.
4. __Courageous__ adults wore __raggedy__ jeans and T-shirts.
5. We enjoyed a __delicious__ lunch.

Score: _____ Total Possible: 8

E. Circle an adverb in each sentence.

1. The wind blew (fiercely) across the sand.
2. The canvas tent flapped (noisily).
3. The air seemed (very) cool when night came.
4. Inside the tent, Anna danced (wildly).
5. She loved the wind and was (too) excited to mind the cold.

Score: _____ Total Possible: 5

F. Draw a delete mark through each incorrect article. Write the correct article above the incorrect word. If all of the articles in a sentence are correct, write C above the sentence. There are four incorrect articles.

1. Abiyoyo was a fearsome giant! (C)
2. Actually, he was a̶ (an) ogre!
3. He danced when a̶n̶ (a) ukulele was played.
4. The boy with the ukulele was a̶n̶ (a) hero.
5. That boy over there is a̶ (the) one who saved the town.

Score: _____ Total Possible: 9

G. Write the part of speech above each word in the sentence below.

article	adjective	noun	verb	adverb
A	fat	frog	croaked	loudly.

Score: _____ Total Possible: 5

REVIEW SCORE: _____ REVIEW TOTAL: 61

127

Lesson 62

Lesson 62 Grammar: Statements and Questions

Writing can be used to ask and to answer questions.

.... **Did You Know?** ....

Most sentences are statements. They end with a period.
The weather is very nice today.

Statements have a subject and a verb. The *subject* tells who or what the sentence is about. The *verb* tells what the subject is doing, or it links the subject to the rest of the sentence. Usually, the subject comes before the verb.
        S   V
We practice our batting and hitting.

In many questions, the subject comes between two verbs.
        V   S   V
What can I do indoors?

....

Show What You Know

Read the paragraphs below. If a sentence is a statement, put a period in the blank. Circle the periods so they are easier to see. If the sentence asks a question, put a question mark in the blank.

We want to avoid adding to Earth's pollution __.__(1) We want to save money on electricity __.__(2) Can we do both at the same time __?__(3) Can saving electricity help avoid pollution __?__(4) The answer is yes, it can! Every time someone uses electricity, a power plant somewhere works a little harder __.__(5) This means it uses more fuel __.__(6) What kinds of fuel do power plants use __?__(7) Many of them use coal __.__(8) Some burn oil or gas __.__(9) Some use nuclear power __.__(10)

Burning any fuel can cause pollution __.__(11) If smoke goes into the air, it makes the air we breathe dirtier __.__(12) Can nuclear power cause water pollution __?__(13) Yes, it can! Heat from a power plant can heat water in a river and kill plants and fish __.__(14) We have good reasons to use electricity carefully __.__(15) Work toward saving electricity __.__(16)

Score: _____ Total Possible: 16

128

Proofread

Read the story below. Use proper proofreading marks to correct the five punctuation mistakes.

Example: We went to the park⊙

Have you ever been lost in the woods⊙ It sounds like a great adventure, but it is not fun. I live near Lost Creek State Park, where I've been about a thousand times⊙ On my birthday, my family went up there to celebrate. We started to hike to the falls. I was at the tail end of the group. Could I use a shortcut and get ahead of them⁇ Suddenly I was in the forest, surrounded by enormous trees, dim light, and weird noises. I had no idea what I could do⊙ It was very scary. Then I heard my father yell my name. I followed his voice and got out. "Was I worried?" they asked me⊙

"Of course not," I answered bravely.

Practice

Write four lines of dialogue for the people in the picture. Use questions and statements.

Review the writing to be sure your child has used realistic dialogue that has been derived from the illustration and correct punctuation for statements and questions.

Tips for Your Own Writing: Proofreading

Review a piece of your own writing. Check to be sure you put periods after sentences that tell something, and question marks after sentences that ask something. The order of the subject and verb will help you decide.

Periods signal that something is being stated. Question marks signal that something is being asked.

129

192 Answer Key

Lesson 63

Lesson
63 Grammar: Requests and Exclamations

Whether you're writing a report, story, play, or poem, the order of the words in your sentence and the punctuation you use are signals for your readers.

························· **Did You Know?** ·····················

A sentence that expresses strong feeling is an <u>exclamation</u>. It ends with an exclamation point. That signals that it is intended to express strong feeling.

I can't believe it! Ready, set, go!

A sentence that gives orders or directions is a <u>command</u>. Most commands have no stated subject. "You" is understood to be the subject. The forcefulness with which the command is given determines whether an exclamation point or a period is used at the end.

Don't throw that trash into the lake.
Don't throw that trash into the lake!

A sentence that tells a person to do something is a <u>request</u>. A request is a polite command and is followed by a period.

Bring my books to the car, please.

···

Show What You Know

In the following sentences, add the correct punctuation at the end of each sentence. Circle the periods so that they are easier to see.

1. Please get back on the bus.
2. Kindly wait for the driver.
3. Oh, no, it's a bear!
4. Oh, dear, he's coming this way!
5. Hey, don't go near the bear!
6. Go back to your seats now.
7. Please move as quickly as possible.
8. Keep the windows closed.

Score: _____ Total Possible: 8

130

Proofread

Read the report below. Using proper proofreading marks, correct the incorrect punctuation marks at the ends of each of nine sentences.

Example: Here I go./Please come with me?

Everywhere we go, signs use huge letters to shout at us. Get your tickets here! Don't ride bikes on the sidewalk. Don't litter! Wait for the crossing light. I feel like I'm in the Army and the drill sergeant is yelling, "Forward, march!"

I think signs in small print look more like polite requests. Check coats here. Have exact change ready! It's like the teacher saying, "Pass your papers to the front of the room."

Of course, when I get home and walk into the kitchen, my sister often greets me with, "Wash your hands!" She should use a sign with very small letters.

Practice

Write one exclamation, one request, and two commands. Punctuate each correctly.

Review the sentences to be sure your child has used the correct punctuation and has shown that he or she understands differences among types of sentences.

_____

_____

Tips for Your Own Writing: Proofreading ························

Choose a piece of your writing that includes dialogue. Look for exclamations that you wrote. Did you remember to use some exclamation points to indicate strong feeling? Do not overuse them. If you use exclamation points too often, they will lose their impact, just like the boy who cried "Wolf!" too often.

Are you using all this important information in your own writing?

131

··

Lesson 64

Lesson
64 Review: Sentences

A. There are fourteen statements and seven questions in the following report. Use proper proofreading marks to add end punctuation that shows which sentences are statements and which are questions. Circle periods so they are easier to see.

The word *library* comes from an old Latin word that means "book." Did you ever wonder why people started building large rooms just for books? Well, remember that books weren't always as common or as inexpensive as they are today. After all, early books were written by hand, weren't they? Even today it's convenient to be able to read all kinds of books that you don't have in your own house.

Libraries are changing, though. What will you find in a library besides books? Most public libraries carry records, tapes, CDs, and videos. Is your public library that well-equipped? Some aren't, of course, but they will be someday.

Most libraries now have computers. Why are they in there with books? Well, a computer is another source of information. Don't you agree that a computer should be in a building thats name means "book"? Libraries are places to go for books and many other sources of information as well.

Along with computers, books, CDs, tapes, videos, and all of the other materials in a library, there are people. Some of those people work there. Do you know which person to ask for help? Librarians are often very well-informed and can help you with a lot of projects. The other people there are readers like you. Libraries make it easy for people to study and learn.

Score: _____ Total Possible: 21

132

B. In the blanks below, identify the type of sentence by writing *E* for exclamation, *C* for command, or *R* for request. After each letter, show the end punctuation you would use.

Annie and Charlie started across the bridge that ran above the train tracks. Annie was scared to death of that bridge, and she knew Charlie didn't like it, either. He even sounded nervous.

"Walk faster, Annie _C ._
                        1 "

Annie held on to the railing of the bridge.

"Please don't hurry me, Charlie _R ._
                                  2 "

Annie was watching every step she took and couldn't look at anything but her feet. She thought "Oh, help _E !_ We are so high up _E !_
                                                        3   4 "

Then Annie realized her brother was standing still. She followed Charlie's eyes and saw a small boy who had slipped on the bridge just ahead of them.

"His feet are over the edge and he looks stuck _E !_ Let's help him, Charlie!"
                                                5

She knew the boy had to be frightened. Charlie started to run toward the boy. "Come on, Annie _C ._ " Annie came.
                      6

Charlie and Annie pulled the boy up. He was shaking. As he stood up, he gave them a weak smile.

"Whew _E !_ Thanks, thanks, thanks _E !_ "
       7   8

Score: _____ Total Possible: 16

REVIEW SCORE: _____ REVIEW TOTAL: 37

133

Lesson 65 Grammar: Understanding Sentences I

If part of a sentence is missing, part of your idea is missing!

.... **Did You Know?** ....

A *sentence* is a group of words that expresses a complete thought.

Summer is one of the four seasons.

Every sentence has two parts: a *subject*—the part that tells who or what the sentence is about—and a *predicate*—the part that tells something about the subject.

SUBJECT   **PREDICATE**

Summer / is one of the four seasons.

A writer uses sentences to share thoughts and ideas with readers. Be sure your sentences have every word that is necessary to get your ideas across to your readers.

Incorrect: A cool way to spend the summer.
Correct: Swimming every day is a cool way to spend the summer.
Incorrect: The girl at the swimming pool.
Correct: The girl at the swimming pool taught me how to dive.

....

Show What You Know

Underline the subject of each sentence below.

<u>Laurie</u> always wanted to be a scientist and search for fossils. <u>She</u> studied with a famous geologist and his friends. In Nebraska <u>they</u> found dinosaur bones buried under tons of ash. <u>A museum named Ashfall</u> was built. <u>It</u> is popular and is visited by many people every year. <u>Visitors</u> can see dinosaur bones as they were found.

Score: _____   **Total Possible: 6**

134

Practice

Use the words below to write complete sentences.
Sample answers are given.

1. barked loudly
A dog barked loudly.

2. the house
The house was huge!

3. in the summer
We go to the lake in the summer.

4. the best time of year
The best time of year is fall.

Review the sentences to be sure your child has written complete sentences with correct subjects and predicates.

Revise

Unscramble the following sentences by writing them in the correct order on the lines. Then, circle the subject and underline the predicate in each sentence. Use capital letters correctly.

Planned Sanchez Mrs. the trip.   The visited kids park the.   Played they baseball. They picnic had a.   Good a time had everybody.   Tired happy they but were.

1. (Mrs. Sanchez) planned the trip.
2. (The kids) visited the park.
3. (They) played baseball.
4. (They) had a picnic.
5. (Everybody) had a good time.
6. (They) were tired but happy.

Tips for Your Own Writing: Revising ....

When you finish a piece of writing, get in the habit of reading it aloud to yourself. You will be amazed at how many incomplete sentences and other mistakes you will be able to fix before anyone else ever reads your work.

Check your sentences for both parts—a subject and a predicate.

135

....

Lesson 66 Grammar: Understanding Sentences II

Sometimes you want to put more than one idea into a sentence.

.... **Did You Know?** ....

One way to combine ideas into one sentence is to join the two ideas with words such as *and*, *but*, or *or*.

Philip is a geologist, **but** he is a college teacher, too.
He searched for fossils in Wyoming, **and** he found interesting ones.
He invites students to work with him, **or** he works alone.

....

Show What You Know

Match the sentences in Column 1 with the sentences in Column 2. Combine the sentences using *and*, *but*, or *or*, and write them on the lines below.

Column 1	Column 2
1. The road was long.	A. Believe me, it was worth the trouble!
2. We ate all day in the car.	B. We played every game we knew.
3. My dad couldn't find the road.	C. I could entertain my twin brothers.
4. Dad said to relax.	D. I felt responsible.
5. I could go to sleep.	E. I lost the map.
6. We finally reached Isle Royale.	F. The drive seemed even longer.

Possible answers are given.

1. The road was long, but the drive seemed even longer.
2. We ate all day in the car, and we played every game we knew.
3. My dad couldn't find the road, and I lost the map.
4. Dad said to relax, but I felt responsible.
5. I could go to sleep, or I could entertain my twin brothers.
6. We finally reached Isle Royale, and believe me, it was worth the trouble!

Score: _____   **Total Possible: 6**

136

Practice

Write two sentences using the pattern of the nonsense sentence below. Write in real words for the nonsense words.

That glurb janded plurpily, but this glurb jands with delight.

Sample answers are given.

1. That bird crowed loudly, but this bird crows with delight.
2. That horse jumped quickly, but this horse jumps with delight.

Review the sentences to be sure your child has written complete sentences that make sense.

Revise

Combine the sentences in the paragraph below into compound sentences using *and*, *but*, or *or*.

A mosaic may be only bits of colored glass and glue. It forms a picture. Old mosaics are beautiful. So are modern ones. You can make mosaics with beads. They won't be as bright as ones made from glass. Make a mosaic with colored paper. Make one with bits of plastic. Try it. You might discover you enjoy it.

A mosaic may be only bits of colored glass and glue, but it forms a picture. Old mosaics are beautiful, and so are modern ones. You can make mosaics with beads, but they won't be as bright as ones made from glass. Make a mosaic with colored paper or bits of plastic. Try it, and you might discover you enjoy it.

Tips for Your Own Writing: Revising ....

Look at something you have written recently. Did you use any compound sentences? If so, look at the sentences you joined together. Are their ideas related? Combine sentences *only* when the ideas in the sentences are closely related.

Combining sentences takes some experimenting, but it's worth the effort!

137

Lesson 67

Lesson

67 Grammar: Combining Sentences I

Avoid short, choppy sentences. They can take your reader's attention away from the ideas you want to share.

.... **Did You Know?** ....

Combining sentence parts when you revise your writing can make a sentence smooth and can cut out extra words as well.
Babe is a video I really like. *Pinocchio* is good, too.
Matilda is one of my favorites.
Babe, Pinocchio, and *Matilda* are three of my favorite videos *or* I really like *Babe, Pinocchio,* and *Matilda.*

....

Show What You Know

You do not need all the words in the following sentences to say what you want to say. Rewrite each group of sentences on the line to make one well-combined sentence.
Possible answers are given.

1. I loved *James and the Giant Peach* by Roald Dahl. I also loved *Matilda* by Dahl.
I loved James and the Giant Peach and Matilda by Roald Dahl.

2. *Oink* was illustrated by Arthur Geisert. Geisert illustrated *Haystack,* too.
Oink and Haystack were illustrated by Arthur Geisert.

3. *Jumanji* is a really weird story. *Bad Day at Riverbend* is strange, too.
Both Jumanji and Bad Day at Riverbend are weird stories.

4. *The Book of Hot Lists for Kids* gave me some great ideas for things to do. *The Kids' Summer Handbook* taught me some things, too.
Both The Book of Hot Lists for Kids and The Kids' Summer Handbook gave me ideas for things to do.

5. Books make my weekends fun. CDs also give me some fun things to do.
Books and CDs make my weekends fun.

Review the sentences to be sure your child has combined necessary parts of the sentences without repeating unnecessary parts.

Score: _____   Total Possible: 5

138

Practice

Picture some people who are important to you. List their names and write a few words that tell why they are important.
Review the list to be sure your child has written with clarity; the
list need not be in complete sentences at this point.

Now choose three of the people on your list who are important to you for the same or a similar reason. Write one sentence about something the people have in common.
Review sentences to be sure your child has written with clear understanding and
correct structure.

Revise

Read the paragraph. Circle the sentences that can be combined. Rewrite them on the lines below.

Steven Kellogg is a well-known children's author. He was born in 1941. He has six stepchildren. He has seven grandchildren. He lives in a small town in Connecticut. His wife Arlene and his dog live there, too. His dog has very long legs. His dog has a big head, too. Steven often includes animals in his stories. Pinkerton is one of his animal characters. Alfonse is another. Pinkerton is the Great Dane. Alfonse is the tadpole.

He has six stepchildren and seven grandchildren. He lives with his wife Arlene and his
dog in a small town in Connecticut. His dog has very long legs and a big head.
Pinkerton the Great Dane and Alfonse the tadpole are two of his animal characters.

Review the sentences to be sure your child has correctly combined like ideas.

Tips for Your Own Writing: Revising ....

Combining sentences can help make your writing concise and understandable. But just because two sentences have the same subject or object does not mean they should always be combined.

Remember, strong writing uses no extra words.

139

Lesson 68

Lesson

68 Grammar: Combining Sentences II

Sometimes writers avoid having too many short sentences by combining verbs.

.... **Did You Know?** ....

If you are saying two things about the same person or place, you can often combine these parts into one sentence. Do this by using more than one verb in a sentence.
Our class **planted** a garden. We **weeded** the garden, too.
Our class **planted and weeded** the garden.
We **found** a video about crops the Inca planted. We **watched** the video.
We **found and watched** a video about crops the Inca planted.

....

Show What You Know

Combine each pair of sentences into one sentence that has two verbs. Write the new sentence on the line.

1. Nancy Ward thought about her Cherokee people. She worried about them.
Nancy Ward thought and worried about her Cherokee people.

2. Nancy talked to the leaders. She begged them to listen to her.
Nancy talked to the leaders and begged them to listen to her.

3. She led her people. She showed them a way to survive.
She led her people and showed them a way to survive.

4. Nancy also talked to the white people. She showed them how they could have peace.
Nancy also talked to the white people and showed them how they could have peace.

Score: _____   Total Possible: 4

140

Practice

List the names of three real or fictional people who interest you. After each name, jot down two or three strong, active verbs you might use to tell about that person.
Review the list to be sure your child has chosen verbs for
meaning and strength.

Next, write two sentences about one of the people on your list. In each sentence, tell one thing the person did. Keep the sentences simple.
Review the sentences to be sure your child has selected verbs accurately and
imaginatively.

Now combine your sentences into one sentence by combining the verbs.
Review the sentences to be sure your child has combined sentences for effect and clarity.

Revise

Circle the sentences that can be combined. Rewrite them on the lines below.

When our basketball players were introduced, the fans stood up. They cheered the team. The cheering was the loudest for Michael. But the game got off to a bad start. The other team blocked Michael's shots. They made him pass to his teammates. But Michael broke free. He grabbed the ball. He raced down the court. He jammed the ball into the basket. The fans yelled. They screamed. They stomped their feet.

When our basketball players were introduced, the fans stood up and cheered. The
other team blocked Michael's shots and made him pass to his teammates. But Michael
broke free, grabbed the ball, raced down the court, and jammed the ball into the
basket. The fans yelled, screamed, and stomped their feet.

Review the sentences to be sure your child has combined verbs in sentences correctly.

Tips for Your Own Writing: Revising ....

You can make a compound sentence by combining the verbs in sentences *only* if there is a close connection between the ideas, and the same subject is doing the action.

Combine sentences to improve your writing.

141

Answer Key **195**

Lesson 69

Lesson
69 Grammar: Combining Sentences III

Strengthen your writing by cutting out extra words. Make every word count.

.... **Did You Know?** ....

You can improve a piece of writing by using one exact word in place of a whole sentence.

The parrot has beautiful feathers. They are very **colorful.**

The parrot has beautiful, **colorful** feathers.

Bats eat mosquitoes and other insects. Bats are **useful** creatures.

Useful bats eat mosquitoes and other insects *or* Bats are **useful** because they eat mosquitoes and other insects.

....

Show What You Know

Combine the sentences in each pair. Write a new sentence by adding a single word from one sentence to the other.

1. My aunt doesn't like this winter weather. It's cold almost every day.
   My aunt doesn't like this winter weather when it's cold almost every day.

2. She often wears unusual winter clothes. She wears colorful winter clothes.
   She often wears colorful, unusual winter clothes.

3. On really cold days, she wears a fluffy jacket. The jacket is purple.
   On really cold days, she wears a fluffy, purple jacket.

4. She also wears a cap with a pom-pom on top. The cap is made of wool.
   She also wears a wool cap with a pom-pom on top.

5. She says she likes her winter clothes. They are warm.
   She says she likes her warm winter clothes.

Score: _____   Total Possible: 5

142

Practice

Read the pairs of sentences. Combine each pair into one sentence. Write the new sentences on the lines.

1. Those long-legged birds are storks. They are strange-looking.
2. No one can say anything good about mosquitoes. Mosquitoes are pesky insects.
3. The wind is blowing hard, with a roar. It is frightening.
4. We are taking a walk on a path. The path is long and winding.

Possible answers are given.

Those strange-looking, long-legged birds are storks.

No one can say anything good about pesky mosquitoes.

The frightening wind is blowing hard, with a roar.

We are taking a walk on a long and winding path.

Review the sentences to be sure your child has demonstrated an understanding of combining sentences without adding unnecessary words.

Revise

Combine each set of sentences into one sentence. Look for different ways to combine the information and choose the best one.

1. Rachel Carson was a biologist. She studied marine life. She was also a science writer.
2. She warned people about air pollution. Pollution is dangerous.
3. She thought that the use of pesticides was destructive. She thought it was hazardous.
4. Carson discovered that pesticides were poisonous. She found they killed many fish.

1. Rachel Carson was a marine biologist and a science writer.
2. She warned people about dangerous air pollution.
3. She thought that the use of pesticides was destructive and hazardous.
4. Carson discovered that poisonous pesticides killed many fish.

Review the sentences to be sure your child has combined sentences in a concise manner.

Tips for Your Own Writing: Revising ....

Choose a piece of your own writing. Try to put related ideas together. Combine the descriptive words into one sentence if they describe the same person, place, or thing.

Weave the ideas together by combining sentences.

143

Lesson 70

Lesson
70 Grammar: Combining Sentences IV

A phrase can help make writing clear and strong.

.... **Did You Know?** ....

You can combine sentences by using a phrase in place of a wordy sentence. A *phrase* is a group of related words that does not have a subject or verb.

My friend taught me step dancing. She grew up in Ireland.

My friend **from Ireland** taught me step dancing.

That man enjoys watching the dancers. He uses a cane.

That man **with the cane** enjoys watching the dancers.

....

Show What You Know

Change one sentence into a phrase and place it in the other sentence. Write the new sentence on the line.

1. We watched our neighbor walk by. She led a beautiful dog.
   We watched our neighbor walk by with a beautiful dog.

2. Our neighbor seems friendly. Her house is that brick one.
   Our neighbor in that brick house seems friendly.

3. The Newfoundland puppy is hers, too! It has a floppy ear.
   The Newfoundland puppy with the floppy ear is hers, too.

4. She and the dog are going on a hike. She wants to reach Carter Lake.
   She and the dog are going on a hike to Carter Lake.

5. She walks the dog every day. The dog wears a leash.
   She walks the dog on a leash every day.

Score: _____   Total Possible: 5

144

Proofread

Circle the sentence that shows one correct way to combine the pair of sentences.

1. **I have read all those books. That is my collection.**
   I have a collection of books that I don't read.
   (I have read all those books in my collection)
2. **We have collected many old records. We give them to my uncle.**
   My uncle has collected many old records.
   (We have collected many old records for my uncle)
3. **Susan has collected many stamps. She takes them from old envelopes.**
   (Susan has collected many stamps from old envelopes)
   Susan takes old envelopes for her stamp collection.

Practice

Read the pairs of sentences. Combine each pair by making one sentence a phrase and placing it in the other sentence.

1. Charlie found a granola bar. The granola bars are in the cupboard.
2. Oranges are Kelly's favorite fruit. She likes Florida oranges best.
3. Melanie wanted an unusual snack. She wanted carrot sticks and peanut butter.
4. Jake loves fresh watermelon. He has a garden full of watermelon vines.

Possible answers are given.

Charlie found a granola bar in the cupboard. Oranges from Florida are Kelly's favorite.

Melanie wanted an unusual snack of carrot sticks and peanut butter. Jake loves fresh

watermelon from his garden full of watermelon vines.

Review the sentences to be sure your child has combined sentences smoothly by including phrases based on the second sentence.

Tips for Your Own Writing: Proofreading ....

Using phrases to revise your sentences can help make your writing smoother and more concise. But do not pack a sentence with too many phrases.

A phrase uses only a few words, so it can help condense writing.

145

Lesson 71

Lesson 71 Grammar: Combining Sentences V

Sometimes you just want to put two sentences together. That may be a good way to make a connection.

.... **Did You Know?** ....

You can combine two sentences with these words: *and, but,* and *or.* The two parts of the combined sentence are separated by a comma.

Many people drive to work, **but** people in cities often use public transportation.

Cars pollute the air, **and** gas for a car may be expensive.

You can choose to fly long distances, **or** you can drive for several days.

....

Show What You Know

Combine these pairs of sentences using *and, but,* or *or.* Write the new sentence on the line. Be sure to add a comma.

1. Trains have crossed the United States since the 1860s. They have moved millions of people.
   Trains have crossed the United States since the 1860s, and they have moved millions of people.

2. Today many people still love to ride the train. Many others think it is too slow.
   Today many people still love to ride the train, but many others think it is too slow.

3. Many families think driving is the easiest for them. It can be tiring.
   Many families think driving is the easiest for them, but it can be tiring.

4. Many people with babies choose to drive. They can fly faster.
   Many people with babies choose to drive, or they can fly faster.

Score: _____ Total Possible: 4

146

Practice

Think of a topic you might write about. Write four sentences. If possible, combine some sentences into compound sentences.

Review the sentences to be sure your child has combined sentences for correct formatting, appropriate punctuation, and understanding of combining related sentences.

Revise

Read the paragraph below. Circle sentences that can be combined and rewrite them on the lines below.

Computers were once rare in homes. Now they are found in many homes. Families use computers for simple tasks such as writing letters. They use them for more complex tasks such as banking. Children use computers to play games. They use them to do homework. In the future, computers will be needed more. Every family will own a computer.

Computers were once rare in homes, but now they are found in many homes. Families use computers for simple tasks such as writing letters, and they use them for more complex tasks such as banking. Children use computers to play games, or they use them to do homework. In the future, computers will be needed more, and almost every family will own a computer.

Tips for Your Own Writing: Revising ....

If you combine two or more simple sentences using *and, or,* or *but,* remember to place a comma before the word that joins the sentences. Do not combine too many sentences with *and's.* This will only make a long, boring sentence.

Combining two short sentences into one sentence can help your readers better understand your ideas.

147

Lesson 72

Lesson 72 Review: Understanding and Combining Sentences

A. Use each group of words to write a complete sentence on the lines.
Sample answers are given.

1. fourth-grade students
   Fourth-grade students enjoy their classes.

2. like many subjects
   They like many subjects.

3. science
   Science interests them.

Review sentences to be sure your child has formed correct sentences with both a subject and a predicate.

Score: _____ Total Possible: 3

B. Write two short sentences using all the words below. Then combine your sentences using *or, and,* or *but.*

closet is feet the length twelve the of width its only inches is thirty
   The length of the closet is twelve feet. Its width is only thirty inches. The length of the closet is twelve feet, but its width is only thirty inches.

Score: _____ Total Possible: 3

C. Combine each pair of sentences.

1. People in Chicago ride buses. Many of them ride subways.
   People in Chicago ride buses and subways.

2. Workers in San Francisco take cars. Others take the BART trains.
   Workers in San Francisco take cars or the BART trains.

3. Older students often drive. Working people often drive.
   Older students and working people often drive.

Score: _____ Total Possible: 3

148

D. Combine these pairs of sentences by using both verbs in one sentence.

1. The drums thundered loudly. They echoed through the hall.
   The drums thundered loudly and echoed through the hall.

2. A horn tooted. Then it stopped suddenly.
   A horn tooted and then stopped suddenly.

Score: _____ Total Possible: 2

E. Use an adjective from one sentence to help you combine sentences.

1. Our guest speaker was very tall. He was thin, too.
   Our guest speaker was very tall and thin.

2. It was easy to hear his clear voice. It was loud, too.
   It was easy to hear his loud, clear voice.

3. His speech was about vacationing in Virginia. It was fascinating.
   His fascinating speech was about vacationing in Virginia.

Score: _____ Total Possible: 3

F. Use a phrase to help you combine these pairs of sentences.

1. We set out for our trip. We went to the zoo.
   We set out for our trip to the zoo.

2. We were told to stay together. There were three of us.
   The three of us were told to stay together.

Score: _____ Total Possible: 2

G. Make one sentence by combining this pair of sentences.

Today I wrote a poem. I was pleased with the results.
   Today I wrote a poem, and I was pleased with the results.

Score: _____ Total Possible: 1

REVIEW SCORE: _____ REVIEW TOTAL: 17

149

Answer Key **197**

Proofreading Marks

lowercase: / ~~S~~ister

capitalize: ≡ o̲hio

delete: ℓ ~~word~~e

transpose: ∿ sheep͜s͜' wool

insert: ∧ beautiful
a͜ sunset
∧

add... **a comma:** ⌄

a period: ⊙

a colon: ⌃

a semicolon: ⌃

a quotation mark: ⱱ

an apostrophe: ⱱ

McGraw-Hill Consumer Products

The skills taught in school are now available at home!
These award-winning software titles meet school guidelines and are based on
The McGraw-Hill Companies classroom software titles.

MATH GRADES 1 & 2

These math programs are a great way to teach and reinforce skills used in everyday situations. Fun, friendly characters need help with their math skills. Everyone's friend, Nubby the stubby pencil, will help kids master the math in the Numbers Quiz show. Foggy McHammer, a carpenter, needs some help building his playhouse so that all the boards will fit together! Julio Bambino's kitchen antics will surely burn his pastries if you don't help him set the clock timer correctly! We can't forget Turbo Tomato, a fruit with a passion for adventure, who needs help calculating his daredevil stunts.

Math Grades 1 & 2 use a tested, proven approach to reinforcing your child's math skills while keeping him or her intrigued with Nubby and his collection of crazy friends.

TITLE	ISBN	PRICE
Grade 1: Nubby's Quiz Show	1-57768-321-8	$9.95
Grade 2: Foggy McHammer's Treehouse	1-57768-322-6	$9.95

Available in jewel case only (no box included)

MISSION MASTERS™ MATH AND LANGUAGE ARTS

The Mission Masters™—Pauline, Rakeem, Mia, and T.J.—need your help. The Mission Masters™ are a team of young agents working for the Intelliforce Agency, a high-level cooperative whose goal is to maintain order on our rather unruly planet. From within the agency's top secret Command Control Center, the agency's central computer, M5, has detected a threat...and guess what—you're the agent assigned to the mission!

MISSION MASTERS™ MATH
GRADES 3, 4, & 5

This series of exciting activities encourages young mathematicians to challenge themselves and their math skills to overcome the perils of villains and other planetary threats. Skills reinforced include: analyzing and solving real-world problems, estimation, measurements, geometry, whole numbers, fractions, graphs, and patterns.

TITLE	ISBN	PRICE
Grade 3: Mission Masters™ Defeat Dirty D!	1-57768-323-5	$9.95
Grade 4: Mission Masters™ Alien Encounter	1-57768-324-2	$9.95
Grade 5: Mission Masters™ Meet Mudflat Moe	1-57768-325-0	$9.95

Available in jewel case only (no box included)

MISSION MASTERS™ LANGUAGE ARTS
GRADES 3, 4, & 5

This series invites children to apply their language skills to defeat unscrupulous characters and to overcome other earthly dangers. Skills reinforced include: language mechanics and usage, punctuation, spelling, vocabulary, reading comprehension, and creative writing.

TITLE	ISBN	PRICE
Grade 3: Mission Masters™ Freezing Frenzy	1-57768-343-9	$9.95
Grade 4: Mission Masters™ Network Nightmare	1-57768-344-7	$9.95
Grade 5: Mission Masters™ Mummy Mysteries	1-57768-345-5	$9.95

Available in jewel case only (no box included)

BASIC SKILLS BUILDER K to 2 – THE MAGIC APPLEHOUSE

At the Magic Applehouse, children discover that Abigail Appleseed runs a deliciously successful business selling apple pies, tarts, and other apple treats. Enthusiasm grows as children join in the fun of helping Abigail run her business. Along the way they'll develop computer and entrepreneurial skills to last a lifetime. They will run their own business – all while they're having bushels of fun!

TITLE	ISBN	PRICE
Basic Skills Builder –The Magic Applehouse	1-57768-312-9	$9.95

Available in jewel case only (no box included)

TEST PREP – SCORING HIGH

This grade-based testing software will help prepare your child for standardized achievement tests given by his or her school. Scoring High specifically targets the skills required for success on the Stanford Achievement Test (SAT) for grades three through eight. Lessons and test questions follow the same format and cover the same content areas as questions appearing on the actual SAT tests. The practice tests are modeled after the SAT test-taking experience with similar directions, number of questions per section, and bubble-sheet answer choices.

Scoring High is a child's first-class ticket to a winning score on standardized achievement tests!

TITLE	ISBN	PRICE
Grades 3 to 5: Scoring High Test Prep	1-57768-316-1	$9.95
Grades 6 to 8: Scoring High Test Prep	1-57768-317-X	$9.95

Available in jewel case only (no box included)

SCIENCE

Mastering the principles of both physical and life science has never been so FUN for kids grades six and above as it is while they are exploring McGraw-Hill's edutainment software!

TITLE	ISBN	PRICE
Grades 6 & up: Life Science	1-57768-336-6	$9.95
Grades 8 & up: Physical Science	1-57768-308-0	$9.95

Available in jewel case only (no box included)

REFERENCE

The National Museum of Women in the Arts has teamed with McGraw-Hill Consumer Products to bring you this superb collection available for your enjoyment on CD-ROM.

This special collection is a visual diary of 200 women artists from the Renaissance to the present, spanning 500 years of creativity.

You will discover the art of women who excelled in all the great art movements of history. Artists who pushed the boundaries of abstract, genre, landscape, narrative, portrait, and still-life styles; as well as artists forced to push the societal limits placed on women through the ages.

TITLE	ISBN	PRICE
Women in the Arts	1-57768-010-3	$29.95

Available in boxed version only

Most titles for Windows 3.1™, Windows '95™ & '98™, and Macintosh™.

Visit us on the Internet at:

www.MHkids.com

Or call 800-298-4119 for your local retailer.

201

All our workbooks meet school curriculum guidelines and correspond to The McGraw-Hill Companies classroom textbooks.

SPECTRUM SERIES

DOLCH Sight Word Activities

The DOLCH Sight Word Activities Workbooks use the classic Dolch list of 220 basic vocabulary words that make up from 50% to 75% of all reading matter that children ordinarily encounter. Since these words are ordinarily recognized on sight, they are called *sight words*. Volume 1 includes 110 sight words. Volume 2 covers the remainder of the list. Over 160 pages.

TITLE	ISBN	PRICE
Grades K-1 Vol. 1	1-57768-429-X	$9.95
Grades K-1 Vol. 2	1-57768-439-7	$9.95

GEOGRAPHY

Full-color, three-part lessons strengthen geography knowledge and map reading skills. Focusing on five geographic themes including location, place, human/environmental interaction, movement, and regions. Over 150 pages. Glossary of geographical terms and answer key included.

TITLE	ISBN	PRICE
Gr 3, Communities	1-57768-153-3	$7.95
Gr 4, Regions	1-57768-154-1	$7.95
Gr 5, USA	1-57768-155-X	$7.95
Gr 6, World	1-57768-156-8	$7.95

MATH

Features easy-to-follow instructions that give students a clear path to success. This series has comprehensive coverage of the basic skills, helping children to master math fundamentals. Over 150 pages. Answer key included.

TITLE	ISBN	PRICE
Grade 1	1-57768-111-8	$7.95
Grade 2	1-57768-112-6	$7.95
Grade 3	1-57768-113-4	$7.95
Grade 4	1-57768-114-2	$7.95
Grade 5	1-57768-115-0	$7.95
Grade 6	1-57768-116-9	$7.95
Grade 7	1-57768-117-7	$7.95
Grade 8	1-57768-118-5	$7.95

PHONICS

Provides everything children need to build multiple skills in language. Focusing on phonics, structural analysis, and dictionary skills, this series also offers creative ideas for using phonics and word study skills in other language arts. Over 200 pages. Answer key included.

TITLE	ISBN	PRICE
Grade K	1-57768-120-7	$7.95
Grade 1	1-57768-121-5	$7.95
Grade 2	1-57768-122-3	$7.95
Grade 3	1-57768-123-1	$7.95
Grade 4	1-57768-124-X	$7.95
Grade 5	1-57768-125-8	$7.95
Grade 6	1-57768-126-6	$7.95

READING

This full-color series creates an enjoyable reading environment, even for below-average readers. Each book contains captivating content, colorful characters, and compelling illustrations, so children are eager to find out what happens next. Over 150 pages. Answer key included.

TITLE	ISBN	PRICE
Grade K	1-57768-130-4	$7.95
Grade 1	1-57768-131-2	$7.95
Grade 2	1-57768-132-0	$7.95
Grade 3	1-57768-133-9	$7.95
Grade 4	1-57768-134-7	$7.95
Grade 5	1-57768-135-5	$7.95
Grade 6	1-57768-136-3	$7.95

SPELLING

This full-color series links spelling to reading and writing and increases skills in words and meanings, consonant and vowel spellings, and proofreading practice. Over 200 pages. Speller dictionary and answer key included.

TITLE	ISBN	PRICE
Grade 1	1-57768-161-4	$7.95
Grade 2	1-57768-162-2	$7.95
Grade 3	1-57768-163-0	$7.95
Grade 4	1-57768-164-9	$7.95
Grade 5	1-57768-165-7	$7.95
Grade 6	1-57768-166-5	$7.95

WRITING

Lessons focus on creative and expository writing using clearly stated objectives and pre-writing exercises. Eight essential reading skills are applied. Activities include main idea, sequence, comparison, detail, fact and opinion, cause and effect, and making a point. Over 130 pages. Answer key included.

TITLE	ISBN	PRICE
Grade 1	1-57768-141-X	$7.95
Grade 2	1-57768-142-8	$7.95
Grade 3	1-57768-143-6	$7.95
Grade 4	1-57768-144-4	$7.95
Grade 5	1-57768-145-2	$7.95
Grade 6	1-57768-146-0	$7.95
Grade 7	1-57768-147-9	$7.95
Grade 8	1-57768-148-7	$7.95

TEST PREP
From the Nation's #1 Testing Company

Prepares children to do their best on current editions of the five major standardized tests. Activities reinforce test-taking skills through examples, tips, practice, and timed exercises. Subjects include reading, math, and language. Over 150 pages. Answer key included.

TITLE	ISBN	PRICE
Grade 1	1-57768-101-0	$8.95
Grade 2	1-57768-102-9	$8.95
Grade 3	1-57768-103-7	$8.95
Grade 4	1-57768-104-5	$8.95
Grade 5	1-57768-105-3	$8.95
Grade 6	1-57768-106-1	$8.95
Grade 7	1-57768-107-X	$8.95
Grade 8	1-57768-108-8	$8.95

LANGUAGE ARTS

Encourages creativity and builds confidence by making writing fun! Seventy-two four-part lessons strengthen writing skills by focusing on parts of speech, word usage, sentence structure, punctuation, and proofreading. Each level includes a *Writer's Handbook* at the end of the book that offers writing tips. This series is based on the highly respected SRA/McGraw-Hill language arts series. More than 180 full-color pages. *Available March 2000.*

TITLE	ISBN	PRICE
Grade 2	1-57768-472-9	$7.95
Grade 3	1-57768-473-7	$7.95
Grade 4	1-57768-474-5	$7.95
Grade 5	1-57768-475-3	$7.95
Grade 6	1-57768-476-1	$7.95